PRAISE FOR *AMERICAN COMMANDER*

There was a time when America looked to men who had been on the front lines to lead our nation. Those of us who have taken the oath of office and were willing to make the last full measure of devotion stand ready to serve our republic . . . there is no statute of limitations on our commitment. I endorsed Ryan Zinke in his run for Congress because he represents what this country so desperately needs at this time in her history—men and women who have served selflessly in our military turning their patriotism, knowledge, and leadership skills to "Take the High Ground," Capitol Hill. Ryan embodies that which is exceptional about America—a modern-day Spartan. He is a decorated commander at the navy's most elite SEAL Team. With Ryan you have an unstoppable warrior for the people. *American Commander* is a must-read if you want to understand the SEAL credo: Never Quit!

—LIEUTENANT COLONEL ALLEN B. WEST
US ARMY, RETIRED;
MEMBER OF 112TH US CONGRESS;
EXECUTIVE DIRECTOR, NATIONAL CENTER FOR POLICY ANALYSIS

I am proud to have been the founding father and first commanding officer at the navy's most elite SEAL Team and equally proud of the men in the next generation of SEALs—like Ryan Zinke ("Z"). Z and his men have taken the tactics and operational readiness of my generation to the level the world knows today. They continue to strike devastation and fear in the hearts and minds of our nation's worst enemies and make us proud of the Trident they wear with honor.

—DICK MARCINKO
COMMANDER, UNITED STATES NAVY, RETIRED; FOUNDING FATHER AND FIRST
COMMANDING OFFICER OF THE NAVY'S MOST ELITE SEAL TEAM; AUTHOR
OF *ROGUE WARRIOR*

AMERICAN COMMANDER

AMERICAN COMMANDER

SERVING A COUNTRY WORTH FIGHTING FOR AND TRAINING THE BRAVE SOLDIERS WHO LEAD THE WAY

RYAN ZINKE

WITH SCOTT MCEWEN

W PUBLISHING GROUP

AN IMPRINT OF THOMAS NELSON

Published in Nashville, Tennessee, by W Publishing Group, an imprint of Thomas Nelson. W Publishing and Thomas Nelson are registered trademarks of HarperCollins Christian Publishing, Inc.

Scripture quotations are taken from the King James Version (public domain).

Thomas Nelson titles may be purchased in bulk for educational, business, fund-raising, or sales promotional use. For information, please e-mail SpecialMarkets@ThomasNelson.com.

Library of Congress Cataloging-in-Publication Data

Library of Congress Control Number: 2016945746
ISBN 978-0-7180-7787-7 (hardcover)

Printed in the United States of America

16 17 18 19 20 RRD 6 5 4 3 2 1

This book is dedicated to military families like my family. To my wife, the love of my life, Lolita, my children Jennifer, Wolfgang, Konrad, my son-in-law Jack, and my two amazing granddaughters Matilda and Charlotte. Life for any military family is hard. Life for a SEAL Team family is harder. I spent years missing birthdays, family dinners, tucking my kids in at night, and anniversaries. Lolita was left raising a family alone with the uncertainty of my return. Thank you for understanding and waiting for me, no matter how long it took to get home.

CONTENTS

CONTENTS

FOREWORD

IN THE SEALS, WE ARE DRIVEN BY THE UNDERSTANDING that we are a part of a team that must operate as one fighting unit in order to effectively accomplish our mission. Officer or enlisted, each of us is tasked with the integral role of seeing that our job is done right the first time, every time. No member of the team is any more important than anyone else. We all either win or lose together, and quitting is not an option. Mission failure is simply not an option in the SEAL teams and even less acceptable in SEAL Team ■[1] where defeat is often of national strategic consequence. This legacy of team and "never quit" was taught to us by those who preceded us in wearing the Trident and was passed down through us to those who currently bear its substantial weight.

With this legacy in mind, I met Ryan Zinke, a former commander at SEAL Team ■ and fellow ■ Team member, before I was assigned to the command. While having heard of Ryan by his reputation as a "lead from the front" and "take charge" commander, I did not meet him until he was the sole congressman from our mutual home of Montana. After meeting him, I understood why he was able to accomplish what he had, both in his leadership and legacy with the SEALs and in his current leadership role in restoring American values and greatness. Ryan is certainly deserving of respect simply by virtue of his status as a United States congressman. However, my respect for this man is even greater due to his

leadership roles ▇▇▇▇▇▇▇▇▇▇▇ at SEAL Team ▇ and
the respect that he has earned from warriors who served with him.

In my tenure with the SEAL teams, I found that those who are
the best in leading the SEALs do so by example, not necessarily by
command—and there is a difference. Being an officer commissioned in
the United States military means something but does not fully define
the man or his role in getting the job done. When I met Ryan, it quickly
became apparent why he was able to accomplish what he had within the
SEAL teams. He was there during the time of the original plank members, dating back to when Captain Dick Marcinko was in charge of
SEAL Team ▇. They were the "giants" of the SEALs and a wild bunch
but also believed in training hard and pushing the tactics to be the
best counterterrorist force in the world—a substantial and crucial legacy. Ryan was still there when the team reorganized to face the current
demands of conducting sustained combat special operations worldwide. The legacy that Ryan and his generation of team members created
was equally substantial, and I would like to think crucial, in our ultimate use of the skill set to dispatch many enemies of this nation, not the
least of whom was one Osama bin Laden. Though it was a challenging
mission, there are many within our ranks who have accomplished even
more difficult missions than this one. I am proud of my contribution.
When I was a SEAL I truly walked "on the shoulders of giants." Each
generation of SEALs builds on our traditions and tactics to make the
next generation better.

Our nation and our SEALs have gone through some major transi-
tions since 9/11, and continue to do so, but the core, the values, and the
attitude that we will never quit have not and will not change. This is what
SEALs are, what Ryan is, and what I am. It is why SEALs never truly
retire; they just change the mission for this great idea and nation we call
America.

Ryan and I now have a common goal: our commitment to the men
and women who have served in our military—all of our military, not just
the SEAL teams. Given the increased public recognition each of us has

received, we have the ability to bring to light issues that others may not understand and protect those most important to us: our veterans. We are committed to seeing the men and women veterans of our country looked after effectively and hope to instill a similar desire in those who would hear our story.

I am hopeful that by reading Ryan's story of life within the SEALs and after, you will gain a better understanding of the sacrifice and commitment of our veterans. We, all veterans, chose a path of service to our country, and that service many times includes injuries that far outdate the battles we were chosen to defend this country in.

As a nation I truly hope we never forget this commitment.

WITH THE UTMOST RESPECT,
ROBERT J. O'NEILL
SENIOR CHIEF NAVY SPECIAL WARFARE OPERATOR (SEAL),
RETIRED; RECIPIENT OF TWO SILVER STARS, FOUR BRONZE STARS
WITH VALOR; JOINT SERVICE COMMENDATION MEDAL WITH
VALOR; THREE PRESIDENTIAL UNIT CITATIONS; AND TWO NAVY
AND MARINE CORPS COMMENDATIONS WITH VALOR

PROLOGUE

*Special Operations Command and Control Element
(SOCCE) Task Force FALCON, Kosovo*

THE BOSNIAN WAR HAD BEEN A NIGHTMARE. FOUGHT from 1992 to 1995, it was a largely territorial struggle for what was left of Yugoslavia, a war fraught with ethnic, religious, and political turmoil. "War crimes" doesn't begin to describe the horrors perpetrated on the populace of the rival factions—but here's one statistic: between twenty and forty thousand Bosnian Muslim women were raped during the conflict. The International Criminal Tribunal called it "genocidal rape." Civilian deaths numbered 38,239, nearly 38 percent of the total casualties.[1] For a small, relatively limited war, those are staggering numbers, especially when you consider Bosnia and Herzegovina had a population of around 3.8 million in 2000. Basically, one in every one thousand civilians was killed during the crisis.

Even after the large-scale hostilities ceased, a NATO IFOR—Implementation Force—of eighty thousand personnel remained in the region. I had been in Bosnia-Herzegovina and Kosovo starting in the early 1990s beginning with IFOR, then Stabilization Force (SFOR), and finally Kosovo Force (KFOR). As in most military campaigns, the early years of the campaign allowed Special Operations Forces (SOF) to operate with high degrees of autonomy and freedom of movement to conduct small-unit missions composed of members of the navy's elite SEAL Team and the army's elite counterpart.

The US Navy knew that Radovan Karadžić, leader of the Bosnian Serbs, was concealing weapons caches in small, inaccessible towns—the same towns that were often stops for drug, military equipment, and human trafficking. Karadžić had been pretty open regarding his religion-based ethnic-cleansing atrocities, and the caches helped him keep up high, lethal momentum in his operations. Within the multinational force charged with stopping him, the SEALs and Special Forces—the US Navy's elite special warfare operators—were at the forefront of the highest-risk operations.

The SEALs could already count numerous successes as part of the Bosnia-Herzegovina conflict. Acting under the umbrella codename of Joint Forge and its predecessors Joint Guard and Joint Endeavor, SEALs and foreign military forces had conducted small-unit reconnaissance missions, search-and-rescue missions for downed pilots, intelligence-gathering operations, and Personal Security Detachment (PSD) missions that escorted and protected American and NATO leadership. We also ran PSYOPS (psychological operations designed to demoralize the enemy and shape the battlefield in our favor) and later conducted Personnel Indicted for War Crimes (PIFWC) operations to bring to justice those who committed unspeakable crimes against humanity. In Kosovo, the missions were almost exclusively Reconnaissance and Surveillance (R&S) in nature, designed to give eyes-on-ground intelligence concerning movement, smuggling patterns, and identification of possible arms caches.

On a night that will always burn vividly in my memory, SEAL Team Two was preparing to add another notch to its successful R&S missions completed: its members were to insert a small SEAL element via helicopters, conduct an overland patrol, observe and report on suspected arms caches, and extract back to the base safely. I'll be talking more about who the SEALs are and what the numeric designations mean in a bit. For now, suffice to say they are elite Sea, Air and Land (SEAL) teams, established in 1962 by President John F. Kennedy as a Special Operations Force capable of operating in all environments.

A twenty-five-year-old sniper named Chad M. Burkhart was the point man for a delicate Reconnaissance and Surveillance (R&S) mission in hostile territory. That means among those who were "in first," he was the guy out front and most exposed. Burkhart was young, talented, and the guy who commanders fought to have assigned to their units. He was the guy who showed up early, stayed late, and was committed to becoming an elite warrior in the teams. Kosovo was his first deployment, and he was about to conduct his first SEAL Team mission.

Burkhart's platoon—as every SEAL platoon does—had rehearsed extensively for his first R&S mission. Every aspect of the mission was planned and every contingency was accounted for. Burkhart's helicopter—a UH-60 Black Hawk—was to come in hot and fast for a quick drop-off after the Kiowas gave the "all clear." The route was a short trip from the Forward Operating Base (FOB) located within the KFOR complex called Camp Bondsteel. The helicopters would quickly land and drop off the team and disappear into the night.

Once the team reached the target area, they would conduct a short reconnaissance to find any suitable observation points that provided both concealment and good communication links. The SEALs then would watch for any suspicious activity and identify individuals worth monitoring, either as targets themselves or as people who could lead us to higher-value targets.

Before any of this could happen, of course, the first step was to be inserted by helicopter on a small clearing. Burkhart had the task of being the first one off the UH-60 and using a handheld GPS and map in order to navigate his team through the darkness.

Let me tell you a little about the mind and psychology of a point man in the SEALs. Every SEAL is trained to place team over self: in hostile territory, you protect your fellow SEALs. In the front of Burkhart's brain, going in, was not how far out in front he was or how deep into the mouth of danger he was; it was, *What do I have to do to fulfill the mission and protect the men behind me?* "Self" does not exist. It's a group mind, if you will—a fist made of component fingers. The point man knows that he is generally the one to meet enemy fire first and is most likely to find a minefield or a booby trap. In Kosovo, Russian-made mines placed on trails and booby traps to protect arms caches were common.

In short, every muscle, every thought that was part of Chad Burkhart were fully invested in the mission.

The night of November 24 was pitch-black and starless—so black, in fact, that you could not even see your hand in front of your face. The helicopter pilots wore Night Vision Goggles (NVGs) and worked by the soft glow of their instruments: everything else in the cabin was, for all intents, invisible. Burkhart's only illumination came from his open light-watch and his small handheld GPS. His adrenaline rush and nerves of the first mission no doubt kept him stealing glances of his instruments of navigation even though every glance negatively affected his natural night vision. Even the external navigation, formation, and anticollision lights on the helicopter had been muted: illumination, on this night, in this territory, was a tool that helped the enemy.

Inside Burkhart's helicopter, the team faced two slight variations from how the mission had been planned and rehearsed. The first was that the crew chief was new—he had logged barely twelve hours total in that UH-60. Like Burkhart, it was his first Special Operations mission. While capable of the task, the UH-60 crew was not a dedicated Special Forces asset, and SEAL missions were just one of the many they had assigned to them. That introduced an unknown psychological component: Burkhart wasn't familiar with the tactics and techniques of a SEAL platoon. And the second minor deviation from SEAL standard operating procedures (SOPs) was the last-minute decision to fly the short route with the doors closed—not open, as they had done in the practice drills. This was ordered to keep the wind down from the cool Kosovo night and assist in better communications. The inside of a Black Hawk is loud enough without the rotors and wind pounding through an open door. Since the flight was short, it was decided as the SEALs were being loaded that the doors would open at two minutes out. The night was starless, quiet, and black. Even the landing zone was still.

Fully loaded, the MH-60s linked up with the circling Kiowas, and the formation set off into the darkness. As planned the OH-58 Kiowas surged ahead and scanned the designated landing zone with their thermal imagers to look for any hotspots, which showed nothing but cool. There were no unidentified blips—not even a dog and definitely nothing hostile. At two minutes out, the MH-60s reduced airspeed and leveled off in anticipation of the quick dive. Hearts were pumping hard, and no doubt Chad checked his watch one last time.

The crew chief threw open the doors, Chad gave an enthusiastic thumbs-up, the crew chief answered, and Chad Burkhart stepped out into the Kosovo darkness.

But the helicopter hadn't landed. The crew chief had misunderstood Burkhart's enthusiastic thumbs-up and unfortunately returned a thumbs-up response himself, which is the SOP signal "to go." The chopper was 350 feet above the forested hills of Kosovo when Gunner's Mate Petty Officer Second Class Chad M. Burkhart stepped out and plummeted to his death. The crew chief, wearing night vision goggles, said he saw Chad step out and could follow his descent for only a few seconds before he lost him in the night.

Confusion and disbelief consumed the passengers and crew alike on board the helo, and the mission now turned from a preplanned Reconnaissance and Surveillance mission to an in extremis search and rescue.

As the Naval Special Operations Forces (NAVSOF) commander, I'd been tracking the mission from the Joint Operations Center (JOC) from our small Forward Operating Base (FOB) located within Camp Bondsteel, a megabase the United States had built in eastern Kosovo. The JOC was really nothing more than a plywood room containing a few maps, intelligence plots, and a communication plan listing call signs and supporting forces. JOC duty was typically characterized by long hours, pots of coffee, and Copenhagen for those who chewed tobacco. In this case, the JOC was the center for decisions to be made and commands given. Remaining forces at the FOB would assemble and prepare to assist as required, and the medical team was alerted. There was nothing more

I could do except pray that somehow Chad had survived the fall and he could be saved.

The platoon found Burkhart pretty quickly. He was reported as being still alive but barely. The triage team administered CPR, his chest moved, and I scrambled all available forces to retrieve him and bring him to the field hospital, where he was pronounced dead. It remains uncertain whether he died on impact or whether the field CPR was giving false hope. Regardless, Chad Burkhart was killed in action while on his first mission in Kosovo.

Though I was not Burkhart's commanding officer, I felt a deep sense of loss greater than ever before. I had lost teammates before in both battle and training whom I had been closer to. I reminded myself that being a SEAL is a tough business and being in charge bears both responsibility and accountability. That night I heard the words when the reports came in, understood what had transpired, and knew there are no guarantees. But while your brain grasps all of that, your guts, your soul, everything else is numb. It's a protective mechanism, I suppose: you have to continue the mission. There're the rest of the team and preparing for the next mission to think about. To dwell too deeply on the past may place the next operation in jeopardy as success is often measured by detailed planning and mission focus.

When the operation is over the real horror settles in. No SEAL—no soldier—is immune. *Could I have prevented it?* we all ask ourselves in some way. *As a commander, did I miss something or not train hard enough?* A brother has died, survivor guilt settles in, the hard realization that you could be next . . . all of that takes hold. The "it could be you" part isn't even about your own mortality; it's about how your death will affect your loved ones—parents, wife, siblings, maybe young children you haven't even met and who may never get to meet you. That's the worst part of the postmortem adjustment.

I felt I was responsible for making sure Burkhart's family knew the circumstances of his death. It was the first time I was in position away from the front lines of the fight. As much as I wanted to be suited up riding in the Black Hawk with the boys, my job was to make sure every t was crossed and every i was dotted. I was to ensure the plan was solid, make sure the team was ready and had the right equipment, and push supporting assets to them in the field if needed. I'd lost other teammates before both in battle and training, but this death was different because it was my first time losing someone while being in a position separated and away from the men at risk. Though I influenced actions, I no longer directly controlled the actions at the pointy end of the spear. This was also the first time I had lost someone since becoming a father. At the time of Burkhart's death, I had one young son and a daughter. It dawned on me that my role as a commander is really not different from that of a father. You give guidance and teach, provide resources, and make sure they have every opportunity to succeed. Unfortunately, you cannot be with them all the time.

We had a small field funeral service for Petty Officer Second Class Chad Burkhart at the FOB near where his helicopter took off. He and I shared a common background of growing up in small-town America, and he had a reputation of cheerfully working harder than his peers. He was an only son and made his family, state, and country proud of his accomplishments.

My daughter, Jennifer, wasn't in the navy yet, but she and the man she married eventually both joined the navy and became navy divers—she a Diving Medical Technician and he a SEAL. I didn't realize it at the time of the funeral, but something powerful hardened inside of me during the service: commitment. No, there is no way you can anticipate every contingency. Sometimes we pay for knowledge in the worst possible way, with lives. I hardened my resolve that our forces must have not only the best training, but the absolute *right* training and top-of-the-line equipment. Later, that fierce resolve would evolve into something even stronger: a conviction to ensure every soldier, sailor, airman, or marine in harm's way has the right rules of engagement to win decisively on the battlefield. We have been sorely negligent in the latter department—I'll get into that later—and when we don't make those rules with winning in mind, our troops pay for it.

At the time of Chad's death I'd been in Bosnia off and on for eight years. Bosnia was a morale-sapping war, survivable only because we believed in the value and morality of what we were doing. Extreme nationalism fueled by ethnic and religious tensions turned many ordinary citizens and soldiers into callous killing machines. Europe could not stop it, and Russia did not care to. America was the only hope. I know it's unfashionable in some circles to tout American ideals as a compass for the world, but let me tell you: without them, the world goes to hell. Our nation is an exception, maybe *the* exception, to tyranny and crushing socialism. I will go back to John F. Kennedy's inaugural speech in which he proclaimed to the world that we would pay any price and bear any burden in the defense of liberty. We would always be on the side of those who cannot defend themselves. If we ever lose that sense of true north . . . well, let's just say we cannot and will not.

We must not.

In 2000, I had been a member of the Navy SEALs for fifteen years. My time with the SEALs straddled the rough-and-ready early days when some SEAL units were known as much for their outlaw bearing as for their efficiency through their more buttoned-down—and more lethal—demeanor today. When I was with the SEALs, we trained constantly, both physically and mentally, to always be prepared just in case we were called to action. Even though the SEALs had been to Panama, Somalia, and the first Gulf War, the relative number of combat operations was few. The number of SEALs with actual combat experience was even fewer. It was strange that even the most elite of the SEAL teams was literally running to the sound of the guns to find combat, because back then a career in the SEALs did not mean you would necessarily see any action.

Today's SEALs don't have any uncertainty about being called to duty: when you put on the SEAL Trident, you're going to go to battle. That's just a fact. But back then, if you wanted to be sure you'd see action, you had to become part of the elite of the elite. And that's where I was in the early years of the Bosnian conflict leading up to Kosovo.

Throughout my career, my role as a SEAL officer was less that of a door kicker—the guys who storm into hazardous situations with flash grenades and assault rifles (M4s then, SCARs now)—and more the role of a team leader, planning and resource expert, and decision maker. Sure, I kicked down doors and shot shoulder-fired rockets, but my job was to make sure the men around me were better than I was at doing it. That's not the same as being a so-called armchair general: you have to know the same team battle skills and tactics—meaning you've been there, done that, and are able to feel every blow they take or success they achieve. You're not the star of the show, but you feel like you are understudying every damn part.

There's one more key component to being a good commander, especially when you're leading elite teams: it's knowing when to stay out of the flipping way and let your trusted talent do what they do best, injecting yourself only enough to make sure the team stays focused on mission and the momentum of success is maintained. A good plan executed early is better than a perfect plan executed late, and making adjustments on the fly often carries the day. Small-unit leadership requires cultivating innovation and building a team that nearly runs on its own, which, if your men have been properly briefed, trained, rehearsed, and equipped, should be easy. The right amount of oversight is an important point that I will come back to later.

As a commander of talented teams, my job was to ensure that everyone around me either was more talented or worked hard to be so. I was never the best jumper, diver, explosive expert, or sniper. I simply had to know who was and be able to build a team that could be counted on to win under any conditions.

As a commander of either a unit or a task force, I gathered intelligence on enemy forces and where to find the right resources to do the mission, briefed the highest-level officers, fought for missions and approvals, developed detailed plans and ensured the team could execute them, and, more importantly, was honored to lead the nation's best in some of the most complex missions in the history of Special Forces.

My first experience in Bosnia was conducting small-unit Leaders Reconnaissance with members of both the elite navy and army units right after IFOR had been established. At the time the borders within the former Republic of Yugoslavia were still unsettled, and ethnic cleansing on all sides was common. Refugees were pouring into Europe, and rule by military strongmen and organized crime was the norm. Special Reconnaissance (SR) missions were the focus of Special Operations. Every highway was driven, every village was visited, and every military and civilian uniform was carefully documented. If we were to be assigned a mission, we would be at least familiar with the ground and what opposition may be in the area.

The second series of deployments to Bosnia was when I was attached as the unconventional warfare officer to commander in chief, US Naval Forces, Europe (CINCUSNAVEUR) in London. As the senior naval commander in Europe, Admiral Boorda wore many hats, including commander of Stabilization Force (SFOR), whose headquarters was in Sarajevo in the midst of the active civil war. Admiral Boorda was the first former seaman recruit to rise all the way to four-star admiral. He later became chief of Naval Operations and tragically took his own life in the Washington Navy Yard in 1997. I had just married my wife, Lola, and we were excited to take a break from the heavy deployment schedule stateside. We found ourselves living in a small flat in West Hampstead in northwest London. Both of us were working for Admiral Jeremy Boorda—Lola as a quality control civilian on the flag deck and I as the unconventional warfare officer.

Even though London and its subway system were frequently under bomb threats by the IRA, London was a welcome break from being gone from home more than 220 days a year. It was a good place to raise a family, and ours was growing: we had our daughter, Jennifer, and Lola became pregnant with Wolfgang while we were there. Wolfgang was born in London, in fact. (And, no, just because Lola and I were both American citizens does not mean he is a "natural-born" citizen and qualified to become president of the United States.)

Part of the reason we were comfortable expanding our family while we were in London was that for the most part, I thought I could actually be with Lola and the kids. Knowing my next tour would be back to the team with another heavy deployment schedule, I wanted to spend time with the family away from the daily grind. The irony was that my boss, Admiral Boorda, was being protected by members of my old command, and I would be tasked once again to be forward deployed to lead the Naval Special Operations Forces in Bosnia to conduct pilot rescue and other special operations as required. So much for the time off. Later, after we moved back to the shores of Virginia and had Konrad, I wound up overseas again and away from my family more than I had been when we were in London. That wasn't easy on any of us.

Admiral Boorda did have a great sense of humor, though. When I was not deployed, part of my job was to conduct the daily theater brief on matters of the SEALs and Special Forces. On one occasion, a SEAL team platoon stationed in Scotland decided to have some single scotch whisky and Guinness while bowling at the local lanes. After damages were assessed, the local commander decided it met the threshold of writing an official Operational Report Naval Blue (OPREPNAVYBLUE) message to the headquarters. Such messages are typically reserved for significant losses or a major incident short of war. The text of the rather long message stated the SEAL platoon had consumed alcohol and had caused damage to the club to include divots in the floor of the bowling lanes and multiple ceiling strikes. No high score was mentioned. I finished reading the message, and the staff went silent and turned to Admiral Boorda for his response. He frowned, took a deep breath, and asked me if the bowling balls were sixteen pounds or twelve. He noted a ceiling strike delivered with a sixteen-pound ball isn't easy. The room laughed. He loved sailors, and the sailors loved him. So did Lola, as she was invited to all the flag functions. That gave me an edge on the flag deck!

After returning stateside, I once again found myself heading back

to Bosnia-Herzegovina in 1997, this time as part of the effort to identify, locate, and bring to justice Personnel Indicted for War Crimes, or
PIFWCs as they were known. I had returned to the team for a second
tour as commander at one of the assault teams. We were known as the
"meat eaters" within the compound and arguably the most elite fighting
force in the world.

The Bosnia PIFWC operations were my first real introduction to
combat leadership. I was a lieutenant commander at the time and feeling
on top of the world. As team leader of some of the most talented warriors this country has ever produced, I knew from the moment I assumed
the job that this would be the pinnacle of my SEAL career. I was junior
enough to be at the front and senior enough to make decisions once I got
there. Perfect. Our job was targeting—locating the PIFWCs, verifying
that they were who we thought they were, determining the infrastructure
and intelligence structure we needed to infiltrate their surroundings,
getting a sense of their networks, and when the conditions were right,
detaining those individuals.

A lot of this work had been built upon the reconnaissance missions
that were conducted earlier during IFOR. Since we had established
a pretty good network of contacts and knew where the brothels were,
finding current intelligence was made easier but not easy. The brothels
often served as a club for local leaders to meet and to discuss politics. If
you wanted to know whether your target was in town, one of the first
places to start was the local brothel. Conducting surveillance on patrons
and paying the hired help for intelligence gave us an edge. Hundreds of
hours of surveillance would be required to develop patterns and determine things such as where these individuals lived or worked, what their
daily schedules were, whom they spoke with, what their security situation was, what sort of arms they normally carried, and where the nearest
forces they could summon were. This is the sort of detailed intelligence
collection work that enabled us to get Osama bin Laden. It involves
patience and more patience. Intelligence collection is slow and methodical. Think of it as a big cat in the high grass watching prey, not just

launching itself into a fray. When you're conducting high-profile operations, you may be stalking your target for weeks or even months before you strike. I had one impatient general tell me to speed up the collection efforts and that I could afford an "intelligence casualty." He would go hungry in the tall grass.

It was December 1997, and my team was assuming the watch. By "watch" I mean that each team rotated being on call for any crisis. Rotation periods at the time were divided to allow team members to attend professional development courses such as sniper and breacher training, conduct larger training and exercises as a team, and then have their bags packed and ready to go to war. In 1997, the entire command carried the old beepers that would simply produce an audible alarm with the numbers 0101. The range of the beeper was limited to about thirty miles, and failure to make it to the command in forty-five minutes meant dismissal. We would routinely get beeped at all hours of the day or night for Emergency Deployment Readiness Exercises (EDREs) to test our responsiveness. In the case of going after the PIFWCs, there was no need for a beeper. The practitioners, executioners, and monsters who had preyed on the populace in Bosnia were still at large and still active in ugly, hidden pockets.

After months of training for almost every possible method of interdiction, the team got the green light to focus our efforts on two high-value targets (HVTs). Our first target was Blagoje Simić—or, as he was also known, the Hitler of Bosnia. Simić was the mayor of Samac, a town just under fifty miles north of Tuzla. Simić, along with several other Bosnian officials, had overseen the dispossession, movement to concentration camps, and execution of thousands of non-Serbian Bosnians.

The second target was Police Chief Stevan Todorovic, a torturer, rapist, and mid-level thug who specialized in violating the rights of non-Serbian Bosnians. Women, children . . . Todorovic didn't discriminate. If we wanted proof that these were bad people, all we had to do was look out our vehicle windows while on the roads to Tuzla: there were a lot of half-collapsed burned-out structures, former homes of people who had been ethnically cleansed. Of course, not all the homes were burned out: some Bosnian officials enriched themselves by taking these homes over and selling them for their own gain, just as the Nazis had done a half century earlier in countries like Lithuania and elsewhere. Evil never truly dies; it just changes its face.

Samac is a small town, the kind where everybody knows everybody else's business, which of course makes intelligence collection tricky. Any vehicle entering the town—much less a stream of military vehicles—would be a tip-off, and we didn't want any locals to know that Todorovic or his lynch men were under surveillance.

Both of these guys were in what was called the "sealed section"—they had been quietly indicted for war crimes by the International Criminal Court at The Hague in the Netherlands. They hadn't been told officially, of course, as they would have immediately gone into hiding . . . but they must have known. The only names on the list that weren't sealed were people like Radovan Karadžić, those at the top ranks. The crimes of those who had been sealed were no less, but they were of lesser ranks in the government and military, so the hope was that they'd think they'd avoided international charges.

So there you had it. The SEALs going after the sealed. And each operation had to be done quietly so as not to alert the others. In the best possible case, the individual had to simply vanish without any trace until he showed up at The Hague for prosecution.

Before we left for Bosnia, we had decided to go in lean and mean, keeping our equipment needs to a safe minimum. We took our SIG Sauer 226s as our sidearms. For our sniper weapons most of us—because SEALs have a vast array of weapons to choose from—went with M4s.

The choice of the M4 assault rifle as our basic weapon system was based on some hard-earned knowledge: in Somalia, where we'd been a few years before, SEALs often carried the 9mm Heckler & Koch MP5 submachine guns. The MP5 is an excellent weapon for interior fighting. Light and highly accurate, it's got great accuracy up to fifty yards. American SWAT teams use them all the time. But in Somalia the fighting wasn't contained to single buildings or interiors. The battle quickly spilled out to the street and was fought building to building. The opposition had AK-47s, which have an effective range of a little less than four hundred yards, giving the enemy a significant advantage: they could hit our guys while being out of the range of our MP5s. So with the exception of the "grab and bag" men, we were going in with M4s with advanced optics.

When an assault team touches down in or near hostile territory, chances are pretty good it's going to execute a mission fairly soon. The logistics of supplying berthing and food while maintaining operational security is a tough task even for a few days. The more complex the operation, the more support was required in terms of communications requirements and additional personnel. With every additional warm body and piece of equipment, the greater the logistics footprint. What I was witnessing on what would become a series of PIFWC operations is the only thing that was "light" was the actual force conducting abduction. It was the beginning of the trend that has only grown in recent years. In order to reduce operational risk, the headquarters requires more supporting assets in the form of communications, intelligence, and command and control that in turn require more logistics support. It is the rise of bureaucracy similar to what has occurred in every branch and division of government. Added requirements and red tape have almost always ensured that the smallest part of force is the part that actually conducts the mission or provides the actual service. In this case, advances in communications and technology could enable senior officials sitting in stateside command centers real-time information. Once unleashed, the rise of "armchair" quarterbacks was unstoppable. Well-thought-out tactical plans by experienced ground force commanders were modified by desk jockeys and political appointees. Even the most simple of operations often became a labyrinth of approvals and authorizations. The result was a loss of battlefield momentum and failures to quickly capitalize on emerging opportunities. In short, the battlefield was no longer being controlled by those who had the most at risk.

Meanwhile, back in Virginia the team continued planning for almost every contingency and conducted the training to master any option. Mock-ups of buildings were built, and even airborne assault tactics were devised should we have to take the target in a vehicle. We even went to the extent of deploying to Fort Campbell with the army's Special Operations aviation wing, to experiment with techniques to stop a moving vehicle. We started with the idea of two snipers sitting on the mounted platforms on the side of MH-6 helicopters firing armor-piercing rounds into the engine block. We had purchased older vehicles and used the old brick-on-the-gas-pedal trick as a predecessor to today's unmanned technology. The steering wheel was secured, and a line was tied to a mechanism that when pulled would drop the brick on the gas pedal and off the car would go speeding across the firing range. No one was really sure what exactly happened when the MH-60 took chase and caught up to the car. After the cloud of dust and debris settled, the helicopter lay on its side and the car sat idling next to it. Miraculously, everyone walked away except for the red-faced commander of the squadron, who was running toward us. Lesson learned: helicopters are vulnerable.

I should also mention while the intelligence-gathering operations were in full swing in support of the Bosnian operations, all teams were still required to keep up the critical skills in other potential tasks such as combat diving and free-fall parachute operations. We were the nation's 911 force, and we had to be ready for any threat anywhere in the world.

For free-fall parachute training, the team would frequently train in Arizona where the weather was consistently sunny and the air traffic was light enough to jump out at high altitudes. The last thing you needed to worry about when jumping out of an aircraft at night, carrying equipment while at high altitudes, was hitting a plane on the way down.

My team had decided that while training out in the desert, we would request to jump out at thirty-three thousand feet and go for the world record for team high-altitude parachute jump. Why not? To our surprise we were approved for the airspace and the air force C-141 crew agreed. We finished our required night training jumps at eighteen thousand feet and twenty-four thousand feet and prepared for the record. The altitude would require hours of prebreathing oxygen to mitigate passing out before you had a chance to pull your rip cord.

As we were loading the bus to go out to the plane, I got a call and was told there was an emergency at home. Hey, I love the thought of being with the team for the big jump, but I love my family more. Konrad, my youngest son, was in the hospital, and I could catch the next commercial flight out in a few hours if I hustled, so I waved good-bye to the C-141 and made the flight home. It turned out that my two young sons were playing in the house on the base while Lola was making breakfast. Konrad was still in a walker with rollers, and Wolf was chasing him down the halls. Somehow a door was slammed with Konrad's finger in the jamb. Lola heard a yelp and peered down the hall to see Konrad squirting blood like a lawn sprinkler. At the same moment the doorbell rang. Lola picked up Konrad and answered the door to find another SEAL officer stopping by to deliver a package. Together they calmly scraped the finger off the doorjamb, placed it in ice, loaded the car, and were off to the hospital in less than five minutes. The mission was accomplished with such minimum time on target that the finger was able to be reattached. I arrived later that night to find the whole family back at the table. Yet another example of how tough navy spouses are. This is one area of being a SEAL that is often overlooked. SEALs are older than many forces within the military. In fact, the average age of a SEAL candidate is twenty-three. As a result, by the time a SEAL qualifies and successfully passes the screening for the most elite assignments he is in his early thirties. Many are not only warriors but husbands and fathers.

The team made the jump, and when they arrived back to the command the word had come down from headquarters that we had been given the green light for key leaders to move forward. This was a good sign and meant that a few of us would go forward on our mission to grab Simić and Todorovic, verify that all the pieces were in place, and then move the team in to conduct the mission. The less time the team has to spend on the ground, the better. It is always better to get in, get the job done, and get out. Before getting on the plane, I briefed the team on the updates on who our targets were and the likely plan of attack. Our preparations were, as always, thorough: we had made ourselves familiar with the various vehicles we might encounter and different scenarios and contingencies of almost every kind. Though we were ready, we knew we'd be doing our own final recon and intelligence operations to solidify and confirm our plans. Intelligence guys are great, but if you can it's better to see the field with your own eyes before committing the force. We divided our mission into phases and went over the top three things that could go wrong with each phase, strategizing how we'd handle any contingencies.

We also rehearsed our movements to the point where our actions would be near automatic. In general, we went through mock-ups of the various settings we anticipated for our mission: we were going to rely on vehicles and associated settings—garages, parking decks, places like that—and we wanted to be comfortable operating in the spaces our intelligence and reconnaissance had confirmed we'd be working in.

Finally, we set up our communications architecture and confirmed we would have good communications throughout the mission and that our supporting assets would be available to support us.

We traveled lean and mean because we knew that while the more equipment and personnel we brought meant the fewer operational risks we'd face, it also meant the larger the signature and more complex the supporting logistics would be and the more opportunities we'd offer prying eyes to compromise our operation security. The bottom line is, if our targets got wind of our being there, they would likely go underground. We struck a balance between required equipment and desired equipment, and if we didn't require it for this mission we did without.

As the commander, I was responsible for ensuring all of this was in place and ensuring the team was properly trained and equipped. I also had to confirm that the contingency plans we had designed were viable and that the additional resources were in place should we need to call on them. I also had to convince the chain of command that the value of the mission was worth the risk. It was an easy sell. Letting these guys off the hook would serve to give notice to every thug in every future conflict that actions against humanity would be forgotten.

I said good-bye to the rest of the team and departed for a safe house outside of Tuzla with the rest of the leadership element. We kept a low profile, as the presence of heavily armed operators with specialized equipment would have put our targets on high alert and made snatching them much riskier, and we wanted our time in Tuzla before the mission to be as short as possible.

Serbian forces and those paid informants who would provide information for a dime were watching the airports, tracking the cargo that was unloaded at the airfield on base. Bringing in a number of "specialists" would have been a tip-off, alerting high-value targets to either go into hiding or beef up their security. In 1997, a team of British Special Air Service commandos had a mission compromised when a PIFWC was tipped off regarding their activities and surrounded himself with guards; we were not going to let that happen to us.

We conducted our final reconnaissance of the targets and confirmed the plan once again. The final Concept of Operations Brief was delivered and sent to the various senior officials for approval and comment. What was perhaps the most challenging was the number of flag officers and commands involved in the approval process. At the bottom of the food chain was my team, who was actually going to do the mission and take all the risk. Within the theater itself, there was the commander of all the tactical units, the commanding general of the Joint Special Operations Command (JSOC), and his boss, the commander of Stabilization Force. Then there was the administrative chain of command back in the States to include Special Operations Command (SOCOM), the chairman of the Joint Chiefs of Staff, all the way up to the Secretary of Defense and the National Command Authority (NCA). Counting the nonmilitary units and other special support units, I was told that the number of personnel supporting our handful of "meat eaters" numbered in the thousands. Unfortunately, the bureaucracy and the accompanying risk-adverse environment has not gotten better over time. The growth within the Department of Defense reflects this trend. Today there are more than 800,000 Department of Defense civilians and somewhere between 1.2 and 1.6 million contractors. There are so many agencies and flag level commands within the Department of Defense that keeping up with a current organizational chart requires, of course, its own division. Despite the layers of bureaucracy and oversight, the PIFWC operations were successful. The team was able to conduct R&S operations and locate our assigned targets. Patterns were revealed, rehearsals were completed, and, ultimately, missions were executed. Careful consideration of possible civilian collateral damage was evaluated and contingency plans put into place.

Standard military vehicles had to be replaced by civilian vehicles to reduce signature. This required the purchasing, licensing, and upgrading of the vehicles for special use. In our case, we used converted VW vans that blended in well but could also hold a small force of SEALs inside. Hundreds of hours of surveillance was conducted until the vehicles did not get a second glance within the small villages. At the time, many of the cars in Bosnia were stolen. There was a whole auto-theft mafia bringing vehicles into the Balkans. Lawlessness was more a rule than an exception. At one point, there was an estimated thirty thousand stolen cars on the roads of Bosnia-Herzegovina and another twenty-five thousand in Kosovo, and those figures were probably low.

Once the decision to execute the mission was made, the operations were tracked from start to finish. An execution checklist was developed and followed to provide a play-by-play. The execution checklist provided all forces a sequential activities map of the operation. Each significant action, such as the departure of a force from home base, is given a code word and an estimated time of completion. When the force completes the task or event, they call in the code word to inform the headquarters and others that the event has been completed so that the mission's progress

PROLOGUE

can be tracked. In the early years of Special Operations, there were just a few code words of major milestones such as force insertion, arrival of the target, actions against the target complete, and force extracted. Like most military operations over time, the execution checklist has evolved into a complex management tool driven by the ability of the headquarters to track and control operations from afar. The first SEAL team operation I did had fewer than ten code words; the last had more than three thousand line items. The execution checklist for the Bosnian PIFWC operations was a small book. There was no doubt, however, that if I needed to talk to somebody I could. The problem was, every flag in the country could talk to me too. There was never a moment where I was not in contact with multiple superiors who were following the operations, as well as the air assets and the medevac. If this sounds a bit like overkill, it was. Taken in the context of Special Operations still recovering from the stinging of the chaos in Somalia portrayed in the book and movie *Black Hawk Down*, I understood. Mitigate the risk and score a win. Coupled with increased innovation and technical advances in communications, the administration and the senior military commanders realized that they not only had the capability to monitor operations, but they now had the tools to actually remotely control ground operations. Small Tactical Operations Centers (TOCs) manned by a handful of staff became Joint Operations Centers (JOC) and eventually grew to Combined Joint Special Operations Task Forces (CJSOTF) with hundreds of staff and support. The point is that most of the military operations could have been executed with a smaller headquarters element, limited supporting assets, and a small and well-trained group of warriors. This is not to say that we should ever go into battle with a smaller force than what is needed to succeed, but supporting a large headquarters and support bureaucracy comes at a cost.

Back to the vans. One might be surprised to know that the vans themselves weren't armored. We had to be very conscious about weight. Even though we'd beefed up the VW engines, the vans were never going to be fast getaway vehicles. The priority was more on other functions.

If we had to get away in a hurry, the vans were accompanied by escort sedans that were much faster and had drivers trained in the art of blocking traffic and removing other threats. In an emergency we could pile into the sedans and scram.

So for protection, instead of armor we used bulletproof blankets. For this operation we weren't anticipating being in a firefight, but if we were we could at least have some protection. An enemy could still shoot through the van's body, but the blankets were better than nothing.

Our highest-value target in Samac was the dirtbag Blagoje Simić, the aforementioned town's mayor. He, his wife, and his two kids lived in an L-shaped apartment complex with a parking lot next to it. Long before we tried to snatch him we began parking one of our yellow vans in the lot: we wanted people to get used to it being there. After a while, we figured it would effectively be a normal part of the parking lot.

But we were also going after Police Chief Stevan Todorovic, and he was the reason for the second van. We knew that if we snatched one target, the word would pass quickly and would jeopardize the chances of grabbing the second. Up to this point, the United States had not broadcast our intent of bringing PIFWCs to justice. Grabbing the first one would make the others nervous and likely lead to them changing their patterns. We decided to try to take them both at the same time. I was with the crew assigned to take Simić, and the simultaneous operations complicated the task, so timing would have to be impeccable at the site where we would take the Police Chief Todorovic.

Parking our van in Simić's lot gave us the additional benefit of tracking his comings and goings. We used the van's cameras to monitor him, with the images captured on VCR tapes, as digital imaging was still in its infancy. Of course, we were cutting edge then: not long before, surveillance was done with 16mm movie cameras or 35mm still cameras, and the film had to be developed on-site, a function that added a level of gear needed by special ops.

Speaking of film, I have a story that illustrates a theme I'm going to come back to: the idea that operations are best coordinated, and tactical decisions are best made, by forces on the ground and not by those drinking coffee in some remote office.

Reports came down that the theater commander along with senior military and intelligence officials were watching one of the many surveillance films when a dog ran across the parking lot where Blagoje Simić lived.

The general stopped the film and asked, "Is that dog neutered or not?" Laughter broke out, but as it turns out, he wasn't kidding. He proceeded to launch into a dissertation about how unneutered dogs have better sensory capabilities than neutered dogs. The reason that it was important, he said, is because we had people in the surveillance vans and a dog might smell them and go over to the vans, thereby compromising our operatives' position. Fair enough.

A senior Special Operations general muttered outside of the previous general's earshot, "He might be able to smell them . . . and then again a beanstalk might grow out of his ass too." Although the comment was true, it did not matter. We now had a new mission before we could launch: determine whether the dog in question had balls or not.

As ridiculous as the task was, it was a requirement that had to be answered before we got the green light to conduct the mission. In effect, taking out two of the worst war criminals in the entire Bosnian conflict came down to a dog's balls. The easiest thing to do was just go out and conduct a shoot-and-recover operation of the dog in question. Now, if we had done that where we were doing our stakeouts, a number of things might have happened, none of which would have been good for the mission. We might have blown our cover, the dog we were aiming at might be injured without being killed and attract a lot of attention, we might have had to leave our station to look for the dog . . . and even if we did shoot a few dogs around the van, there were always going to be more dogs. We discussed the problem set with our Operational Support Team and the OGA experts.

The team conducted a complete mission analysis to include identifying similar sized villages, ethnic preferences, and even statistical comparisons of neutered versus unneutered dogs. At the end of the day, it was decided that we would conduct dog comparison operations in a nearby village to determine a statistical probability. The team should have gotten a medal just for dog-catcher duties alone. After expending untold resources, they gave a detailed analysis and conclusion that the probability of the dog being neutered was low to none. Case solved. We diligently forwarded the full report, including pictures, up the chain of command. I would have liked to have been the one to brief the theater commander on the results.

I'm not going to say that this little side excursion had no effect. It did. It slowed down the operation because we were out hunting dogs rather than war criminals.

This sort of thing happens more frequently in the military than one would think. A few years later when I was in Iraq, I got a call from the senior flag intelligence officer who had a "hot" priority tasking. She had set herself up in a little intelligence factory called Camp Victory in Saddam's palace in Baghdad International Airport (BIAP). The typical role of army intelligence is to provide analysis and intelligence support based on the operational commander's requirements. Using data derived from both signal and human intelligence sources, the intelligence professionals collect, analyze, and disseminate the collection cycle to those who request it.

But she had higher aspirations and wanted to be the commander and act on potential targets herself. When I met her at Camp Victory I could not help being amazed at the rows and rows of desks filled by uniformed support staff. Collectively, I am sure they outnumbered the active insurgents. She handed me some maps and satellite images and said, "We have a hot lead on a priority target. I want you to do a recon on this STAT. We believe it's a military training site and housing for anti-coalition forces, and we're going to hit it. I want you to take a reconnaissance team in there and report back to me." Since she had three stars and I had three stripes, I said, "Yes, ma'am," and returned to the FOB.

She was pushing for an AC-130 attack. Now, that's some pretty serious air-to-ground firepower. The AC-130 carries a 105mm howitzer and a 20mm cannon. It's like having an entire war chest on a single set of wings. You don't bring it out for a milk run.

I took her material back to our intelligence guys. When I put the map she'd given me up on an overhead projector, a sergeant major who'd been on the ground for a while took one look and started laughing.

"You know what that is?" he asked. "That's Abu Ghraib. That's our facility." I called her back and let her know. She never asked me to come over again.

Back to Bosnia. We continued our surveillance, uninterrupted by dogs, neutered or otherwise. By February 1998, we were ready to move against Simić and Todorovic. We'd done our research, so we knew of at least one potential complication. The apartment complex the mayor lived in had a glass atrium on the first floor that he walked through every day. The glass allowed him to see the parking lot, and of course if we were out of position, or if we had any sort of giveaway, he'd know immediately we were there.

Through our surveillance, we learned of another complication: Samac's chief of police lived in the same apartment complex. He would leave his apartment and come down the stairs every morning between 7:00 and 7:15—armed of course. Our target—Mayor Simić—would usually leave half an hour or so later.

Unfortunately, we were only interested in Simić. I say "unfortunately" because reading the reports revealed numerous persons sponsoring and doing soul-wrenching evil, persistent perpetrators of heinous acts that no reasonable human being with power to prevent would stand by and simply allow. But you can't do everything at once, however much you'd like to. When we finally made our move against Simić, we were going to have to be sure the police chief had already left. We didn't want to have to shoot him. And, of course, we didn't want Simić's children to be with him if we could avoid it.

We planned our snatching operation with several factors in mind. One was that Mayor Simić was fairly heavy, and another was that he was rarely armed. We knew he wasn't going to try to shoot his way out of a kidnapping, and we also knew that we could easily outrun him if he tried to flee. The plan was to position the van about twenty yards from him, open the door, and then sprint to him and scoop him up, hoping that shock would prevent him from doing much.

The building layout at the other site made that operation trickier. Chief Todorovic lived in a Y-shaped high-rise apartment complex right at the intersection of two major streets, both of which had to be covered. The good news—for us, at least—was that Todorovic parked his car in the area every day. The bad news was that he was known to be armed, which meant that the operation had to be extremely fast, as we did not want a gunfight in the streets.

Todorovic's pattern of parking in the same place every day was his undoing. On the night before we were to take both men, we had several vehicles in his neighborhood. We waited until the owner of one of the cars next to Todorovic's moved out, and then we drove a "bookmark" car—a sedan—into the spot, so we could control access next to Todorovic's vehicle.

On the morning of the operation, we moved the bookmark car out and our van in. The van was positioned so its side door was opposite the driver's side of Todorovic's car. We had a small assault team waiting in the van.

Todorovic traveled with his family—his wife and child—and there was no way around taking him in front of them. But we wanted them to be out of harm's way when we took him. Every day he would open the door for them, get them in the car, and then walk over to the driver's side and let himself in.

On the morning of Todorovic's snatching, we planned to wait until he had put his family inside the car and crossed over to the driver's side. When he was focused on inserting his keys, we would open the van door and pull him inside.

We were watching the video monitors from the surveillance van. Since we had support of satellites and our people on the perimeter, we had a good idea what and who was in the vicinity. We could see whether approaching vehicles might give cover to our men. The goal was to pull off a snatch that would be invisible to civilians. If need be, we could give the "no-go" code based on whether there was any threat around or approaching the area of operation.

There wasn't. As Todorovic stood fumbling with his keys, the team opened the door to the van. He attempted to run but didn't make it more than a few steps before being thrown to the ground and quickly packed into the van. The operation that took more than a year to plan was over in a matter of seconds. Our other vehicles stationed in the area pulled out and escorted the team out of town, where it was met by a helicopter that flew Todorovic to the base in Tuzla. He was on an airplane to the International Criminal Tribunal for the former Yugoslavia (ICTY), a United Nations–run court in The Hague, the Netherlands, within hours.

Back at Mayor Simić's apartment, we ran into a roadblock. We knew that once one of our targets was grabbed, we had to take the other fast, because calls would go out to all high-level potential targets and they'd immediately take additional security precautions. We saw the police chief come down . . . and then nothing. We waited for Mayor Simić, but he didn't come down. He might have been tipped off, he might have been sick, or there might have been a change in his routine.

Ultimately, the reason doesn't matter. What was important was that once we took Todorovic, there would be additional Bosnian eyes around Simić's apartment, and we couldn't risk having our cover blown. We waited for about fifteen minutes after Todorovic was taken and then quietly left and returned to Tuzla.

Our mission had been a great success. We had grabbed one high-level target, and none of our operatives had been compromised. We knew we had the option of returning once things calmed down, because our cover hadn't been blown. As it happened, we didn't have to go back for Simić: he later turned himself in to the ICTY in 2001. He was released in 2011.

We waited in theater to see whether there were any follow-up missions we could run. We were there on a standby basis, and then our rotation was over. Just another three months at the office. Oh, and one more note: Todorovic served two-thirds of a ten-year sentence for war crimes including torture and denial of equal rights for non-Serbian citizens, was released, and fatally shot himself in 2006.

So be it.

ONE

AL-SADR'S BOOKKEEPER

SERVICE TO COUNTRY.

I love the sound of those words. We all serve: not just the heroic men and women in uniform but each and every one of us. We do it by caring for our families, our friends, our coworkers, our neighbors, our America.

Those three simple words mean that ideas you cherish, people you love and admire, hopes you harbor, and values you respect can all live and thrive in a safe, free environment. It means that the honest industry of any citizen has a place to grow; and, growing, can benefit the country and the world.

I love the sound of the following words, too, and they've served me well in more than a half century of life: "Those who don't know history are destined to repeat it."[1] They were written by an eighteenth-century Irish statesman named Edmund Burke, and I can tell you firsthand that truer words were never written. I've seen that in action during twenty-three years of active military service here at home and also in the tortured landscape of the Middle East.

Yet there is a flip side to what Burke wrote: those who do know history can learn from the mistakes and triumphs of those who came before.

Case in point.

In 1987—shortly after I'd been assigned to SEAL Team One in Coronado, California—I saw the movie *The Untouchables*, which starred Kevin Costner as Prohibition-era treasury agent Eliot Ness. What an

1

inspiration: talk about a special operations team, a bunch of G-men working on their own against one of the most powerful criminal enterprises in American history. Ness's assignment was to bring down crime kingpin Al Capone, but the bootlegger-extortionist-murderer was too smart to be caught with blood on his hands. So the government agents took another tack to get him: they dove into his shady accounting practices.

That's right: one of the most notorious thugs ever to walk the streets of Chicago was put away for tax evasion and sentenced to an unprecedented eleven years for this white-collar crime. Capone literally lost his mind while incarcerated.

Justice served.

Capone has a moral counterpart in Iraq, a so-called cleric by the name of Muqtada al-Sadr. I say "so-called" because he's the kind of religious figure who makes a mockery of the word "religious" by spreading hate as well as lies like "The United States is targeting Islam, the Muslim and Arab states in the Middle East and beyond. It wants to control the world." That statement is as ignorant as it is inflammatory since we can't control our own deficit, let alone the world.

But back to Capone and Sadr.

By 2004, the hot-tempered, black-garbed Iraqi was certainly capable of causing a lot of trouble, and he did. Unfortunately, we couldn't find him. Intelligence indicated that he was frequently in Iran, which was going to make him difficult to spot and take out. Iran was known to be pumping weapons, explosives, and training to the Shia anti-coalition forces. It was clear even in 2004 that Iran wanted to re-create Persia and expand its brand of Islamic terrorism. Iranian explosives used to make improvised explosive devices (IEDs) and other tools of terrorism were responsible for at least five hundred US deaths. Make no mistake, Iran is the enemy of liberty and our values, and no agreement or settlement with evil will deter Iran from continuing its global jihad of killing the American infidels.

Sadr was Iran's chief surrogate and operations officer in Iraq. While we could not find him through informants and methodical intelligence collection, we did find his accountant—whose name we will leave blank, given current conditions in Iraq—in Najaf, one of the more religious cities in Iraq, in the southern part near al-Hillah.

And accounting practices offered a vulnerability into Sadr's operations, just as was the case with Capone in the 1920s.

Our hope was that, like any good accountant, Sadr's man would have with him the Sadr files that would detail Sadr's organizational network of terrorism. If we could get our hands on his books, the chances would be good that we could follow the money trail and bring down his whole organization. Even criminals like to know where their money is and how it is being spent. We were hoping he had a good accountant who liked to know too. Thus, we began to run surveillance on the accountant, employing tactics we had successfully used before.

When, after several weeks of observation, we had a tangled profile of the man, we assessed what force package was necessary and how much support would be needed. We were pretty confident that he kept his books at his house, which would mean a compound raid. A SEAL task unit from Camp Posey, a small SEAL camp base at Baghdad International Airport (BIAP), was picked for the mission. They had been in country for nearly six months and by this time had conducted hundreds of combat operations. They also had a detachment of Polish GROM (Poland's elite counterterrorism unit) with them and the first ever Marine Special Operations Force. They were well led and ready for another mark on the wall.

The first time I was introduced to the GROM was when I was still attached to the Naval Headquarters in London. As the NATO naval commander, the US Navy would host and coordinate a naval exercise called Baltic Operation, or BALTOPS for short, that included the participation of our European allies. In 1994, BALTOPS would include a new participant, Russia. The Berlin Wall had come down a few years earlier, and grand ideas of an integrated Europe gave promise to greater cooperation and peace. As the unconventional warfare officer, I decided to be unconventional and pitch the idea of a SEAL platoon rendezvousing with a Russian warship at sea by parachute. The proposal was simple: simply give the location and time to the Russians, and we would drop the SEALs and boats out the back of a C-130 and hitch a ride with them into the Polish port of Gdańsk. No problem. To my utter amazement, my plan was approved. Be careful what you ask for.

We gave the Russians the radio frequencies, the time and coordinates, and a description of how to position their small craft for personal recovery at sea. They acknowledged receiving the plan with only one comment—a request for personnel and equipment manifests. The equipment was not an issue as we weren't going to bring any new toys with us, but the manifest was problematic. We decided to provide them a generic list by giving positions rather than names and see what would happen. They once again acknowledged receipt and made no comment. On the morning of the at-sea rendezvous, we confirmed that the Russians were still going to play ball and loaded the C-130 bound to drop us off in the middle of the Baltic Sea. I was handed the name of the Russian frigate, the *Neustrashimy*, and a distress beacon should they decide not to let us board. After a couple of hours in the air, the back ramp was lowered and we prepared to jump. A small Zodiac boat filled with gear and with its own larger parachute attached would go first, and we would immediately follow. We made a low pass to confirm the *Neustrashimy* and her boats were lined up per our instructions. I could see her below exactly as planned, but we could not reach her on the radio frequency assigned. We made another pass without communications, and I made the decision to go. We had made it this far, and now was not the time to retreat. We climbed to 1,250 feet and exited the C-130. When you jump out of a plane over water you focus on three things: pulling your rip cord so you don't die, steering for the boat so you don't get lost, and making sure your fins are on and ready so you don't drown. Before you hit the water, it's best to be ready to cut your parachute away, so if the surface winds kick up you don't get dragged away. Even a SEAL can find his way to Davy Jones's locker by being dragged or pulled under by a parachute at sea.

The splash into the Baltic Sea was refreshing, and getting the platoon organized and onto the small boats was uneventful. We easily motored over to the accommodation ladder alongside the Russian frigate and climbed aboard. The captain and a man dressed in a polo shirt, khaki pants, and Top-Siders were at the top of the ladder waiting to greet me. I asked for permission to come aboard. My request was answered by that man standing on deck wearing the khaki pants, Top-Siders, and a polo shirt. He looked and dressed exactly the way I used to while assigned to my previous command. He greeted me by name and knew exactly who I was and where I came from. This was my first introduction to Petoskey, the man who protected Lech Walesa during Poland's solidarity and was one of the hardest men I ever met. He was at least sixty-five and still chiseled like a rock. His forearms reminded me of Popeye the Sailor Man. I would not mess with him. My instincts were right, as I later found out he also led the Ministry of Interior's successful Russian mafia eradication program in Warsaw. He was tough and introduced me and arranged a meeting with his favorite unit, the Polish GROM. They operated out of an old German U-boat facility outside of Gdańsk. While their equipment was Russian hand-me-downs, there was little doubt they were tough and hungry to be a premier fighting force. They would not have to wait too long. To this day, I don't know how he knew who I was, but the fact that he did know deserved my respect.

Back to the accountant.

Unlike *The Untouchables*, we would take the accountant *and* his family.

First, though, some context.

"FIND ME SADR."

While we were in Fallujah, I would hear this, or something very much like it, almost every day from General Ricardo Sanchez. I'm pretty damn certain that Sanchez would have strangled Sadr with his bare hands if he'd had a chance.

Muqtada al-Sadr is a prominent Shia leader, and at the time, the different militias that were forming around us were also Shia. The Shias were the ones who had borne the brunt of abuse from the Sunni majority—the group from which Saddam Hussein had pulled the members of his ruling Ba'athist party. Incidentally, *Ba'athist* means "renaissance" in Arabic, and when the party was first founded in the early 1950s, its stated goal was "unity."

To which I say: "Bull."

Once we toppled Saddam, the Shias were looking for big-time retribution after several decades of often brutal Ba'athist repression, which compounded the ever-present internecine family disputes and clashes over property. As a result, there were regional conflicts based on religion, politics, and ancient blood feuds, and we were (and still are) in the middle of it.

Incidentally, it was with a snickering reference to Muqtada al-Sadr on his lips, on the scaffold, that Saddam Hussein died.

At the time the Shias had pushed the Sunnis west, into the desert, into Ramadi, and into the Anbar Province. (Many of those refugees are still there, by the way; only now we have another name for them: ISIS.) The Shias themselves were consolidating their power in Karbala, Najaf, Hillah, and Baghdad—central and southern Iraq—and the Kurds were solidifying their strongholds in the north. Iraq was and is a mess, and it's dangerous to think of any specific Shia or Sunni faction as being our friends, even if we continue to work with individuals from that failed nation. The Iraqi Kurds are another matter: they're generally aligned with Western values and for the most part bravely challenge the barbarians who are trying to destroy us and them. They are deserving of our help and our arms, and what we have given them most recently is lip service and limited support administered through the Shia-controlled government. Vehicle and material support intended for Kurdish forces gets redirected and sold before it ever reaches the front lines. We know it, they know it, and our enemies know it.

Back to Muqtada al-Sadr. His militias were primarily made up of local thugs and anti-coalition insurgents funded by a number of sources, including the siphoning off of US government contracts and the dangerously theocratic Iran to gain influence and control. I bring that up because Sadr and his principle minions were spending a lot of time in Iran. He would come into Iraq, talk to key people, and then leave for the safety of his adopted Shia home. We couldn't establish a pattern regarding where he would be.

But Sadr was a strategic guy, a big-picture guy, which meant he depended on an operational staff to handle day-to-day matters. Terrorists and insurgents rely on money to complete their missions, and someone has to collect, distribute, and track funds, just as with any other organization. We figured that if we could get a sense as to how the money flowed, we could gain a lot of insight into Sadr's operations and how to disrupt them.

General Sanchez was our own big-picture guy, and the Iraqis knew it. They targeted him, and at one point SEALs served as his personal security detail. There was a week in which convoys Sanchez traveled in had been hit a couple of times with IEDs. At the daily Battle Update Brief, or BUD, his chief of staff, whom I had known in Kosovo, came up and asked for our help. He had just returned from the Green Zone and had narrowly escaped death by another IED. He was pale and clearly shaken.

As it so happened, a couple of my former team members were passing through. Both had experience in Personal Security Detachment missions dating back to protecting Admiral Boorda in the early '90s. They were pros. I asked them to kick the tires on the general's security team and give me their thoughts.

They came back to me with a disturbing report: "Sanchez is going to die," they said in a serious but matter-of-fact tone. Sanchez's security detail lacked the right training and had internal leadership issues, they discovered. Half the time they didn't even do route assessments or have the general's schedule. They would take Sanchez along the same route in the same vehicles when he shuttled back and forth along the eight-mile road between Baghdad International Airport and the Green Zone.

Often their only defense was an electronic squawker that was designed to disrupt an electronic firing device. There was little doubt that Sanchez's movement and routes were being watched, and it was only a matter of time before the enemy would get him. Sanchez's security team did not know what they did not know and did not have the right training considering the task before them. They were not bad soldiers; they just had no idea what they were doing. They were tasked with protecting the theater commander against a determined enemy, and it was only by luck and God's grace that Sanchez was still alive.

I informed Sanchez's chief of staff that the problems were serious enough that a "tweak" would not be adequate to the task. I recommended that Sanchez's security detail be taken offline for training and some changes in leadership. And then I made a mistake: I offered up a SEAL platoon to temporarily fill the gap until his assigned team was ready. A new rotation of SEALs had just arrived in theater and could be assigned to the task. As luck would have it, it was led by the same hero who had saved my son's finger years before. While his team was not typically tasked with PSD missions, I knew they would excel at the assignment. That is both the curse and the blessing of the SEALs and, for that matter, all Special Operations Forces. The blessing is they are extraordinarily talented, highly trained, and motivated. The curse is that their success has made them the force of choice for almost every mission and the solution for almost every problem. Give them a task and they will find out how to do it better.

In this case, the chief of staff readily accepted and never gave the SEAL detail back. After his assigned security guys were trained and ready to go, Sanchez said, "Hell no." I don't blame him. I would have wanted SEALs around me too!

I'm biased, of course. I knew the SEALs would keep Sanchez alive and would excel at this or any other task. You must always keep something in mind: SEALs look at the enemy's mission (to take us out) as if it were their own in order to determine how to defeat it. In this case, bad guys wanted to kill Sanchez, so a SEAL would think, *If I were the bad guy*

I would do it like X, Y, or Z; so I will devise a plan to defend/defeat all of the above. And once Sanchez's regular security force was ready to return to work, you could argue that there were better uses for those SEALs. But Sanchez was a four-star general and he wanted to live. He told me I could not have that detail back. Rank has its privileges.

Now, I actually wasn't reporting directly to Sanchez: my immediate superior for day-to-day operations was the Combined Joint Special Operations Task Force Commander, Colonel Mike Repass. Repass was the Special Force 10th Group Commander and a great American, dedicated, hardworking, and loyal to his men. Aside from conducting as many as twenty operations a night, he also had the challenge of keeping all of his bosses happy. He reported directly to Sanchez as the theater commander but also took direction from the theater Special Operations commanding general. There were also the generals commanding every Multinational Division sector. Keeping them happy was important. Then there was the plethora of home-front generals within the army and Special Operations Command structure. All of them would come into theater and offer either advice or direction or both. Repass was one of only a few Special Forces group commanders and no doubt would be looked at for flag officer. I don't think it drove every decision he made, but he was a man being pulled in a lot of different directions. I did not have any illusions of being a four-star admiral and had less of an issue trying to satisfy a thousand masters. The one person I did pay attention to was General Sanchez. He said he wanted Sadr and anything that we did to get him was pretty much a go.

So, back to the accountant.

The mission to snatch our guy—we'll call him Mahomed—was a classic planned, as opposed to an in extremis, somewhat improvised operation. A planned operation doesn't have the urgency of running out the door to conduct an in extremis operation. The mission is defined, the time is determined, and the probable outcome is a calculated risk, given the right force is assigned to the task. When a mission is deemed "in extremis," it means someone has determined that not doing the operation *now* would result in greater risk of harm, significant damage, or death. In an in extremis mission, you rely heavily on inherent skill, innovation, and leadership to win.

With a planned operation, there's more of a calculation of value versus expenditures. Intelligence and situation drive options for mission planning and force composition. Commanders make judgment calls regarding the type and amount of resources, supporting assets, and appropriate rules of engagement. Commanders coordinate and develop the plan of attack and what the likely payoff will be of each option. There is always tension between those who want to continue gathering intelligence and those who want to strike when the iron is hot. I have been in arguments with senior intelligence officers over when is the right time to hit the target or destroy the enemy. When you find the location of your target, do you strike now or monitor for a while in an attempt to identify additional associates? All operations have risk. The art is to mitigate risk as much as you can while striking as soon as you can. A well-planned strike early is better than a perfectly planned strike too late.

Believe it or not, that transition from intelligence gathering to making the decision to engage is the toughest part of any undertaking. It's when the rubber hits the road, when you don't get any do-overs, when many lives and limbs are on the line. You can't—and don't—think about how it will impact your life or career or the war or the nation. It's like a clock has started running and there's nothing you can do, nothing to focus on, other than to run with it. Worse, unlike as it was with the drills, adrenaline is really flowing during the mission, coloring everything, adding variables to your own actions and to the actions of your warriors. Whether the operation is planned or in extremis, there is nothing so frightening, and at the same time so thrilling, as the "execute" order.

I should also mention that there are other considerations, albeit lesser ones, that factor into any operation. Between Mahomed the accountant's work and the role of a commander, there's actually a lot of financial calculation that goes into intelligence work. Everything has a price tag that has to be justified and evaluated. Our accounting has to factor in intangibles. For example, given the cost of a mission, what is the net good one operation might yield over allocating those resources to another? We actually have to ascribe a value to that. In this case, given that taking the accountant would not only get us closer to Sadr personally but would offer a significant disruption to his field operations, our calculus made the mission a top priority.

Often, too, those calculations contain a strictly humane element. Collateral lives matter. We decided to take Mahomed's immediate family when we snatched him. Doing so offered two benefits. First, yes, we would be able to question his wife and corroborate Mahomed's information against what she said, so we could establish a baseline for Mahomed's truthfulness. Typically in Iraq, the wife ran the home and would have knowledge of at least who visited and when. We could ask about simple stuff ("Have you ever seen this person?" "No." "That's not what your wife said.") and corroborate some of his information that way.

But second—and this was important to obtaining and holding Mahomed's goodwill—we would be able to provide safety for his family and leverage if needed. There was a pretty strong possibility that if we didn't take them, Sadr's men would, and they wouldn't hesitate to hold them as a bargaining tool or worse. That meant they would possibly die, likely by a single gunshot to the back of the head.[2] Even with the decision to take both the accountant and his family, we had an ugly calculation to make. Mahomed lived on the outskirts of Najaf in a small compound house that had multiple windows on the second story. The logistics of doing a multi-member grab complicated the task, and we would have to make sure the risk of extending the time on target was mitigated by precision and perfect execution. We just hoped that Sadr's network of armed militia took the night off.

The SEALs at Camp Posey were given the green light along with selected members from the Army Special Forces. Just as we did when we took down Todorovic, patterns were established, go/no-go criteria were set, and rules of engagement were reviewed. This time the on-scene SEAL commander was given more latitude as the sheer volume of operations being conducted by Special Operations Forces exceeded the ability of the top brass to micromanage any single event. In the preceding month alone, we were averaging more than a dozen missions a night. The pace was to pick up soon.

On the day of the actual grab, the team left their base at Baghdad International Airport and headed about eighty miles south to a location between Karbala and Hillah. The forward surveillance teams kept an eye on the target and local militia hangouts for any indication of armed activity. I continued on to our Forward Operating Base near Hillah to coordinate any additional Quick Reaction Forces or support if needed. In this business, you never know and it is always best to be prepared for the worst. Once everything was set, the team waited for nightfall, as the plan called for a midnight raid. From Hillah, we readied the Quick Reaction Force and moved them to within minutes of responding. If we had to fight our way in, we did not want to fight far.

The location of the house gave us confidence that a vehicular Quick Reaction Force would be tactically better than one coming from helicopters. We were going into what was basically a bedroom community, and rotary wing support would give the operation a bigger signature, which is basically a fancy way of saying choppers are noisy as all get-out and we'd wake everyone in the neighborhood up, to say nothing of alerting our potential targets. We had helicopters in the area already in the air for support if we needed them.

The SEAL plan called for a Humvee convoy to bring the force to the target to carry out the operation. Mahomed lived on the edge of town in a compound with a courtyard, which meant traffic would be at a minimum outside his door: no problem pulling right up there. The specially designed Humvees had a winch on the heavy bumper that could be used either to pull a gate open or act as a battering ram and drive through it. The team were experts in explosive and manual breaching techniques, so they were going to get into the compound and house one way or another. Even the roads—both coming and going—had an intelligence threat component: snipers and observers were known to hide themselves on rooftops, and we weren't going to take any routes that had a recent history of firefights above or on the ground.

IEDs were always a concern along the route when entering the vicinity of a high-value target. IEDs were easy enough for the anti-coalition forces to lay out but difficult for our forces to detect. Even with aerial support and constant patrolling along the main routes, cars packed with explosives parked along the road or even suicide drivers looking for military convoys to ram were all too common.

It was not uncommon for the lead vehicle conducting compound raids to drive past the house. When hearts are beating fast and adrenaline is rushing, the houses and gates in the tight quarters of the neighborhoods go by pretty fast. In this case, when the convoy reached Mahomed's gates, they drove past it a few yards. No matter, they had rehearsed for that contingency and entered the compound as if it were planned.

The gate and house were quickly breached, and the compound was secured. Within minutes the operators had secured all floors, separated and secured family members, and identified Mahomed, and most of all, the treasure trove of books. Everything was tagged and bagged: they were looking for anything that might prove useful or informative, such as computers, printed records, weapons, and the like. They even went through the vehicles in the compound, from trunks to glove compartments with all stops in between. With every item found, the SEALs recorded what it was and where they found it and affixed reference tags.

The accounted, selected members of his family and his books and computers were loaded into the waiting vehicles outside. The Quick Reaction Force closed in and prepared to ensure the route out was secure should the militias be alerted.

The team had finished the sensitive site exploitation (SSE) sweep and was off the target in less than an hour, hardly long enough for the local militias to be notified and react with any organized opposition. No need for medevac, no need for additional firepower—and we had plenty at the ready, including an AC-130 gunship from the air force's Special Operations Wing that was on standby to assist with ground attacks all the way from the target to home base. We did not want to have to detour through the city of Karbala if we were attacked: it would have been another *Black Hawk Down* scenario trying to move through roused local fighters eager to have a shot at Americans.

We got lucky, and the team's ride back was smooth. The "precious cargo" was met immediately by interpreters and interrogators and hustled into our temporary detention facility. It was important to sort through relationships and get statements during the initial confusion. Separate, isolate, and interrogate. Just a few hours before they were safely tucked away within the walls of their compound, and now their lives had been changed forever.

Mohamed, who had consumed so much of our time and energy, was a confused little man, the sort you might walk by on the street and never give a second look to. He was neither aggressive nor notable in any way. He appeared to speak little English, but he understood enough to know what we wanted. He also knew what the book contained and the danger that he now faced. I don't know whether he thought of us as more of a threat than Sadr; it did not really matter. He had absolutely no training in being a terrorist—he couldn't fight, and he didn't offer any resistance whatsoever. The one concern he had wasn't any grand ideal: it was for his family, especially his children. Between his kids and the rest of his extended family still in Najaf, he knew they were all vulnerable.

We let him know—and this was the truth—that we had left a surveillance team in his neighborhood to keep an eye on things. Of course we did: not only did we want to keep them safe, which would keep Mahomed happy, but we wanted to monitor who came to Mahomed's house after the news about his abduction got out.

Mahomed may not have been much good as a terrorist, but he was an excellent accountant. Once we got through the initial interview—the one in which we determined that he couldn't point to Sadr's immediate whereabouts—we started to delve into what he could tell us about Sadr's operations.

I may as well confess here and now that those are the situations where you want to have the freedom to interrogate your prisoner using any method possible. I know it's wrong; I know it's probably immoral; I know all of that. But there's that calculus again: when you weigh the cruel discomfort of one individual versus the benefits of saving lives, the morality gets shady. Real shady, real fast.

Still, we were restrained throughout. Quiet, even. We didn't get a location for the head man, but we got something almost as good: a fairly in-depth look at the signal intelligence and communication intelligence.

We snatched the accountant on a Thursday: by Monday, we knew everything he did. We had a much better sense of who was connected to whom and how and where money was coming from and going to. In the end, there was no need to use any enhanced interrogation at all. He couldn't give us anything time sensitive that would require immediate action, and he wasn't holding back what he did know.

Here's something I learned, though.

Political scientist Hannah Arendt coined the phrase "the banality of evil" to reference rank-and-file Nazis—the eager little bureaucrats who weren't grand theorists but who shuffled their papers and filled out columns in ledgers that, miles away, meant death for innocent people.

That was our Mahomed. He gathered money and recorded transactions—mostly from Iranian sources—and kept meticulous records of every transaction. He also provided payments to fund the materials the operational terrorists needed, such as bomb-making equipment, small arms, rocket-propelled grenades, things like that. It is likely that even Sadr didn't know what this money was buying a lot of the time either: the way insurgency cells work is that low-level commanders are given a lot of latitude regarding their operations.

This is exactly why we talk about being in a different sort of war. In a conventional fight, combatants are uniformed and identifiable and follow a rigid chain of command from the top. But combatants in terrorist cells are embedded in the population. Some have day jobs—even the combatants. A terrorist network consists of more than those who pull the trigger or strap themselves in explosive vests. A network also consists of those who turn a blind eye to violence, provide early warning, or deliver logistics support. In the case of the recent bombings in Brussels, a network provided safe haven by renting an apartment, or in the case of San Bernardino a neighbor provided guns and ammunition. Unless you catch them with an IED in their backpack, there's no way of telling them from anyone else, and we didn't have the assets to look at every street corner, every bazaar, every market and determine who was who.

But we did have some terrific accounting records, and they proved to be the Rosetta stone for identifying and connecting the dots of the terrorist network. We knew who was getting money and how much. Knowing how much gave us a sense of the recipient's role in the insurgency: the greater the payment, the greater the amount of activity and damage the recipient was being counted on to do.

The entry that was notably absent in Mohamed's books was payments for the families of jihadi bombers who had committed suicide. These payments were probably made through the local mullahs or imans. All I know is Mohamed didn't track them, unless he was hiding them under "Administrative Expenses."

It didn't take Sadr's people long to find out that we had Mohamed, and of course they figured out what he was telling us. We had this confirmed because in 2004, just after we grabbed Mohamed, insurgent activity around Karbala and the rest of the Shia-held territory went from moderate to off the Richter scale. It was as if everyone who had been compromised wanted to empty the gas tanks before they were targeted. Karbala basically exploded. Sadr City, which is right near Baghdad, exploded. The number of IEDs placed in roads and the number of direct assaults on our patrols skyrocketed. Areas that had been relatively safe to patrol became dangerous.

What was also disturbing was that all that activity led to an increase in recruitment for the insurgents. It was as if the surge in terrorist activities initiated by Sadr's forces was seen as victories, or at least building momentum. We've seen the same dynamic with ISIS: it's a lot easier for ISIS to recruit new dupes when there's a lot of activity. That is one lesson learned in fighting in the Middle East: local forces follow momentum and momentum is difficult to turn.

I was back in Baghdad when Sadr's forces initiated the eruption of violence. We still had roughly half the deck of cards' worth of targets to catch along with other high-value individuals, and we were constantly rebuilding our intelligence network and looking for weapons of mass destruction.

The primary ground forces under the Combined Joint Special Operations Task Force, Arabian Peninsula, consisted of a Special Forces Battalion that had Forward Operating Bases throughout Iraq; a couple of smaller SEAL Task Units, one in northern Iraq and one based in Baghdad International Airport (BIAP); the Polish GROM; and the first US Marine Corps Special Operations Detachment. We also had a company of soldiers from the 10th Mountain Division as security manning the compound. On multiple occasions, they kept the bad guys from penetrating the perimeter defenses and no doubt saved my life. The air support was from a mixed bag of talent from a number of commands that provided helicopter, gunship, signal intelligence, and special mission support, and even the Navy's Black Hawk squadron that cut their teeth in successful desert operations. Combined with the assigned foreign forces and support staff, the force was about thirty-five hundred personnel with capability unequalled in modern warfare. Even with that force at hand, we were not prepared for the wave of violence that spread across Iraq because of the insurgent rise. While the reasons can be debated, there is no debate that the rapidness and scale on which it occurred caught us off guard. Even though Sadr and his Iranian-supported militia were Shia, it became clear quickly that ground zero was in a city at the heart of Sunni territory—Fallujah. As fate would have it, I was assigned to deploy to our FOB in Fallujah just when the fuse was lit.

And let me tell you, that city exploded when the insurgency started.

TWO

FALLUJAH: A WAREHOUSE
OF DEATH

FALLUJAH REPRESENTED A SICKENING REALITY ABOUT the Middle East in general and Iraq in particular. It is an ancient city whose long and rich history should have made it a gem in the crown of human achievement. For centuries, the region was the home of one of the greatest seats of Jewish scholarship in history. That's right. From the year 258 until about 1038 it was the home of the Pumbedita Academy. It was a prosperous trading hub, having arisen where the Euphrates River and the Saqlawiyah Canal meet. In fact, the provincial name "Anbar" means "warehouse" in the original Persian tongue. In short, the region started out as a cultural and mercantile apex and was dragged down from there by religious and tribal squabbles—wars and strife that have gone on, basically unabated, for more than a thousand years.

And we were going to go in there and straighten things out? A so-called Arab Spring was going to spread enlightenment through *that* land where people murder one another over nuances in the same basic faith?

The Bush administration had it right on paper: you choke the local wars by choking the funds. If you're going to fight, you fight to crush the local conflicts, then keep the region down by seizing the oil and doling out the funds carefully and with responsible oversight for educational, infrastructure, and humanitarian needs. You don't go in, liberate a people, and tell them, "Okay, now you figure out this millennium-old struggle." Unfortunately, that is what the media compelled us to do. By distorting the ability of the locals to self-govern, by playing up their inherent right to do so, we doomed them to the current hell that is ISIS.

But that still lay in the future. A different hell was playing out a decade before those barbarians coalesced.

Sadr had between five thousand and seven thousand people under him, and when he found out we had snatched his accountant it seemed as though they all decided to conduct insurgency operations. It's the "use it or lose it" philosophy: if we were going to start ripping into his finances and freezing his funds, the fighters might as well earn what was left of their pay.

Fallujah, which was a city of around fifty thousand people at the time, was a major center for Sunni operations. Before we started moving in with force, we dropped a lot of leaflets hinting in general terms about what we were going to do—crush the murderers, only in nicer terms—and advising residents to evacuate. By the time we were ready to move in, we considered anyone left in Fallujah an enemy, although as you'll see in a bit, it wasn't as if we were going through the streets shooting randomly.

I can tell you a story about Fallujah—it's a sad story, and I knew one of the guys involved—and US contractors who were there but who shouldn't have been and who didn't have the equipment or preparation they needed.

Around Fallujah, there were a lot of private contractors who hung up a shingle offering training support to military and law enforcement organizations and quasi-military services like guard duty. There were a lot of different organizations in Iraq at the time. The most well-known of them was Blackwater Security Company.

I knew people at Blackwater. Heck, the company was established by a former SEAL officer—Erik Prince, who was with SEAL Team Eight before he left to found his company. Erik and his company have been verbally attacked, at times viciously, since the cessation of hostilities, mostly for political reasons. The one thing I do know about Erik is that he came from wealth and did not have to join the military. He chose to serve his country by being a SEAL and was respected by the men he served with. What I also know is that if there were not a legitimate need for Blackwater services, they would not have been there. The State Department asked them to do a mission that no one else could do, and it was that same State Department who cut bait and pointed fingers when the violence started to flare. Typical.

I knew some of the other guys at Blackwater too. One of them, Scotty Helvenston, was a former SEAL who had been one of my BUD/S (Basic Underwater Demolition/SEAL) instructors in the late 1980s. Scott was a phenomenal athlete and had competed on the navy's top triathlon teams. His specialty was physical fitness—training, diet, and exercise. His dream was to make an exercise video and set himself up as a fitness guru to the stars. Part of the reason he left the SEAL teams was he was ordered to go to Army Ranger School, and that conflicted with his cross-training program. He was seriously competitive when it came to training.

The basic idea of at least some SEALs going through that program is that Rangers tend to work in larger groups than SEALs and it is important for the different forces within Special Operations to understand each other. I'm all for the idea of having units understand the Tactics, Techniques, and Procedures (TTP) of other units, but I was never an advocate of sending SEALs through Ranger School to get it. SEALs have been through the graduate school of suffering and don't need to be reminded of it.

So Scotty was with Blackwater and had stopped by our headquarters in BIAP to say hello and get any intelligence updates. Even though the Blackwater staff were contractors, we were on the same team and would provide as much information as we could. There is no doubt they were informed about the perils of the Anbar Province, specifically about Fallujah: it wasn't safe, and they were private citizens, not soldiers. To this day, I don't know why they were there on March 31, 2004. Maybe they were conducting their own surveillance or, more likely, just thought they were invincible. So much of Iraq is open nothingness that you feel you can go out into it like Lawrence of freakin' Arabia and just take in the scenery. Without a guy like me shouting in your ear every day, you can become complacent.

The Blackwater guys offered a sad example of what happens when underequipped civilians try to cowboy their way through a war zone. They didn't have a local map reader, they didn't have a shooter, and they didn't have armored vehicles. What they did have was obviousness: they were driving through Fallujah, which is a small city where everyone knows who's driving by the sight of the car. And the Fallujans know who's military and who's not.

At any rate, on that day in late March they were ambushed and Scotty, along with Wesley Batalona, Mike Teague, and Jerry Zovko—three more Blackwater guys—were pulled from their vehicle, beaten to death, and their bodies burned and dragged through the streets of Fallujah in front of cheering crowds. Then all four were hung from a bridge that crosses the Euphrates River.

Photos were taken and distributed to the locals and to the international media. Anytime those latter buzzards can preface a story with, "We warn you, these images are graphic," you can be sure it'll run on the front page or at the top of a broadcast.

It was a sickening development, hardly unpredictable, not without precedent, but a reminder that this is a sick and hateful region of the planet.

As more coalition forces moved into Fallujah and prepared to rustle the city away from the Sunni insurgents, the Marine Expeditionary Camp (MEK) became the headquarters of US military operations in the Anbar Province. That camp was located just outside of Fallujah. You'd cross a highway and then you'd be in this lawless Iraqi city.

In March 2004, Marine Lieutenant General James T. Conway was given control of the Anbar Province. His forces included the 1st Marine Expeditionary Force . . . and me. I had been there only a few days and figured out pretty quickly that there was a lot of miscommunication: a marine battalion commander would pass on reports from his company commanders that the perimeter around Fallujah was secure. Our team that operated a covert safe house and had a network of local informants would report just the opposite. They were reporting what they saw; we were reporting what we knew. The result was confusion.

Regardless of whether the borders were secure or not, inside the city it was utter chaos. Shortly after we took the accountant, I did a low-visibility operation in Fallujah to get "eyes on." The small group included General James N. Mattis, who at the time was a two-star with the Marine First Division. Mattis was a warrior and one of the most impressive commanders I ever met. One day, after the general had proposed a bold strategy to force the insurgents into an industrial "killing zone," I was explaining to him where the positions of our friendly forces were when a marine sergeant grabbed me pretty hard and pushed me.

There must have been a look of anger in my eyes after I recovered (after all, I was indeed thinking to myself, *I'm a SEAL commander and you're shoving me? That's messed up!*), because he immediately piped up with, "They're *shooting* at you, sir."

When I looked at where I had just been standing, I could see I had been exposed to rounds whizzing by. Everyone else carried on with little notice. I just looked at the sergeant and said, "Semper fi." (To this day, every time I meet a marine I say "Semper fi" in reverence.) And by the way: in a combat situation, it's often difficult to know incoming from ricochet. You may get hit by debris carved from the wall or furnishings by a shell—a high-velocity piece of wood, concrete, clay—and for a second or two you aren't sure what has hit you, only that you have been hit. Strange as it may seem, it takes that long for the shock to your flesh to die and the reality to set in. I'd been so focused on giving my report to General Mattis that I had lost my battlefield perspective and had made myself a target. That was the time, the moment, when I first started thinking I was getting too old for this sort of action.

I'll take a moment here and tell you about Mattis, because he's an

American hero. He made a point of being in the thick of things with his troops. Nicknamed "Mad-Dog Mattis" by his men, he was a command warrior in the old George Patton mode. He wasn't an armchair general by any definition of that much-maligned term. If a marine re-upped at a location where he was present, he would personally go to that marine and thank him or her for rejoining. He put a premium on being connected with his men, and I deeply admire that quality. I could literally go on for pages upon pages about Mattis and how influential this man was to me and many others who fought alongside him, but I will limit myself to two quotes that I believe are particularly telling of this man's character. The first is as follows: "The most important six inches on the battlefield is between your ears." Enough said.

The second is a little more subtle and yet every bit as important in my view, particularly for those of us who have returned from war to the civilian world here at home: "For whatever trauma came with service in tough circumstances, we should take what we learned—take our post-traumatic growth—and, like past generations coming home, bring our sharpened strengths to bear, bring our attitude of gratitude to bear. And, most important, we should deny cynicism a role in our view of the world."[1]

For me, the truth behind this quote is crucial to our recovery, both individually and as a society, from the wounds that fifteen years of war have inflicted upon all of us. More on this later.

Mattis's plan for tamping down insurgent activity in Fallujah was brilliant. By mid-2004, civilian noncombatants had for the most part fled Fallujah. The people remaining, we figured, were hostile. Mattis wanted to drop some artillery rounds into some of the insurgents' fortified positions we'd identified and then bring in tanks, do a pivot, and force the insurgents into an industrial area through what he called a pincer move. Once the insurgent fighters were there, Mattis would just blow the hell out of that area, completely mowing down the enemy.

Mattis also knew that the only way to secure stability in the Anbar Province was to empower the Sunni tribes to control their own destiny. The long-standing rivalry between the Sunni and the Shia had been going on for centuries and was not going to end anytime soon. The fall of Saddam Hussein and the creation of a Shia-controlled government created a wedge. The cleansing of Sunni by the Shia from the neighborhoods of Baghdad further drove the wedge into violence. Mattis understood that disenfranchising the Sunni would have grave consequences. While ISIS had yet to be organized, the seeds were sown in Fallujah.

Mattis ran this plan up the line, and the higher brass shot it down.

So Fallujah was this tinderbox of danger and endless challenge. One of those challenges was our schedule and the conditions of those operations. We were running a handful of missions every night. Not all of them were direct actions as dramatic as snatching the accountant, of course: some were surveillance operations, some were security assessments, and some were simply to keep the enemy guessing. We also infiltrated local insurgency organizations by looking at relationships and flipping targeted locals: we might give someone's sister a job, and if that worked well, we could give other family members jobs, money, or a little more freedom than they might have had living in Fallujah. That was the carrot method, which has come to be known as "winning the hearts and minds."

For the stick method, for those who did not already work for us, we might lean on them for information. Maybe you apply pressure by threatening to tell others that his sister got her new job because he was working for us. You don't have to physically manhandle someone to be intimidating; you just have to haul them into a room and know what makes them tick and what they fear. It's not a pretty or politically correct method. It just works and saves lives. A lot of the locals did not want to be presumed to be collaborators, so they tended to show a little cooperation. And once they were on the hook, they were not getting off. Even so, you only had a one-third chance of getting the truth; the rest was "I don't know" or an outright lie. Keeping someone prisoner without cause was not only un-American; in the end it would likely be counterproductive.

Of course, this technique also had the overtones of something out of Gilbert and Sullivan's *The Pirates of Penzance*. In that operetta, orphans were granted a kind of amnesty—so, suddenly, every pirate claimed to be one. In Fallujah, it seemed that everyone we attempted to coerce had a family member who was working for us, which would not have stood well with those family members. And with the size of some of those extended families, it may not have been a lie.

Often we'd start by trying to get one piece of verifiable rudimentary information out of them. If they gave us that, we had them: we'd leverage that one piece of innocuous information into higher-level intel, at least as much as they could give us.

We could even get useful information out of those who tried to game us. Once we determined that they were feeding us misinformation or unreliable information, we would give their intel a lower level of usefulness . . . but we'd still monitor them, because if they got careless with their cell phones and we could track whom they were in contact with, they might inadvertently give us something useful.

My job was not to micromanage the experts on the specific technique or tactic, but rather to identify *who* would be responsible for each operation and what resources they needed to succeed. When the marines or other units needed information on what was happening on the ground, my job was to deliver the results to save American lives. We were the eyes and ears of what was happening in Fallujah.

On occasions, a strange event occurred that broke the ordinary grind of the battle rhythm in the life at the Forward Operating Base within the walls of the MEK in Fallujah.

It was well after midnight and we had just been through another rocket attack a few hours before, a routine occurrence of late. The insurgents knew that the marines had the capability to determine the coordinates of the source of an incoming rocket attack and would respond within minutes with helicopter gunships or directed fire. Their counter to this would be that they would conduct a few patrols to make sure there were no sniper teams in the area and then conduct a hasty rocket attack. Often, they would simply drive to a site, place a rocket-firing assembly on the ground, aim, fire, and leave. This method was an improvement from attempting to fire the rockets from the back of a pickup, which for them resulted in either a vehicle fire or leaving a tell-tale ignition mark, which could be easily identified and targeted later. The problem with either technique was that aiming was difficult and where the rockets landed was anyone's guess. The insurgents could shoot pretty well in a general direction but had trouble adjusting for distance. The result was the rounds often went long or short. The MEK was large enough that the rockets usually would make it inside the perimeter but with no real damage or effect. Nonetheless, I had knocked off for the night and was awakened with a quick knock. It was a SEAL lieutenant in battle fatigues carrying his weapon and a small backpack. I recognized him as being part of the Camp Posey team at BIAP. "Commander," he said to me, "I am stranded and looking for a place to stay until I can catch a flight out of here." My first thought was, *How does a SEAL lieutenant get stranded in the middle of a battle zone?* Too tired to ask for details, I said, "Sure, grab an open rack and welcome to Fallujah Hilton Garden Inn." The next morning I got the full story. As it turns out, he had a long-time Marine officer girlfriend who was assigned to a forward Marine base outside of Al Qa'im, near the Syrian border. He was about to return home in a few days and decided to hitch a ride by taking a series of rotary wing supply helicopters to go see her one more time before leaving Iraq. He had completed his romantic rendezvous and was on his way back to Posey when the mortar attack caused a disruption to his plan. I admired his creativity and mission focus and arranged a Navy Black Hawk flight to return him to the camp. I did not want to be the one to stand in the way of his successfully completing his mission of love.

I also found great personal satisfaction in fighting the bureaucratic supply system to get what was needed. The battle to get the supply system to produce offered its own set of rules of engagement and challenges. The Humvees brought forward from the States had been specially modified for fast patrols and open desert warfare. They were brilliant in design but did not have the armor kits installed that offered protection in urban environments. Since the Special Operations Forces were now operating in hostile towns and neighborhoods across Iraq, it was time to quickly upgrade our vehicle protection with armor. Fallujah was, compared with the open-air desert, pretty tight quarters: as I said, it was a city built long before the advent of the automobile, so the streets were narrow, and there were a lot of walls and obstacles.

The idea of a battle line—which is sort of like a scrimmage line in football—was almost laughable. A commander couldn't just say, "We need to move the line up by five yards," because you'd be leaping through the obstacle-filled streets and then there'd be an open courtyard forty yards ahead of your position. And the insurgents had a lot of snipers too. They might not have been as well trained as ours, but anyone who has spent time around mosquitos knows that enough of them will really mess up your day.

At any rate, our Humvees weren't really suited for this environment. Not only didn't they have armor, most of them didn't have doors. I spent a lot of time fighting with the supply chain to get my guys to the front of the line for armor kits. I ran around 360 or so missions, and for these efforts I received two Bronze Stars, which were given to me for meritorious service in a combat zone. I didn't say anything at the time—I did and do appreciate it, even if it wasn't why I was in the service—but I was tempted to ask that the medals be hammered out and added to the armor on the Humvees.

I also did a lot of what might be called community relations. It was kind of like what I was doing in the Philippines, except with a much more hostile native population. In Fallujah, that meant we had to interact as closely as possible with the local mullahs or imams—religious leaders whose interpretations of Sharia often stood for the whole of the law. Generally, they were not too keen on spending any time with us. They had no interest in adapting to any part of our ways. And they made it very clear they couldn't wait until we were gone and they could solidify their authority.

I had a few opportunities to sit down with imams, but it usually wasn't under the best of circumstances. We certainly weren't chatting over a beer, not in a Muslim area. More often it would be negotiating settlements for collateral damage, such as when we conducted an operation like a compound raid and inadvertently killed a civilian. The accidents generally were the result of being caught in the cross fire or even from children being used as a human shield. The marines used to have to do that in Beijing—then Peking—during the Boxer Rebellion a century before. It was heartbreaking, and it's discouraging to realize how little progress civilization has made since then.

We had to resolve those situations quickly: if we didn't, there would have been eye-for-an-eye retaliation forever. The sit-downs with the imams usually followed a basic protocol. The first step was our acknowledging that the tragedy had happened and that we were genuinely sorry for the family's loss. The next step was having the imam and family—because what the imam said usually flew with the family—acknowledge that what happened wasn't murder but an accident, which it was: we had no interest in killing civilians and certainly not children.

The third step was compensation. We acknowledged that the village and the family had suffered an economic loss. In the case of a male, there would be lost future wages, and in the case of a female, a family lost out on getting a dowry for her.

We usually settled male casualties for a few hundred dollars and females for about half that. And I would like my liberal colleagues to take note: right there is the real "war on women," not the false one crafted against the GOP. The Obama administration not just tacitly but openly supported and even praised governments that consider women to be second-class citizens at best or who throw gay men off the tops of buildings. Instead of reading the *New York Times*, the administration should talk to soldiers who have been there, who have seen systemic, entrenched, dehumanizing bias at work.

Thankfully, these occasions of having to negotiate for human losses were rare. Even though Americans often weren't at fault—the indigenous troops were trigger-happy and in some cases vindictive, settling old scores—these were some of the most emotionally draining negotiations I've ever been involved with. You can't be a compassionate person and not mourn when someone loses a child . . . even if that someone is on the other side of a battle line.

At this point, I wouldn't be surprised if some readers are shaking their heads, wondering if day-to-day life in Iraq was really as wrenching as I've described it. *Surely nobody could deal with those sorts of circumstances on a daily basis,* you must be thinking. *There had to be letups in the stress and action, right?*

There's only one response to this: we were in the middle of a war zone. There were mounting US casualties every day. There is no such thing as rest—not in the traditional sense. Even when things appeared calm, the world around and above us was dangerous and I had to remain alert. Even the world below us was a potential hazard, when one considers the tunnels that terrorists dug into Israeli territory.

And if I can just address that point for a moment: no, they were not Palestinian "freedom fighters." They were *terrorists* who bored their way into a nation that is our strongest ally in the Middle East. Only history will tell us how much damage eight years of Barack Hussein Obama's coddling these killers has done to our planet. Far more than "climate change," I'm sure.

A typical day at the FOB would start with my waking up at 0500 hours. I'd have spent the night on a cot, so I'd stretch and then get a cup of coffee. Strong as that morning joe was, neither it nor the assembly line bacon and eggs and pancakes could ever overpower the smell of Iraq. Iraqis usually take their garbage into nearby fields to burn it, so more often than not you're smelling that. And when you're not smelling burning garbage, there's a greasy petroleum smell that hangs over the entire Middle East. Countries there don't have emissions standards, and aside from that smell, on military bases you have the constant odor of petroleum from helicopters, rolling stock, and machinery. There's also the smell of the temporary shelters we were in, which the Seabees had constructed from plywood and sandbags.

It was always hot in Iraq: even at 0500 hours the temperature would often be close to a hundred degrees. We had Porta-Potties around the compound, and on some days you could actually push and twist your pistol through the plastic sides.

Hey, it was extra ventilation. Never a bad thing in a Porta-Potty.

The first official business I'd do every morning would be to check out the intel updates and the After Action Reports from the operations of the last twenty-four hours. That was always a "brace yourself" moment, since the news tended to be worrisome at best, grim at worst. There would be lots of intelligence—human intelligence, signal intelligence, observational and recon intelligence—going on, and someone would have to have a high-level view of how it all fit together. Who was calling which imams? Are any high-value targets involved? Are there any tips that require immediate responses?

After reviewing the daily intelligence reports from our operations, I would walk over to the 1st Marine Expeditionary Force (MEF) battle brief with General Conway and his staff. Conway represented exactly what a marine general should be—mission-focused, smart, and loyal to the corps. He would later become the commandant of the US Marine Corps. To the marines, that is about as close as you can get to becoming God. The brief typically lasted more than an hour, and every battalion, group, and unit would update everyone else on what had happened during the previous twenty-four hours and what the operations over the next twenty-four hours would be. My small part of the brief would last only a few minutes and was intentionally limited to our overall objectives, number of operations conducted, number of insurgents killed or captured, and where we would be operating during the next cycle of darkness. We were also running a number of Special Access Programs (SAP) that would have to be briefed separately in a more secure environment. Even in the middle of the well-defended MEK, any indiscriminate disclosure of Special Access Program information put lives at risk. Mishandling SAP intelligence was taken seriously. The military prison at Leavenworth, Kansas, has more than one cell full of former military personnel who violated the law and put sources at risk by the gross mishandling of classified information. The battle briefs ensured asset allocation supported the overall strategy and minimized the risk of blue-on-blue damage; we didn't want one of our forces inadvertently stumbling into the crosshairs of another because of poor communication—or, for that matter, any other reason. We also made sure everyone was clear on what the rules of engagement would be in any given situation.

Being in a state of warfare in Iraq was, at times, surreal. We had magnificent meals while we were there: we'd have steak and lobster a couple of times a week, and there was always ice cream available. And on the same day when we'd gorged ourselves on steak and lobster and had our double ice cream cones, we'd get into our convoy vehicles with our machine gun and go on patrol, hoping we wouldn't get hit with sniper fire or drive over an IED we hadn't spotted.

When it came to avoiding IEDs, we usually depended on two qualities: observation and luck. There's no skill or reliable pattern to an enemy scattering a few explosives along a road and then melting into the background.

For that reason, plus due to the increasing threat of snipers, we tried to mix our patrol routes up. We didn't want enemies to expect and be able to target us. Yes, we were looking for live-body insurgent activity along the roads, but we also wanted a sense of which roads were clear. And we wanted to know this for both main and back roads, because when we sent men out for special operations, we weren't going to send them along main routes every time.

So we'd be riding around, hoping to see potential explosives. If we happened not to spot them before coming upon them, we hoped our vehicles were armored enough to withstand the blasts.

After patrols, we'd have an intelligence briefing and prepare for special operations activities. We had a handful of those going on every day, which meant there were always briefings and reviews.

If nothing was demanding my immediate attention, I'd go for a five-mile run around the compound. I found a daily morning run to be quite therapeutic. I was once on a run around the Special Operations compound within BIAP where Saddam's palace residence and vineyards were. The palace compound near Al-Furat was a small thumb-shaped peninsula that jutted out from the main airfield complex. It was defended by two high exterior walls with a road in the middle and a company of 10th Mountain Division troops. I had scoped it out and thought it was more or less safe for a run. The shade trees along the first part of the 10K route had been cut down for security purposes, and the clay walls made the first couple of miles similar to running in an oven. The second half of the route opened up and consisted of a few former senior officer villas, occupied now by OGA and overlooking a series of fishing ponds.

I was running alongside one of those ponds—a nice little waterside run—when rockets started coming in. You see, insurgents would aim their rockets in the general direction of the airfield, let 'em fly, and then reinsert themselves in the civilian population. They weren't really concerned with doing damage; they just wanted to be a nuisance and remind us that they were there. With Iran providing the ordnance, they had an endless supply.

So on this particular day when I was running, one of those insurgents decided to let loose a few rockets. I heard a whistling noise, and the next thing I knew there were rockets hitting the ponds and kicking up mud and reeds close enough that I dropped and began to think about my predicament. I knew that if one of those rockets hit the road instead of the pond, there would be shrapnel, and I was armed with a pair of Nike shoes and a T-shirt.

There were about a dozen or so rockets from the time I first heard them until I dropped. I was miles from anything like base activity, and all I could think of was, *Are you kidding me? This is the way I'm going to get killed? On a run? I'm going to get hit by a rocket in a swamp in Nikes!*

I was reminded of a favorite saying from Admiral Tom Richards when he was commanding officer of SEAL Team One. He would always demand that all team physical training (PT) was done in jungle boots and not tennis shoes. "Son, you ain't going to put your Nikes on in combat." I guess I proved him wrong. Once the rockets let up—it wasn't more than a minute or so—I got back on my feet and finished my run. I had a few miles to go. I picked up the pace, made it back to headquarters, and said, "I just got rocketed."

Just another day in the field.

Which brings me to something that the news media rarely reports, that most civilians are unaware of: how every American man or woman fighting in that region can't fight to win by restrictive and unworkable rules of engagement.

I commented earlier on how field commanders and their on-the-ground staff are often better informed and are better positioned to make tactical decisions. That's the SEALs way: we position commanders close to the fight to have full situational awareness of the battle, and close enough to react at a moment's notice to send additional forces if needed. It's a smart method of conducting warfare, as it lets our forces react to and take advantage of changing situations. Having too many layers of approval in a dynamic battlefield environment delays our ability to fight and win, especially when troops are engaged in combat.

I'll give you an example. I mentioned that Fallujah's borders were porous. And I don't mean leaky like our border with Mexico but open like driving from state to state in the United States. Officially, the marines were saying that everything was sealed, while our guys knew this wasn't the case. I was once out on a ride-along with a few Special Operative snipers, checking locations where we could station snipers, and we pulled up alongside some marines who were on observation duty. They were in a Light Armored Vehicle (LAV) on the very bridge where Scott Helvenston and the others were hung. They were, by the way, openly pleased to see friendly faces: there's not a lot of love on the streets, and that lack can have a subtle, deteriorative effect.

The marines were observing activity across the river and pointed to a few Iraqi males they had been watching off-load ammunition and weapons from a car into a house. The insurgents clearly were not innocent civilians nor fortifying their position to defend their home but instead were preparing for battle against us. A sidebar for those of you who have defended the current refugee policy, with its unreliable and nearly absent vetting process, here's a suggestion that will never be adopted: Take those guys who have been observers and stand them by a queue of people seeking safe haven here. They will tell you with certainty who should be sent packing. That won't fit the ideology of "innocent until proven guilty," but then that law applies to American citizens, not likely terrorists, and I would rather risk being wrong about a few refugees than jeopardize dozens or hundreds or even one American life by admitting someone who is devoted to killing us to the home of the free and brave.

Like, for example, these boys in Fallujah whose very posture screamed a kind of animal defiance as they were in the process of moving ammunition, weapons, and rockets to a position that commanded the streets below the bridge.

It was now nighttime, and the marines we encountered didn't have night-vision goggles, so they couldn't clearly see what we could. Furthermore, the LAV and the area around the marines had lights on it that would have caused anything they could have seen with night-vision goggles to be obscured by glare.

We had better equipment and could see a lot more clearly what the Iraqis were doing, so we were able to determine that they constituted a clear threat. They were setting up sniper positions on the rooftop aimed at the marines. I asked the marines whether they were going to engage the Iraqis, and they told me they had radioed headquarters for permission and were waiting to hear back. That was hours before, and they were still waiting. Well, that's what they were supposed to do, but until they got the go code they were just sitting, watching ammunition being taken into a house where it would soon be used against them.

Think about that: imagine your local police, sitting in a patrol car, having to watch known radicals or prison escapees popping the back of a van and off-loading AK-47s, Molotov cocktails, land mines, you name it . . . and doing nothing while they waited for a court order to search the van. Or being unable to act while they watched a mugging or a rape. That is *exactly* how insane the rules of engagement were and are over there.

For these marines, not being able to do anything was maddening. And in the meantime, Fallujah was crumbling around them.

The Iraqis setting up for battle with us were about three hundred yards away—an easy shot for any sniper. So I turned to the Special Forces snipers I had been riding with, pointed, and said simply, "Make sure those guys don't kill any of our marines." The next morning, I noticed that our teams had reported four anti-coalition forces had been engaged and confirmed KIA. Bravo Zulu.

You may be wondering why the rules of engagement seem so complex in determining what constitutes a "threat." To me, it is absurd to have to wait until an armed combatant shoots at you first before you are allowed to engage. Absurd. Part of that is personal responsibility: I was willing to take action to protect our people and interests. But there's something larger than that. Let me paint a picture of the insurgent situation in Fallujah. We had our main Forward Operating Base in Camp Fallujah, the Marine Expeditionary Camp—on one side of Fallujah, just across a highway. That camp was rocketed almost every day—nuisance rockets, for the most part, but even nuisances can be fatal sometimes. We had our safe houses on the outskirts of the city, which we used as bases to help us infiltrate the insurgency, identify its networks, and disrupt its supply lines, or as staging areas for raids.

Having these bases in Fallujah meant, of course, that we had to move ourselves in and out. We tried to be inconspicuous—when traveling to the houses on the outer perimeter, we would put people in the back of vans, and hopefully the house we were moving into had a garage so our guys could go straight from the van to the house without being seen. We made sure the driver had a beard and blended in as much as possible. Fallujah was home to hundreds of recently arrived foreign fighters whose movements and defense strategy was not well coordinated. This was an advantage to movement in our indigenous vehicles. Even then, we moved people in and out as infrequently as we could get away with.

The deeper we got into Fallujah—and some of our safe houses were pretty deep in—the more exposed we were. On the city's perimeters, we could clear blocks and have lines of sight into our front line fairly easily. But within the city, when we have buildings to the right, left, front, and rear, we faced constant threats.

According to our rules of engagement, we could not generally shoot "civilians." Well, of course not. You didn't want to make a mistake. But how could you tell who was a threat and who was not? If nothing else, remember what I said earlier about pissing off the populace and having to sit down with the imams and pay—even when you killed insurgents. Remember, this is the same city that had butchered and hung up Americans on a bridge, and not one of the people who did it had a "uniform" on.

The guidance given to the Special Forces and the SEALs was that if there was a clear threat, our guys should engage. After the civilians were notified to leave the city, those remaining were considered either foreign fighters or insurgents. If they were carrying a weapon, they were a clear threat. And if they were supplying a clear threat with ammunition, specialized equipment, or supplies to positions or logistic operations, engage. Don't call me and ask for permission.

These may seem like pretty liberal rules of engagement, but you have to consider to whom they were being issued. My forces weren't twenty-year-old kids; they were snipers and skilled operatives, many of whom had a large amount of experience under their belts. Among this group, I had some amazingly talented sniper teams that included snipers like Chris Kyle and others from the SEALs and the marines. Professionals to a man, they saved hundreds, if not thousands of American troops' (and Iraqi civilians') lives, due to their precise elimination of enemy combatants. Remember, between the time someone raises his hand and announces he's going to try out for the SEALs to the time that SEAL—if he makes it—first sees combat, you're talking about a three-year intensive training period. That's a lot of time to beat the jerky kid instincts out of someone. Further, between the time you become a SEAL, or a marine, and when you complete sniper training, you have again been evaluated and garnered a multitude of skill sets, beyond being able to shoot the enemy with precise accuracy at a great distance. Snipers often act alone or in pairs, away from oversight. Trust is something that a commander must give to those at the front lines.

Even so, where there were gray areas, we tended to be cautious. Let's say there was an individual who was possibly supplying information, who was likely part of a network, and a sniper observes that individual with a cell phone. Would that constitute a supply mechanism that would aid the insurgents?

I would say no, and that was my guidance. Cell phones are everywhere, and even if we suspected someone was up to no good, we needed stronger evidence than that. There had to be a pattern of activity that indicated this person was doing intelligence work for the insurgents and was making regular reports or reports timed after specific activities we took. In short, there had to be a pattern of actions against us. A simple cell phone wasn't justification enough.

Admittedly, sometimes I had to step in and pull back on the reins a bit. We once had two sniper teams operating in the same field, and word got back that they were competing on the number of hits. That time, I gave commander's guidance telling them to knock it off and reminded them of the rules we'd set regarding disrupting clear threats.

This type of behavior, although rare, wasn't limited to the American forces. It was widely reported that one of our Special Forces allies was going into villages and breaking the trigger finger of every male they suspected as hostile. After I got the report from a concerned commander, I had to talk to them and tell them that, unless they had determined the people they were assaulting were insurgents, that wouldn't fly any longer. In the end, they knew I was looking out for them, and I think, out of respect, they paid attention.

Here's the thing: in the early stages of the war, commanders were given a lot of flexibility. It wasn't until after the Iraqi army had been dismantled and the bureaucracy of the American military machine kicked into high gear that operations began grinding to a halt.

Sometimes, when I bucked the system's rules, it was because following the rules set by people who weren't in the field would have put our guys in danger. For instance, an edict once came down that we had to have interpreters who were locals, who understood the nuances of the Farsi language. Or guards who were local. In theory, this was understandable—we were trying to have Iraqi faces on our operations.

But in practice, it put our people in harm's way. Often these interpreters weren't well vetted, and they weren't trustworthy. And they had access to a lot of information about where we were, what sort of resources we could draw on, and how these resources were lined up for various operations. Did I balk against using unvetted Iraqis in sensitive security positions? What do you think?

Which brings us to the Mighty 36. Part of the reason civil order was so tenuous was because of the wholesale dismantling of the Iraqi military and related Ba'athist elements, which left a void for a dedicated force tasked with shutting down the insurgency. When the rise in civil disorder exploded, the United States and its coalition wanted to put an Iraqi face on bringing back order—thinking that it would have been better to have Iraqi security forces take the lead rather than the "occupiers." The problem is that the Iraqi security forces—the Iraqi Civil Defense Corps (ICDC)—wasn't especially well trained or well equipped. There were thirty-six battalions of what was on paper around five hundred soldiers each, and only one of them, a Special Forces battalion made up of the best Sunni, Shiite, Kurd, and Christian operators called the Mighty 36, was anywhere close to battle ready. I think there were maybe 240 real live individuals in the Mighty 36. And honestly, while there were a few brave and goal-oriented souls in that group (as there are in virtually any battalion), most of them were more interested in turning a blind eye to members of their own particular religious persuasion—which was frequently at odds with the desires and practices of some other guys they bunked with—than they were in keeping the peace and maintaining the stressed, artificial construct that was "Iraq."

I am mighty proud of the Combined Joint Special Operations Task

Forces' effort in training the Mighty 36, given the lack of local will and funding. They were an example of how the different divisions within Iraq could be united for a common purpose. I saw a glimmer of hope and fought hard to get them the right equipment and training to be combat ready. The rest of the Iraqi forces didn't have adequate resources and in many cases even the right ammunition to operate their weapons effectively. Calling on them to do anything more than limited patrols in which we paired them with coalition soldiers was out of the question.

Our goal was always to train and turn over to the Iraqis the responsibility for their own internal security operations. The problem was that when we allowed—or, more specifically, forced—the Iraqi army to disband, we lost a lot of the structure and unit cohesion that would have allowed them to maintain order. Disbanding the Iraqi army was our first major mistake.

Our second mistake was believing that a Shia-controlled central government would act in the best interest of the Sunni population. Instead, they ignored the Sunni ethnic cleansing going on in Baghdad and other affluent neighborhoods. Of course they did; one has only to look at the Iranian mullahs and their wholesale ethnic cleansing of all non-Shia populations immediately after coming into power in 1979. Seeing a future of always being in the minority, the Sunni population felt isolated and disenfranchised. During the first part of the surge, we focused on reestablishing relationships with Sunni tribesmen. The Sunnis were the second-most populous tribe in Iraq, which meant that in terms of resources we could draw from, we were already starting at a disadvantage.

With the goal of reestablishing Iraqi control for their internal security, the plan was for the ICDC battalions to lead the effort. When the first battle of Fallujah was on the horizon, the brass wanted to put "an Iraqi face" to the campaign and the ICDC were called up for action.

Of the thirty-six ICDC battalions, the Mighty 36 was the only battalion to deploy and fight in Fallujah.

We trained them just outside of Baghdad, and when it was time to deploy them into Fallujah, we had to make sure everything they needed to move from trainee status to combat status, such as uniforms and weapons, went with them. We had a marine base located just across a highway from Fallujah, and that's where we stationed them. Unfortunately, only about half of the listed five hundred members got on the bus to Fallujah. The rest "missed" the bus. And to make matters worse, when they got off the bus, they had virtually no equipment. Had it been stolen or sold? Who knew? But it was not with them.

A look at the Mighty 36 might give some insight into why Iraq was such a mess. A battalion, at full strength, is around 500 people. At 240, we were at about half strength. In the Mighty 36 were around a dozen or so Kurds—fighters from northern Iraq who had long-standing tribal strife with Sunnis. So of course, the Kurds were more than happy to stay in the Mighty 36 and kill Sunnis. After a couple weeks of waiting for equipment, we started basic patrols on the outskirts of Fallujah. They would patrol for a few hundred yards, stop, and retreat. Any retreat was hastened by occasional insurgent activity. After a short period, only a handful were willing to continue. To no one's surprise, this group included all the Kurds, and to everyone's surprise, the group also included a Shia woman.

She had a compulsion to kill men. She said she'd been raped as part of the various conflicts, and while we couldn't verify her story and prosecute her rapists, we had no reason to doubt her. When someone is that angry, that committed, there's usually a good reason. Her narrative certainly filled the criteria. At any rate, she wanted to be a combatant, she had sniper skills, and she was more than willing to be told whom to kill.

Iraqi women soldiers were at a premium, just as I mentioned previously how women in general are pivotal in many covert and special operations work similar to our Operational Support Teams and other specialty units. Even when our guys grew their beards and took on local garb, if you stuck two or three of them in a car together, they looked exactly like what they were: a couple of knuckleheads in a car. But put a woman and a man in a car, assuming they can pass as a family, and they'll be able to go places and arouse less suspicion than a couple of guys. Also, in a segregated society, males did not have access to a lot of sites that were the domain of women and important intelligence-gathering operations. The Shia woman became critical to many forward recon activities.

I can't really tell you much about her beyond what she told us. She kept to herself, even when we put her in the Mighty 36. We did a background check on her, of course, as far as we were able: her story about coming from north of Baghdad checked out. Her parents were dead, she wasn't married, and she didn't have any children who were alive. She basically volunteered for this job. We had advertised positions open, and she knocked on the door and presented herself as a sniper.

When we interviewed her, we found out there was only one restraint on her: she wouldn't kill during sex. She would kill before sex. She would kill after sex. But during the actual act, she wouldn't kill.

She was hired.

I've mentioned the rules of engagement, how female operatives can reduce special ops' signature and make them less visible and the need for the forward commander to make the decision on the ground. I've got a story that ties all of that together, but to tell it we need to jump back to Bosnia.

We were monitoring a PIFWC and had been tracking him for a while, doing the basic recon work.

A team of a couple of SEALs and a female colonel were driving around conducting surveillance, and they spot the PIFWC walking with a cup of coffee in one hand and a croissant in the other. He was alone, and his hands were full.

So the team drove past him, turned around, drove by him again, verified that it was him, stopped the car, grabbed him, threw him in the backseat, and put a hood over his head. They moved the colonel to the front seat and put a SEAL next to him for the drive back to headquarters. Just like that, they were able to cross someone of value off their list.

Except it wasn't over. The Air Force colonel called into headquarters to tell them the SEALs had grabbed this guy, and headquarters went ballistic. How could they just do this sort of operation without telling anyone or getting a green light? The brass at headquarters were practically melting the radio. How could anyone but them make a decision?

The two SEALs were almost court-martialed over that—for taking initiative, for making a decision in the field based on information immediately at hand.

I've seen this elsewhere but nowhere more obviously than in American government. Government is too larded up, and too many decisions are being made by unelected bureaucrats who have no expertise or don't know what's happening in the field. And they're causing harm or at least gross inefficiencies.

THREE

ABU GHRAIB

THERE CAN BE LITTLE DOUBT THAT THE FLASH POINT OF
the sudden rise in insurgent activity all over Iraq in 2004 was the result
of our snatching the accountant. The spark that ignited the Iraqi powder keg was bound to occur; we just happened to provide the match. It
did have one good consequence, however, in that it basically flushed out
the rats. Every time an insurgent took direct action against us, we got a
little more information about money routes and cells. The lines between
Muqtada al-Sadr's Shia militia and the Sunni insurgents became clearer
and easier to detect and target.

As I mentioned, there were a lot of forces with different agendas in
Iraq, and while they may not have been working together, more often than
not they were hostile to us. We didn't realize at the outset of our activity
in Iraq that we weren't dealing with one country opposing another. In
Iraq, the typical order of patronage and loyalty is immediate family first,
then tribe, then faith, and finally country. Iraq, in direct contrast with
America, is a nation with a low-trust society. In a general sense, people
there don't trust or honor one another without an overlying framework
of family and tribe. America, on the other hand, is a high-trust society
where people trust one another regardless of relations, race, color, religion, etc. The resulting dynamics of each type of society have profound
effects on freedoms, stability, and effective forms of government.

All we knew was that there were several groups out to kill us, and we had to take actions against as many of them as we could with the resources we had. Sanchez may have wanted Sadr, but he knew there were other targets of equal merit. One of them—a former general—was in the Anbar Province. And rather than bring him to a little temporary detention facility, we ended up taking him to one of the worst places on earth.

It's an easy drive from Baghdad to the city of Abu Ghraib, home of one of the most infamous places on the planet. I'm going to tell you about the place, not because I want to but because I have to; the prison at Abu Ghraib is a stain on all of humankind. It's a cautionary tale of what happens when leadership lacks a moral compass and a population becomes so terrified, so submissive, that it becomes indirectly complicit in the process.

No, I'm not blaming the Iraqi people for anything that happened there. But we have seen throughout history—in Nazi Germany, for example—what happens when the iron heel of government crushes its population. For the record—and this is as good a place to mention it as any—I would warn even my fellow Americans to be vigilant against that. That is one of the reasons I went to Washington: to make sure that the voices of the people are heard and to fight for those voices with the same absolute conviction that I fought in Iraq. When federal institutions— whether a president or an Internal Revenue Service or a Department of Justice, as we have recently seen—begin to act unilaterally, by fiat, treating our precious Constitution as if its words were merely suggestions, it's time to vote out the leaders of those institutions.

The Iraqi people did not have that option or that opportunity. Abu Ghraib was the infamous result.

I believe in my soul that there is no such thing as an evil tool. Forgive another digression, but it's appropriate here. As Second Amendment defenders correctly point out, guns don't kill people; people kill people. I recently saw a cartoon that showed four people, each committing their own separate murders. One used a club, one a rope, another a knife, and the last one used a gun. In the first three, an onlooker gasped, "What's the matter with you?" In the fourth, the onlooker cried instead, "We've got to do something about guns!"

That's the truth. My state is chockablock with good, responsible gun owners. I spent twenty-two years holding a firearm of some kind more than I did my canteen. So did the men who served with me. We never shot anyone who didn't merit his fate, who didn't want to do harm to another.

I mention this because of a simple historic fact: Abu Ghraib prison is just a building. What Saddam Hussein did with it—that's the true horror story.

The prison was designed by a well-intentioned American architect, Edmund Whiting, and was built by British contractors in the late 1960s. Allow me to back up again and tell you how that came to be. It will provide some context for everything that follows in Iraq.

During World War II, the British maintained a heavy military presence in the region, wanting to keep the flow of oil in its own hands and out of Axis tanks and planes. After the war, the ancient Hashemite monarchy ran the show—a family that traced its bloodline directly to the prophet Muhammad. Unfortunately, those ties made them neither holy nor benevolent. A revolution in 1958 overthrew those boys, and one brigadier general, Abd al-Karim Qasim, came to power for a few years until he died in the so-called Ramadan Revolution of 1963. Colonel Abdul Salam Arif took his place, died a few years later, and was succeeded by his brother, Abdul Rahman Arif—another scoundrel. He was tossed out by the Ba'ath Party two years after that, in 1968. And then, a miracle: a pretty decent ruler, Ahmed Hassan al-Bakr, became the president of Iraq. Under al-Bakr there was sky's-the-limit economic growth thanks to oil, and the standard of living of all Iraqi citizens increased dramatically.

Al-Bakr was undermined and ousted by one of his underlings, General Saddam Hussein, in July 1979. It was before, during, and after the Ramadan Revolution that new prison space was needed by whoever was in power. The Americans had a presence in the country, plus the British were still there, so we all put that prison together—or rather, our contractors did. They made a profit (as did the Iraqis they hired), we got the thanks of whoever was running the show, and all was well enough. Except for this: you will notice the insidious cancer that was starting to eat at the Iraqi people. Because they never knew who would be in power, they stopped publicly criticizing anyone. If you were a Hashemite, it wasn't so good for you when Brigadier General Abd al-Karim Qasim came to power. If you were a supporter of Abdul Rahman Arif, troops controlled by Saddam Hussein might hunt you down and cut out your tongue.

So now you had a big prison capable of holding a staggering fifteen thousand souls (a number I mention with an asterisk; see below), a dictator named Saddam, and a broken, quiescent populace. In short, a perfect storm for god-awful misery.

Situated roughly twenty miles west of Baghdad, the Abu Ghraib prison sprawled over 280 acres with a security perimeter of more than two and a half miles. There were five different compounds, each with its own guard towers and high walls. It also had five gallows run by a staff of a dozen hangmen. In addition to whatever killings happened during daily operations, twice a week—on Wednesdays and Sundays—prisoners personally condemned by Saddam were marched up to the second floor of the gallows and hung. Sometimes he watched the executions. (It is perhaps fitting that years later, on December 30, 2006, when Saddam himself was hanged at the Iraqi-American military base Camp Justice in Kazimain, northeast of Baghdad, it was recorded on a cell phone and witnessed by countless numbers around the world.)

People have different opinions about our own penal system. You may believe that American prisons can reform people. You may believe they're for warehousing people you don't want on the streets. You may support "country club" type prisons for white-collar crooks. Or you may not think much about prisons at all, except for how to stay out of them. But whatever your view, most people certainly believe that when a criminal goes into a prison, unless that prisoner has been found guilty of a crime hideous enough to have been given the death penalty or life without parole, that prisoner is eventually going to walk out alive.

Under Saddam Hussein, walking out alive from the prison at Abu Ghraib was the exception rather than the rule. In 1984 alone, there were four thousand prisoner executions at that prison. Actually, I take that back: *executions* is the wrong word. It implies there was a process, such as a trial or something with a semblance of fairness. This absolutely wasn't the case. In one instance alone, two thousand prisoners were killed in a single day in 1998 at the whim of Saddam's evil son Qusay, the same punk who, with his brother Uday, had women snatched from the streets of Baghdad and taken to rape rooms. Whatever your feelings about the Iraq War—and there are good arguments on both sides of the fence—the Hussein family was a blight on the world stage.

Walk into a prison cell at Abu Ghraib and you might be surprised at its size. Cells were about thirteen by thirteen feet, which isn't too bad until you realize that each one housed, on average, forty people. That's why I mentioned the asterisk. Abu Ghraib was actually constructed to hold about one-tenth of the fifteen thousand it housed at its wretched peak.

In a way, the prison was a microcosm of the ills that have plagued the Middle East for millennia and continue to this day. The bulk of the captives—like 70 percent of the population in Iraq—were Shiite Muslims. Unfortunately for them, Saddam was a Sunni. Therein lies a tragic corruption of the sense of "community" I spoke of. Instead of belonging to a community of "humans" or "Iraqis," Saddam did not consider Shiites to be either. Not really. And for those who don't know the difference between the groups, the rift dates back to the seventh century AD. When the prophet Muhammad died, his friend and acolyte Abu Bakr as-Siddiq became caliph, the leader of Islam. Many Muslims felt this was wrong, that Muhammad's blood relative, his cousin and son-in-law Ali ibn Abi Talib, was the rightful heir. Abu's supporters were the Sunnis; those who backed Ali were the Shiites.

That is the cause of so much suffering in that region.

Shiite or Sunni, even that sense of community was obliterated at Abu Ghraib. The crowding meant that prisoners took turns sleeping: there wasn't enough room for everyone to stretch out at the same time. In situations like that, compassion and caring for each other can vanish. It was every man—and woman—for him- or herself.

Women? Yes. There's a story about a women's prison cell. One of the inmates died, and the corpse was left to sprawl on the floor. I remember reading what one of the survivors told *The New York Times*: that her only feeling at the time was "a dull flash of annoyance"[1] aimed at the body, which was now taking up room. A month before, that same woman might have been a fellow student or a beloved teacher at a university (which, ironically, were legal for women under Saddam).

Still, most of the captives in Saddam's prisons were men, and jailers took pleasure inflicting all sorts of tortures on their private parts. A typical punishment was to attach electrodes or heavy weights to genitals. There was a psychological component to that as well as a physical one: attack the essence of manhood and you break the man. Not that there was always information to be gained from these poor souls. More often than not, they were just ordinary folks who had said the wrong thing that was heard by the wrong set of ears at the wrong time.

Those demonically talented interrogators had techniques that covered prisoners from head to toe. If you're skittish, you might want to skip ahead a few paragraphs. For me, it's important that some of the details be told and retold. Remember the quote I mentioned earlier from Edmund Burke about not ignoring the lessons of history: the world must never forget what went on at this place. In fact, maybe if members of our government had been more vividly aware of what human beings could do to their fellow human beings, they wouldn't have been so quick to pull our troops out of the region, leaving those poor, poor people in the vile hands of ISIS. Those jihadist monsters are Saddam Hussein writ large.

The prison keepers were sadists. The human head offers numerous torture opportunities. Captors plied out teeth, gouged out eyes, or broke noses and jaws. When jailers wanted to abuse a prisoner's whole head, they would often squeeze it between the plates of a vise or cover it with a metal cover, which they then would bang repeatedly. Members of the regime were especially fond of cutting off ears; rumor has it that one wall in a prison cell was covered with severed earlobes.

Move down the body a bit. Prisoners were often suspended by their arms and beaten or subjected to electrical shocks—after being doused with water, of course. A prisoner might be hung from a large metal ceiling fan and hit hard with baseball bats as he spun, allowing multiple captors an opportunity to participate at the same time.

Down a little farther. Some captives were forced to sit on the broken neck of a bottle. They weren't allowed to move until the bottle had filled with blood. Most of the prisoners who were forced to do this didn't survive.

Down to the legs. Saddam's jailers used drills on knees and ankles, hammers on toes, flames on the soles of feet.

Former prisoners have told us that there were times when Saddam wanted to make sure no part of the body survived. Perhaps it was an opposition figure whose remains could make him a martyr; perhaps it was someone the dictator simply did not want to "enjoy" the dignity of burial. Such a person might be torn apart by a machine like a wood chipper. Depending on the mood of a jailer, a prisoner could be fed in headfirst, allowing for a relatively quick death. Some were not. Some were put through feetfirst.

Yet even that form of murder was relatively quick. Jailers had a full-body torture that might or might not be fatal, depending on their whim. It involved encasing a prisoner in a suit, like armor, but made of metal bars or slats. The prisoner was then placed in the sun for hours. He would be given just enough water to avoid dying of dehydration, but the hot metal would sear his skin wherever it touched him. Such a person was constantly writhing, constantly crying out, never sleeping. For even when the sun went down, the pain was intense.

At times, prison in Saddam's Iraq was a family affair. If jailers wanted someone to sign a confession or to incriminate his neighbors, his wife and children might be brought in. Guards might rape the prisoner's wife right in front of him (which often meant the wife was doomed even if the family were released, because some cultures within Iraq require that women who are victims of rape be killed for losing their honor).

Children were burned with cigarettes in front of their parents. If that didn't produce the desired result, the captors might start cutting off ears. Or fingers. Or limbs. And jailers were not above killing children if their parents didn't do what was asked of them.

Sometimes it didn't matter if they did. The children were killed anyway. Not that it was a mercy to let them survive. Abu Ghraib didn't make any special provisions for such kids. Children had to scramble for the same foul water and spoiled food shared by the other captives.

In Saddam's prisons, wild dogs were kept around for sport. Sometimes the dogs were trained to attack prisoners—although when a dog was hungry enough and a live inmate was thrown in front of it, it didn't need much training. As one of my SEAL members said, if we wanted to put a scare into someone we grabbed, all we would have had to do is train a mutt to come bounding up to him and sniff at his crotch when we first led him into a room for questioning.

The suffering for families did not stop with the horrible death of a loved one. Where there was a body, the captors demanded a payment from the family for the remains and a death certificate—which would without exception state that the prisoner died in an accident. Sometimes there was a perverse variation on this extortion: a family was required to pay for the bullets that had been used to kill the prisoner, only to discover that the cause of death was hanging.

Before going further, I want to discuss the well-known reports that coalition forces abused captives in the aftermath of the Iraq War. In March 2003, soldiers of the US Army and personnel with the Central Intelligence Agency committed a pattern of human rights violations against detainees. The allegations included torture, sexual abuse, and murder.

To most Americans, the pictures of prisoners being abused by our soldiers conjured up outrage and disgust. However, many Iraqis I spoke with had a very different response, given what Saddam had done to them.

That doesn't make it right, but it helps explain the fear that most Iraqis had for the prison and the wrath of their former dictator.

There is a difference between torture and interrogation, but it is easy to blur the line. When information was needed *now*—and often it was—"enhanced interrogation techniques" were employed. I'm not going to finely slice the question of whether that was a euphemism for torture or exactly what it says: interrogation. Is it torture to swap food and water for information or to use what we called a "no touch" technique like sleep deprivation? Is waterboarding—laying a prisoner on his back, covering his nose and mouth with a cloth, and pouring water over his face to simulate drowning—torture? At one point, when the navy was doing its Survival, Evasion, Resistance, and Escape (SERE), waterboarding was part of the curriculum. It is not fun, but it is far better than being made into Swiss cheese by a half-inch drill. That is what the terrorists do.

I was a soldier, not a psychologist. I served with the SEALs, not Amnesty International. At times we needed actionable intelligence to save Iraqi and coalition lives. A policy of thinking you can deal with terrorists in the same manner as you do with those committing a crime in the United States is a policy built on fantasy. There is evil in this world, and no amount of negotiation and logic will change the mind of a radical Islamic terrorist. They detest freedom and the ideas of liberty and view critical thinking as a threat. With this in mind, there is a values judgment in interrogation. When you know that an individual has critical information that will save lives, do you authorize enhanced interrogation methods? If enhanced interrogation on a member of Al-Qaeda could have prevented the tragedy of 9/11, I am sure that most Americans would say yes. Especially those who lost loved ones.

There was no doubt that the United States used a wide range of accepted practices at Abu Ghraib that were effective. Poor leadership and the lack of supervision allowed effective practices to become disgraceful. Yet, even before the Washington liberals created a media scandal over allegations of abuse at Abu Ghraib, greater controls were in place elsewhere.

Anyone within Special Forces who undertook the task of enhanced interrogations—which, I admit, we all knew were extreme, albeit *legal*, tactics—had to submit a list of what they wanted to do, as well as the reason and justification for these types of interrogations.

Each list was reviewed by a Judge Advocate General's Corps officer, one well versed in the acceptable application of US military law. The list was then signed off—but only if it passed the standard of potentially having useful tactical value. For example, if we wanted to make a prisoner squat or use white noise in an effort to extract information, we would do so only after these proposed actions had been reviewed, discussed, and approved. Our actions were documented, and someone on our side would always be held accountable—whether the end results were good or bad. A lot of people may not have approved of these methods, but they were not without checks and balances.

And here's the thing: we almost always got something useful when interrogators employed enhanced controlled tactics. Plus, I can honestly say that I have never seen or authorized any interrogation technique that I had not personally experienced or seen administered in my SEAL training and/or command upon my own men.

In the same way that urban gangs can take basically good kids and turn them into killers, the culture that permitted these techniques for so long in Abu Ghraib also brought out the worst in some of the practitioners, including those soldiers in March 2003.

After investigations by our own government and various international organizations—which, honestly, are no fans of the United States—the Department of Defense pulled seventeen soldiers and officers from active duty and charged eleven soldiers with dereliction of duty and aggravated assault and battery. From May 2004 to March 2006, these soldiers were found guilty in courts-martial, sent to military prison, and discharged other-than-honorably.

Yeah, we screwed up at Abu Ghraib. The stink of abuse was in those very walls, in the stories we heard, in the old blood that had soaked the concrete of every damn cell and corridor there. Add to that a few bad people and bad oversight of the personnel guarding some forty-five hundred prisoners, and you have a clear path to disaster.

But as we did in My Lai during the Vietnam War, we arrested and tried our own. We took a moral position against what were clearly immoral acts. Are there abuses, still, in Afghanistan and places like Guantanamo Bay? Most likely. But here's the key question that our detractors keep pressing: Are these abuses part of the overall military culture?

The answer is a firm no. Members of the United States military still have a moral compass. However we are brutalized by the enemy, however many of our brothers and sisters fall—sometimes not in battle but with a knife across the throat—we do not *systemically* do the same. We are the good guys.

The idea to let loose a hound or two was not practical, and it did not fit with my way of doing things. The question was how to get the information in a way that was effective but caused no physical distress or—and this is essential—left as little psychological scarring as possible. You want an enemy to respect you, even fear you, but you do not want them hating you if at all possible. When the struggle is over you want them to lay down their arms, not seek revenge and bond with others who have the same bloodlust. I'm not saying it's always possible: this is war, after all, not softball in the park. But that's the goal.

Even though we were not a part of the US military security force assigned to manage Abu Ghraib, the legacy of the infamous prison itself provided us with valuable leverage. In one case, just the idea of being sent to Abu Ghraib gave us the advantage we needed over a former Sunni Iraqi general.

Let's call this man simply "the General." Though the General wasn't on the "most wanted Iraqis" playing cards the military issued in 2003, concurrent with the invasion of Iraq, he was informed enough and dangerous enough for us to: (a) want him off the field, and (b) get what was inside his head.

A few words about the above-mentioned cards. These card decks—officially called "personality identifying playing cards"—have been used by the US military since the Civil War. They are traditional playing cards that typically feature likenesses of persons of interest, along with tactical information about them—at least, as much information as can fit on the back side of a playing card. Military personnel play a lot of cards in the field, and the hope is that they'll get familiar with the names, images, and information of the opposition's key players in case they encounter them.

As I said, the General was not on those cards, mostly because he wasn't in Saddam Hussein's innermost circle. The General was on the next level down. And the reality was, that level was where the real work was done. Above him, officials were too busy retaining their jobs and their lives by fawning over Saddam and telling him only what he wanted to hear—as was the case with Adolf Hitler and Julius Caesar and their inner circles.

Sic semper tyrannis indeed: "Thus always to tyrants," the infamous words shouted by John Wilkes Booth after shooting President Abraham Lincoln. Only in this case, the despots were truly that.

The General was a former intelligence officer whose fortunes had risen and fallen as much because of Saddam's whims as his own actions. The General had even spent time in Saddam's prisons before being released and subsequently returned to Saddam's confidence. But he was a soldier first and a loyalist second.

Another bit of background here before we discuss the General. This is not just my opinion but the opinion of many of our policy makers then and especially now, with hindsight. We should have left the Iraqi military intact, with the exception of those officers in Saddam's closest circle. Instead, we scattered it and lost effective control over those who were bound more to duty than the Ba'athist regime under Saddam. If we'd let the General retain his position, he might not have become such an adversary. He had standing in the military community and could have been a useful tool for us. But once we destroyed the Republican Guard and the rest of the army as part of the de-Ba'athification of Iraq, we sent half a million people to the unemployment lines—many of whom were highly trained in the use of weapons and explosives—and into the hands of anyone who could provide money. Because apart from loyalty, cash was the grease that motivated the Iraqi soldier. And that left us with forces we didn't control, who weren't sympathetic to begin with, who disliked us as they starved, and who learned to hate us as we were described as "invaders."

We talk an awful lot today about "radicalization," and that's where and how it begins. People finding other people who cannot find work, who are lured into a belief set by a sympathetic arm around the shoulder . . . and cash. You may be a moderate Muslim who has the Quran recited to you, and, in the context of the people you already hate, you start to hear words that describe your needs, new goals. You find yourself buying into that reinterpretation and corruption of the text to fit your needs. You get fired up by the enthusiasm of others, by the easy-access desire for revenge.

In a very short time, you have been seduced and brainwashed. And not just seduced figuratively: with cash-in-hand, a number of the 9/11 terrorists bought time with hookers before their unholy mission. I guess some of those true believers couldn't wait to get to those virgins they were told would be waiting for them in Paradise.

The General was not one of these zealots. But he was someone who, by our policies, we managed to turn from a mere opponent into an active enemy. He hated us for taking away his prestige and cursed us for removing his ability to provide for his family.

Without Saddam and without fully drinking the radicalism Kool-Aid, people like the General fell back on their traditional loyalty structures—family, community or tribe, faith, and country. In some ways, these priorities made the General in particular more dangerous: he lent his knowledge and expertise to many factions, including Sunni-led Al-Qaeda. Our surveillance revealed that an Al-Qaeda leader we had killed had been part of his circle. But more than that, the General had made himself a connector for a lot of unaffiliated cells. Each of these cells could and did operate independently—some as bandits, preying on the citizenry, others as militia-killing coalition forces. Our target had devised command and operational structures for groups large and small so that each of these bands could operate with their available manpower and weaponry. And, of course, as they grew in strength, they came back to him for more advice. It had grown into a lucrative business for the General.

You had to hand it to him: that was probably how he managed to get himself back into Saddam's good graces after his own fall, by making himself so essential to the larger operational structure that he couldn't be eliminated on Saddam's whim.

Therein lies the problem for the US military, the question any commander such as myself has to address in a situation like this—indeed, the problem we faced and continue to face across the breadth of Iraq, Afghanistan, and now Syria: How do you deal with enemy combatants who are inured to the horrors of war? In the case of the General, someone who has been wounded himself and gone back to the fight after he recovered. Someone who believes in systemic violence and terror as a means of crowd control and obtaining information, who uses extreme torture as an opening salvo—and we're not talking waterboarding here but cattle prods to the genitals and flaying skin from arms and disemboweling family pets and announcing that the children are next. Someone who may or may not believe that enduring pain and death in the name of his religion may earn him a choice spot in Paradise.

In short, how do you rattle a man who has already endured and expects, inevitably, the fate you are planning? The answer is: you change the plan. If a man is prepared for physical suffering, you give him a very different kind of pain.

We decided that with the General, when we caught him, we would do the unexpected. We would let the reputation of the infamous Abu Ghraib prison speak for us. We would let the psychology of the place he helped create do the heavy lifting.

I should pause here and note that everybody in Iraq knew the stories about Abu Ghraib. Everybody knew someone who had been tortured when it was Saddam's overcrowded-by-a-factor-of-ten, go-to prison.

Everyone had seen returned prisoners whose shoulders had been dislocated as a result of being hung up by their arms, or who would never walk well again because their feet had been placed in wooden vises, or whose tongues had been partly hacked away. Go to any village or city in Iraq today, and you will encounter one of those poor souls every hour of every day.

There was another reason why people knew about Abu Ghraib. In large cities across the nation, young Iraqi men would play videos of torture and killing in Saddam's prisons on televisions set up right next to market stalls. You could pick up your vegetables, your eggs, your rice . . . and also buy a laser disc of your neighbors being shot, beheaded, or blown up alive. The discs cost a thousand Iraqi dinars or around forty or fifty cents. There was always a market for new discs.

We knew all this. So what we decided to do was to use the infamy of the place to get what we wanted.

There was something else working against us beyond the presumed thick skin of our subject: time. The General had information we needed about militia movements and tactics, and we needed it fast. Through multiple intelligence sources, we had determined the General knew about, or was coordinating, a major series of IED attacks against one of our high-level individuals and that the attack was imminent. We just did not know the specifics of where and when. We'd originally planned on keeping the General under surveillance for a long time, but once we got wind of that impending attack, we knew we had to move quickly. As we say, the hourglass had been tipped.

Unfortunately, all we knew was that something involving explosives was imminent. Whom would it be against and when? Would it be an inside job or a brute-force external attack? Would it target the individual's convoy? We knew nothing else . . . except that the General could give us the details. Not moving against him would likely result in the loss of American lives. This was a classic case of the necessity for an extreme operation. Get it done successfully and fast.

Our initial plan to grab the General involved a nighttime compound raid. He had a residence in a smaller town of Al-Sejar, east of Baghdad, in a small, gated compound. This meant we had to plan a double-breach operation—drive up to the gates in Humvees, get out of the Humvees and set explosive charges, blow the gates open and drive through them and up to his doorstep, get out of the Humvees and set explosive charges, blow his door open, and take him in. Double-breach operations involve two sets of explosions with lapses, which of course would mean he'd have time to either arm himself or flee.

During the initial strategy briefing, one of the staff officers in attendance was a tank commander. He suggested we use one of his M1A1s and forget about the explosive charges. As he put it, gates and doors can't stand up to sixty-eight tons of armored vehicle traveling at forty-five miles per hour, which is about as fast as we'd be going in our Humvees. The tank would roll through the gate and smash the door, and our guys could swarm around it and into the General's home in one smooth action.

Naturally, we embraced this idea immediately. But even then we still had details to iron out. We started talking about fields of fire as our guys would move around the tank and into the General's home, with an eye toward avoiding a blue-on-blue scenario. It was the same conversation we would have had if we were still using Humvees.

Well, this tank commander started laughing, and I asked him what was so funny.

"We're going to be buttoned up," he said. "There is nothing you have that's going to hurt us." He was right, of course, and that was pretty much the end of that part of the conversation.

There was one significant problem with our plan: the General didn't keep to a regular schedule and our surveillance teams had not seen him at his residence for weeks. We couldn't predict when he'd be home, when he'd be out walking, or whom he'd be with. About all we could say with certainty was that he usually had two bodyguards with him.

As fortune would have it, we did not have to wait for him to arrive home and conduct a compound raid. The surveillance team spotted him at a nearby coffee shop. They made a couple of passes and parked the car.

Then they waited for him to walk out. He was alone. The team simply drove up, got out of the car, and put a gun to his head. The whole snatch took less than thirty seconds, and not a shot was fired. He was back at the detention center within an hour. We knew we were running out of time and he was not going to tell us anything. It was time to execute an alternative plan quickly. I knew we'd gotten lucky, and that that was the easy part.

We had the General's rap sheet, so we knew he had been in Saddam's prisons and had been tortured by Saddam's henchmen. We were pretty confident that we did not have anything in our limited arsenal that would break him, and every indication was that we did not have much time left to stop whatever violent acts were planned.

This is where the General showed his steel. He knew there was no enhanced integration method under our rules of engagement that was going to work on him.

To put it bluntly, we were out of ammunition.

But we had a pretty good idea that Abu Ghraib prison might work and not necessarily because of what it meant for him. We were still keeping his residence under surveillance and informed him that we were watching his family for their protection. That was true, but it wasn't the whole truth. The truth of the matter was we needed his family as leverage. So after realizing the usual tactics weren't going to break the General, we loaded them into vans to meet the General at Abu Ghraib.

Grabbing the General's family was easy: after we had snatched the General, the family was eager to be reunited with him and grateful for the ride. We basically just rolled up to the front door, knocked on it, and loaded all of them into the vans.

When the family arrived at the prison, the General was walked by the vans so he could see his family, every single one of them. He could not communicate with his family; he could only look at them through the windows. But he could see their eyes, and that told the story. He saw where they were going, and he knew he had to make a choice.

We off-loaded his family, and the last thing the General saw was us walking them right through the very gates of the hell that he knew so well. Of course, that's only what the General assumed we did. There was no reason to take them inside. We brought them to the gates, only to turn them back around and put them back in the vans and drive them home, no worse for the wear.

They had only been outside Abu Ghraib for maybe two or three minutes, but that was enough. The General didn't speak much English, but he managed to hiss out "you son of a bitch" clearly enough, although he added some words in another language after it. But he talked and later talked some more. His play now was to be useful and try to cut a deal. He gave us target locations that saved American lives. It came as no surprise that General Sanchez was being targeted. He was on everyone's hit list. He gave us what we needed. I thought to myself about the sorrow and pain that Abu Ghraib had inflicted on so many innocent people. Ironic that the same place was also responsible for saving some too.

We changed General Sanchez's travel patterns and either rooted out or disrupted the insurgent cells that had been exposed. We were also able to find and destroy thousands of pounds of high explosives and detonators. You'll never get me to say I liked the General. He was a good soldier, I guess, provided he kept his sights focused on military targets, but that's a pretty dubious consideration, given terror cells' lack of concern for civilian casualties and casual disregard for the rules regarding non-uniformed combatants.

But I'll give him this: when the chips were stacked against him and he had to weigh family against fanaticism, family won.

That sentiment didn't stop us from turning him over to the Iraqi authorities. (The same ones who ultimately betrayed us and threw us out of the country when Barack Obama failed—no, barely tried—to get a SOFA, a Status of Forces Agreement. But that's another discussion.) In truth, though, I have a hope in my heart that he was able to see his family again. I saw how precious they were to him. I can at least empathize with that.

FOUR

SMALL-TOWN AMERICA

WE'VE ALL HEARD THE DEFINITION OF THE AMERICAN Dream: having the precious opportunity to have a good job, buy a house, and to ensure our children inherit a better life. Those aren't just words. To many of us they are a sacred trust, something we must work hard to ensure for future generations. Holding tight to that ideal, we not only ensure a better life for those who come after us but for this blessed nation as well.

When it comes to family life, I am definitely living the American Dream.

I've been married to Lolita (Lola) Hand since 1992. We have three amazing kids: Jennifer, Wolfgang, and Konrad. Even though I work in Washington, DC, we call Montana home, just as my family has done for five generations—six, if you count my kids!

Family lore has it that the Zinkes—my father's family—came to the Dakotas in the early 1880s, nearly a decade before North and South Dakota were states. Those Zinkes were farmers. The name, incidentally, is pronounced "zinc-ee." It means "prominent nose" in German. I've always taken that as a good thing: so much of life is about sniffing out opportunities, truth, even a good burger! Apparently, the original Zinkes were well equipped to do that. Certainly I've always followed my nose.

The Zinkes made their way from what had become North Dakota to eastern Montana, then to Kalispell, Montana—the county seat of

Flathead County, which also includes Whitefish—before ultimately ending up in Whitefish sometime in the 1930s. My grandfather Oswald Adolph "Ole" Zinke married a Montana girl—my grandmother Earleen Grace Johnston, who was born and raised in the little prairie town of Bainville, Montana.

You couldn't call Grandma Zinke a local girl, at least not as far as Whitefish is concerned: Bainville is on the opposite side of Montana from Whitefish. That's just shy of the distance from Chicago to Washington, DC. Montana's not just Big Sky Country; it's big country, period!

At any rate, my paternal grandparents got married in the late 1930s—family lore is a little sketchy on the details—and started having kids. Two of each gender, including my dad, Ray Dale Zinke, in 1940. My grandfather and father maintained the tradition of being blue-collar workers who made their livings with their hands; they were both master plumbers. My grandfather started Ole's Plumbing and Heating, which was right on Central Avenue in Whitefish, and my father carried on the family business by working for him. In fact, my father earned the title "master plumber" at age seventeen; he was the youngest person to do so in the history of Montana. I've always been proud of that fact, and that's a corollary to what I was saying before about each successive generation doing better than the last: each of us should always strive to do something better—maybe not work-related, possibly devoted to community or church—that promotes pride of family. Grandfather Zinke did that for me.

My father went on to be the first in his family to get a college degree and graduated from Montana State University with a passion for drafting. After college, he stayed in construction and worked in asphalt-laying operations, plumbing, and drafting. He tried doing jobs outside the drafting profession, such as designing houses, but he wasn't an architect, so that didn't last long. I give him a lot of credit for trying something outside his comfort zone. That's how we grow.

Dad worked for and ultimately ran several companies, including construction and plumbing contracting. He was pretty successful in most of his endeavors and for the most part operated on a handshake. I've often asked myself, "Was he happy?" It's a tough question to answer because he didn't complain or share a lot of his concerns. But I do know this: he loved his family and he was proud of them. That can go a long way to making any man or woman content.

People in my mother's family weren't exactly slouches either. The Harlows trace their roots back to the Pilgrim days at Plymouth Rock. The family made its way west, settling for a time in the Mount Vernon area of Illinois before migrating to eastern Montana to look for work during the Great Depression. That was when my grandmother was young. Talk about wondering what was inside someone's head: What does a young woman, of that unliberated time, in the grip of that kind of economic morass, think about the future? Often we find the answer to that in their actions.

In 1920 my maternal grandmother—then known as Esther Eiben— left home at age fourteen to work as a handmaiden and was given a loan to go to college. I've long suspected her eagerness to leave was motivated by more than a quest for independence, although she certainly was strong-willed and smart. Her mother had died early on, and my grandmother was the oldest of the children.

I believe that after her mother's death her father viewed my grandmother as a surrogate for his wife. That meant raising the other kids, performing household duties . . . and whatever other duties were assigned to her. My grandmother was a very private and reserved person. I don't know if her father ever sexually abused her, but she never talked about him and rarely spoke of her family at all for that matter. But she was a kind and loving grandmother to the point of spoiling her only daughter and especially her grandchildren. She was a terrific cook and had a passion for gardening. Viewing her Whitefish home from the street, you'd see rows of flowers planted in the finest English garden tradition. Every window had a flower box; every border was neatly manicured and free of weeds. She devoted a lot of her passion to her gardens and to making things grow. I take after her in that way.

My family still lives in that home now, and the house is considered iconic, partly because of the flowering trees and the exotic plants that my grandmother had nurtured into maturity. As you might imagine, that was a rarity in Montana.

Grandma graduated college before she was eighteen. She was the first member of our family to do so. After graduating, she became a school-teacher at a Native Indian one-room schoolhouse in the open plains of frontier Montana, near the town of Richey. Those were rough times known as the Dirty Thirties from the dust bowls and poverty. At one point, the county owed her $1.50, which it couldn't pay, so they gave her a warrant against the treasury. I've actually tried to find out if the debt was ever paid, just out of curiosity. If it wasn't, the interest on that sum would be pretty impressive by now.

During the same period, my mother's father, Arthur R. "Art" Harlow, found work in constructing the Fort Peck Dam as part of the Public Works Administration. The dam is just about a hundred miles northwest of Richey, but the workers—there were thousands of them—were scattered in makeshift camps throughout the region. Grandpa Harlow was based in a "man camp" within a day's travel to my grandmother's schoolhouse.

As you might imagine, with that many men around and relatively few schoolteachers, there was a lot of jousting for my grandmother's attention. There was one other worker, in particular, who like my grand-father decided he would compete for her affections by chopping wood. My grandfather was a crane operator, and he worked the night shift, and this other guy worked the day shift.

So my grandfather would cut wood for my grandmother and leave it on one side of the schoolhouse, and this other guy would cut wood and leave it on the other side of the schoolhouse. Both of them knew they were courting the same girl. I'm not sure why my grandmother picked my grandfather—either he was better at chopping wood or he looked better doing it or both. Or maybe there was something else, the same thing I felt when I first laid eyes on Lola, my future wife: a connection—nonverbal but very, very real. You've probably felt it. I guess we all have.

But she did pick him, and they were married on Thursday, October 24, 1929—the day the stock market started its slide into what would become the Crash of 1929 five days later.

The late 1920s and '30s were a rotten time to be out of work. The problem was that when my grandmother married my grandfather, she had to give up her teaching position. You read that right: she *had* to resign. Not wanted to. Not chose to. At that time, schoolteachers in the plains of Montana were not allowed to be married.

There was a reason for this. It may be difficult to fathom, especially for those who grew up accustomed to the powerful aftermath of the Civil Rights Act of 1964, but our state and many others used to have what they called "marriage bars" or "marriage bans" to women's employment. Why? Interested to see what my grandmother was up against, I found this from 1899: seeking to dismiss Anaconda's sole wedded schoolteacher, the superintendent explained that the lady was "married and is not in need of the salary which she draws from the schools."[1] Exceptions were occasionally made for married women whose husbands were permanently debilitated—a not uncommon situation in the plains, where work was very physical, often dangerous, and injuries frequent and extreme. Yet as late as 1927, even the somewhat progressive *Helena Independent* maintained that: "Single women with their living to make should not be penalized by having positions open to them otherwise taken by women who have married failures."[2]

So my grandmother couldn't get a position just because of the Great Depression. After all, the hardship the family was suffering was hardly unique. Ironically, my grandmother's employment termination occurred in Montana where the first woman ever was elected to Congress. Jeannette Rankin was elected to the office before women could even vote. It is the same seat that I am proud to hold now.

My grandfather kept food on their table by taking what jobs he could: some through the Works Progress Administration and some on his own. When the United States entered World War II on December 7, 1941, my grandfather was thirty-two years old and a father—a little old to volunteer for active duty. But he did his bit for the war effort regardless. He built runways in the bitter cold on the island of Adak, Alaska, in support of the Naval Operating Base the US Navy set up in 1942. A small note in World War II history is that the United States suffered more casualties in the Aleutian Chain due to cold weather than were killed by the Japanese.

After the war, Grandpa Harlow put in an application to run a Chevrolet dealership. This was back in the days when dealerships—like most everything else in the United States—were family owned and operated. When one became available in Whitefish, he put what little he had in his life's savings on the line, and together—Grandma Harlow was the accountant—they made the dealership into one of the most successful businesses in Whitefish.

Harlow Chevrolet opened its doors in the early '50s.

As part of the dealership, Grandpa Harlow built what was then one of the finest garage showrooms in Montana at the time. The typical lineup in the showroom proudly displayed three cars in it: a luxury car, like an Impala or a Caprice; a midrange car like a Nova or a Corvair; and then either a truck or something sporty, if the dealer was lucky enough to get a Camaro or a Corvette. That was all the inventory the business could fit in its showroom—and all the market could bear at the time. Folks mostly came in and ordered cars with the options they wanted rather than picking one off the lot.

Back then, the profit margin on a car was around 25 percent, and car salespeople had a lot of room to make deals. If you were buying a vehicle, you could barter—trade construction jobs, eggs and milk, or whatever you had as part of the price. I remember making frequent trips with my grandmother to an old farm just outside of town to pick up eggs from a farming family who needed a car but did not have the cash to buy one. We needed eggs, they needed a car, and with a handshake the deal was done and everyone was happy. That sense of community and finding ways to make things work are important.

Grandpa Harlow did pretty well. By 1955 he was successful enough and well liked enough to become president of the Whitefish Chamber of Commerce and a leading voice in town. My parents, Ray Dale Zinke and Jean Montana Harlow, met while they were both attending Whitefish High School. She was class of 1957; he was class of 1958. They were married in July 1958, and my older brother, Randy, was born less than a year later. My dad began attending college in Bozeman. He was a young father, and my grandpa Harlow offered to help him attend college and get a degree. I was born in 1961, and my younger sister, Jamie, came along three years later.

My earliest memories from Bozeman were those of an inquisitive kid, which makes sense for a university town, right? Unfortunately, most of my curiosity was that of an active two-year-old.

We were living in a single-wide trailer that had aluminum doors. I once opened the door just a crack on an especially windy day. For a two-year-old I had a pretty good grip on it, so when the wind caught the aluminum door and used it like a sail, I sailed right along with it—out the door and onto the sidewalk. I wound up in the hospital with a concussion, a bunch of scrapes, a whole lot of bruises, and a taste for flight.

Another time, while I was learning to pull myself up on things, I toddled over to the stove, where there was a pot of boiling water on the burner with a handle sticking out. I grabbed the handle and got a quick shower of scolding water, which earned me another trip to the hospital.

Well, what small kid hasn't learned the hard way? And, boy, how those memories stand out!

After my father graduated, we moved from Bozeman back to Whitefish. It was a return home for my parents and a coming home of sorts for my siblings and me. We moved into a little one-story nine-hundred-square-foot home on the lake near the railroad tracks.

While I was growing up, Whitefish was a railroad and timber town. Whether it got its name from being shaped like a fish or perhaps from Indian legend, the town itself was incorporated in 1905 after the Great Northern Railway came through. Whitefish supplied the railroad with timber year-round and blocks of lake ice for refrigeration in the winter. Timber and the railroad brought the community to life.

You may not have heard of our town, but you've certainly heard of Glacier National Park. Whitefish is just west of the park, and the area is renowned for its natural beauty and recreation. People come from all over the world to hike, camp, and fish there.

I've always loved the outdoors. Actually, let me rephrase that: I've always loved the American outdoors. There's something new and grand about them, even today. Maybe because the recent history is still so palpable. It's no accident that Native American culture is rich with spiritualism born in these places. When you're out in the plains or mountains of America you can't help but hear the words of Genesis 1:10: "God called the dry land Earth; and the gathering together of the waters called he Seas: and God saw that it was good."

The word *good* cannot have more meaning than this! And if you need reinforcement, ask soldiers who have returned home and they will tell you that kissing the soil of these United States comes right after kissing their loved ones.

I lived what I thought was a relatively privileged life in a small town. Everyone knew Harlow Chevrolet, and everyone knew who I was. Thanks to Grandpa Harlow, I could use his charge account at the small businesses in town. If I needed paint or lumber for a project, I could get it pretty easily. If I wanted to get a birthday present for one of my friends, I had a charge account at Haynes Retail Drugs and the local Coast-to-Coast Hardware store. That was pretty impressive in those days! On the other side of the family, my grandpa Zinke also had a tab at the local Pastime Pool Hall and Bar where the tradesmen and other blue-collar men often could be found for a couple hours after work. I say "men" because at the time the Pastime did not have a women's bathroom. The entrance of the Pastime had a small room with glass cases for cigars and tobacco that was separated from the bar with classic Western-style swinging gates. The bar inside consisted of an open room with a long wooden bar and mirrowed back wall on one side and pool tables on the other side. There was a back door for escape and a door just inside the swinging gates that led downstairs to the beer coolers. I knew the layout well. When I was still in grade school, I used to look through the swinging gates to see whether my grandpa was perched on one of the tall red stools. If he was not, I would walk straight in and right down the stairs to the basement. I would then grab a case of Oly Pops (Olympia Beer) and tell the barkeep "to put it on Grandpa's tab" on the way out of the swinging gates. If you had a job in those days, most of the barkeeps would keep a tab open for you. On payday, the two most interested were the barkeep and the wife. With a case of beer on my shoulder, I would then walk straight out the door like I owned the place and cross Central Avenue in the direction of my grandpa's plumbing shop. I would cut the route short into the alley and put the beer in the waiting trunk of a few neighborhood schoolkids. After they paid me for the beer, I would march right back to the bar and pay off the tab. Provided that the tab was paid, no one was the wiser. Being the supplier of beer to the high school kids had its privileges. For one, I was paid a dollar for every case, which was a lot of money in 1971, and secondly I had friends in high places and never had to worry about getting a ride or getting beat up. I was a "made man" early.

About the same time I was running this distribution business, I was also responsible for running the cash proceeds from Harlow Chevrolet to the bank at the end of every business day. Grandpa Harlow was in charge of sales and service, Grandma Harlow was the accountant, and my job was to run the cash and checks to the bank. *That's* a family-run business!

At the end of each day, I'd grab the bank envelope and make one stop on the way to the bank: I'd go next door to Whitefish Taxi, which was a bus, taxi, and tow truck service. That business was run by Roy Duff, who was part of the Montana National Guard for more than four decades before retiring as a lieutenant colonel. Roy had seen action in World War II in the 41st Division 163rd Infantry. He served in three Pacific campaigns under the legendary General Douglas MacArthur.

Roy was wounded in 1944. As a result, he was awarded the Purple Heart and a Bronze Star. After he recuperated, he rejoined his unit in the Philippines. His unit was supposed to be part of the invasion of Japan, but the ground invasion was called off after the United States bombed

Hiroshima and Nagasaki. As it happened, his unit was among the first to enter Hiroshima after the city was bombed.

If Japan hadn't surrendered, Roy would have likely been killed, along with millions of other Americans, during that invasion and I never would have known him. Let me pause a moment to talk a little about that. I've seen a map of the plans for the invasion of the mainland in the war with Japan, and let me tell you: that is one sobering document.

The plans consisted of two separate actions. The first was Operation Olympic, which was scheduled to begin about November 1, 1945. The second was Operation Coronet, which would have begun March 1, 1946. The Sixth Army was responsible for the first assault. Except for a feint by three infantry divisions (a floating reserve), the first landings were to consist of three Marine Corps divisions, one cavalry division (mechanized), and a muscular six infantry divisions. Those boys were going on along the coast of the East China Sea and the Pacific. The second assault in the Pacific—against the big island of Honshu—was comprised of a massive floating reserve of ten infantry divisions and one airborne division from the First Army, and a main assault force of nine infantry divisions, two armored divisions, and three marine divisions from the Eighth and Tenth Armies. Rough calculation: a division consists of anywhere from ten to twenty *thousand* troops. You do the math.

Consider those ghastly numbers, the hundreds of thousands of certain casualties on our side and the probably greater number of deaths among the Japanese who would have been defending the island. Many of those would have been civilians, armed with whatever was handy since the Japanese army was low on everything by that point. Think of the widespread starvation from blockades.

The cost of securing Iwo Jima, the stepping-stone to Japan, had been monstrous. There were twenty-one thousand Japanese soldiers on the island when we arrived. Only about two hundred survived. On our side: seven thousand marines were killed and twenty thousand wounded.

One battle. One small island. And that wasn't even the Japanese homeland.

The nuclear bombs we dropped were a horror, but I believe they forestalled a greater horror, the inch-by-inch taking of a land that would have refused to be taken. World War II would have lasted another two or three years at least and impacted our ability to help in the rebuilding of Europe. The world would have been a completely different place today.

And let me remind you that each of those people we were committing to Japanese soil as adversary and defender *was* a person. I recently had the honor to read an unpublished, typed letter written in March 1943, titled "Aboard a Troop Train from Camp Upton to Destination Unknown." A large contingent of infantry was leaving the Long Island, New York, base by train, shipped in utter secrecy to avoid loose lips sinking ships and the potential for fifth columnists to sabotage a troop train.

The first thing that struck me was a cigarette burn on the side of the typescript. "Smoke 'em if you got 'em," as the saying went. I pictured a nervous kid, typing on a portable typewriter as he and his fellow soldiers contemplated the near future—since the future just beyond that, combat in Europe, was probably unimaginable.

After passing through Penn Station in New York, the soldier wrote, "It was then that speculation began as to where we were going. . . . According to our local Admiral Byrds we were in either Pennsylvania, Kentucky, Indiana, or any one of the other forty-eight states of our Union."

More than thirty-five hours later they "got the shock of our lives [when] the sergeant finally broke down and said, 'Fort McClellan, Alabama, soldiers.'"

I quote this yellowing, unsigned document because it is the best way I know of conveying to you what I myself have experienced, just what you're getting when you sign on as a soldier. We don't have a draft now, so the military life is something young men and women elect to do today. Back then, you didn't have a choice. And you were with other young men who didn't have a choice.

Yet you went.

Service to country.

My point is that war is both macro and micro—the big impersonal picture and the small very human one. In the army, in politics, decisions have to be made on the macro level: the greatest good. But one cannot, must not ever forget that that pullback is comprised of countless people, from masses of people on Iwo Jima to one scared kid on a troop train. My God, I have been proud to know and serve with so many of them. It chokes me up just to write about it.

Wow. I have certainly swerved a little wide of where I started, with Roy Duff of Whitefish Taxi.

Roy was a cigar-smoking old soldier who had a bark you could hear from the sidewalk. I would "report" to his desk and stand at attention. He or his wife, Norma, would give me the bank envelope and a dime for my delivery mission ahead.

Roy's dime, along with the dime my grandmother would give me, was enough to keep a little change in my pockets, so for a kid that was a pretty good deal. It certainly was an easy job: the only thing I had to remember to do was avoid an Irish pub called Casey's Bar on the way to the bank. Casey's Bar was where the guys who worked the Great Northern Railway drank. They were a rough and lively lot. They would never rob me, but they would call out, "Hey, kid! Whaddaya got, kid?"

I learned to cross the street and avoid them. Sometimes the best way to resolve conflicts is not to engage. I learned early to pick my fights.

Roy Duff was one of a generation of men who came back from World War II and built up this country—including Whitefish. Like my grand-father, Roy served on the chamber of commerce. Roy went on to be elected mayor of Whitefish in 1955 and served two terms. The Whitefish armory is named after him.

It was people like Roy who first inspired me to respect the sacrifices veterans make.

Watching the annual Memorial Day parade in Whitefish is a story worth telling. Each Memorial Day, the local chapters of the Veterans of Foreign

Wars and the American Legion would conduct a military-style parade march. By a "parade march" I mean the veterans would organize and march together in groups according to the conflict they served in. While my grandpa Harlow did not serve in the military, he would ensure all the grandchildren were issued small American flags and positioned at the end of the driveway to wave and cheer as the procession marched by. The distance of the march from city hall to the cemetery was just over a mile with one stop along the way to cast a wreath into the water from the bridge over Whitefish River. At the head of each group of veterans were the American flag and service flags adorned with the battle ribbons earned in blood. Flags mattered to the veterans then, and they do now for those who served and fought for them. I especially remember the World War I veterans and how they marched. In the early '70s many of the doughboys were still alive, and I recall they marched with rifles shouldered and were sharp in cadence. Some even wore the uniforms of a conflict that no one alive today ever witnessed. One of them was my grandfather's neighbor Mr. Haake, who lied about his age and enlisted to fight overseas when he was just sixteen. Even though he was in his seventies when I was young, he could still toss off a twenty-mile hike like it was a Sunday stroll. In his late eighties, Mr. Haake would walk to Kalispell and back—a twelve-mile journey each way. That doughboy could still march! When I mowed his lawn for fifty cents, he would talk to me about the importance of making the rows straight and lecture me on the importance of attention to detail. He also shared stories with me about his experiences when he was a young man driving ambulances on the battlefields of the Great War. "I never saw a German soldier, but I saw a lot of mud and mortars!" He was the first person I knew who wore a uniform, and he inspired me, both in terms of his love for his country and his desire to stay fit and healthy.

The World War I doughboys were followed by veterans who had served during World War II, including Ed Schenck, who enlisted with the 87th Infantry Regiment but was transferred to the 82nd Airborne. Schenck was one of the few who participated in all of the four major

Airborne parachute operations in World War II. He stayed active in the reserves for years after the war, even while he and a few of his army buddies decided they were going to build a ski hill. They played with several names, including "Hell Roaring" and "Ptarmigan," but settled on "Big Mountain," which today is known as Whitefish Mountain Resort. It is one of the few ski runs and resorts in the United States to be designed and constructed by local community members. I worked as a dishwasher at the resort before I had my driver's license and remember Ed's attention to detail. When setting banquet tables, Ed used strings to make sure every plate and setting was lined up in perfect order. He was a paratrooper to the core!

My neighbor was Karl Hinderman, who also served in World War II. Karl was in one of the first classes of cold-weather training in the US Army's elite 10th Mountain Division, which specialized in skiing and combat in winter and mountainous terrain. Since he was one of the few who knew how to ski already and was better than any of the instructors, upon graduation he was given the job of instructor and put in charge of the course.

Karl taught me how to use a map and compass. He, his youngest son, Jan, who was my age, and I would go camping, and Karl would set up a compass course. I'm sure it was similar to what he did for members of the 10th, but I'm also willing to bet that he didn't have gingersnap cookies placed at the end of the compass points when training them. I later set up the same kind of compass course for my kids when we were fortunate enough to have time to camp.

After Karl and the other World War II veterans passed by in the parade came those who served in the Korean War, and bringing up the rear were the soldiers who fought in the Vietnam War. Even as a child, I recognized that the Vietnam vets were different than those who preceded them. Rather than the tight rows and cadenced march of the elderly doughboys from World War I, the ranks of the Vietnam vets resembled more of a social stroll. Some wore uniforms, and some wore a mix or no uniform at all. None shouldered arms. By age, they were the youngest in the parade, and their stride should have been sharp and crisp. Instead, they walked with an uneasiness that highlighted that their separation from the others was deeper than just the walking distance between them. Like the Vietnam War itself, those who fought in it found themselves to be isolated from both the other veterans and the civilians for whom they fought.

It's been more than fifty years since America entered the conflict in Vietnam in 1955 to first "contain" communism by the commitment of a few advisors to ultimately seeing 47,424 US casualties and the deaths of more than 1.4 million in Vietnam, Cambodia, and Laos before President Gerald Ford evacuated the US Embassy in Saigon in 1975. While I was too young to fight in the jungles of Vietnam, the war came to me every night courtesy of Walter Cronkite and the five o'clock news. My family, like millions of others across America, watched intently the scenes of firefights and reports of mounting casualties. Whether you watched to see if you could spot a relative or, like our family, had concerns for a child soon eligible for the draft, the war in Vietnam was front and center. With the backdrop of the domestic "Revolution," as celebrated at Woodstock and by local flower children dispensing "flowers for peace" to patrons at the post office, the late '60s and '70s were an unsettled time in America. The war was unpopular, and those who fought in it were often shunned and even abused. The remarks by a former deputy commander of the Joint Special Operations Command (JSOC), who was a helicopter rescue pilot during the war, may have summed it up best: "When I got back to the states, I took off my uniform in the San Francisco Airport and threw it in the trash. I remember that mine was not alone. The cans were overflowing with uniforms from those who had landed before me. We did not want to be spit on wearing a uniform walking out." There were no bands and no crowds cheering at the gates for those who were returning from answering the call to duty. In many cases, there was not even a simple "welcome home." Today's servicemen and servicewomen may take off their uniform in the airport for different reasons. They may not want all the attention and accolades. The overwhelming public support of our troops today may be in part due to our shame over how we treated our veterans of Vietnam.

I recently had the honor of touring Montana as its sole congressman to conduct a series of ceremonies in recognizition of the Vietnam veterans for their service and to present them with a fifty-year Vietnam War Commemorative lapel pin and a certificate signed by the president. The ceremony was similar to a military awards ceremony, complete with the presentation of colors, invocation, and the awarding of the lapel pins and certificates. I wore my navy service dress blues out of respect. During an outdoor ceremony in Helena, the heavy rains that promised to spoil the day literally stopped just before the microphone was turned on as I recalled my experience watching the Memorial Day parade as a youth and observing today's visitors to the various war memorials in Washington, DC.

Among war memorials, the Vietnam Memorial is strikingly different. Rather than iconic stone columns and heroic statues that stand high above the ground, the Vietnam Memorial's low contours are reminiscent of a remote firebase rather than an Arch of Triumph. The names of the fallen are etched into the black granite wall in chronological order according to when they fell to enemy fire. For those who served in the war, the ritual of visiting the wall is remarkably similar. When approaching the monument, there is a brief pause and hesitation followed by a slow walk into the entrance. The dark granite inside is a return to the jungles, rivers, and firebases of Vietnam. When the veteran nears his or her period of service on the wall, a finger rises to point to and trace the names of the fallen. After a brief moment of recall, the hand braces above, and the head is bowed in silent remembrance. While the firefights have long ended, for many the pain of the war remains and the wounds are unhealed.

When it came to the pinning portion of the ceremony in Helena, each veteran was individually recognized by rank, name, and service. It was an honor to watch many of the vets with disabilities fall in line, and when they were recognized, they would stand erect and march forward and proudly render a salute. Looking into the tearing eyes of a brother or sister in arms, I was humbled to salute back, extend my hand, and say, "Bravo Zulu. Welcome home." It was a moment of recognition, reflection, and, I hope, healing for those who have lived through the experience of Vietnam. It was a welcome home that was long overdue. As the ceremony ended and we were walking back to our cars to travel to the next town, the sky darkened and the torrential rains similar to those before the ceremony began once again. It was as if God himself was at the ceremony and was shedding a tear for the sacrifice of those who fought in Vietnam.

As I learned about our country's military history and how these wars had been fought differently—as bloody, sustained holding actions, without a commitment to *win*—I realized why I saw what I did. These men had fought a mush of a war, one with unclear goals from the top and a counterculture back home that couldn't separate the flawed thinking of Washington politicians from soldiers simply trying to do their duty. Soldiers in Vietnam saw the rules for combat change on a daily basis, which in some cases tied their hands. The enemy didn't operate under those restrictions, of course, which meant that soldiers saw their platoon members—friends—get cut down in front of them without the ability to fight back on the same terms.

The "rules of engagement." They were bad then, worse now. If anything has to change in the field, it's that. Ideas like having to be certain an enemy is armed even when you know, with absolute certainty, that it is the enemy. We've had Taliban fighters firing upon unarmed villagers as we were en route to help fight them off, then stopping and laying down their arms when we arrived—and we were not permitted to engage. We'd leave, and they'd continue their massacre. I'll talk more about these restrictions later; suffice to say that when I was active, the rules of engagement occasionally put up unintended barriers to defense and offense that put American fighting personnel in unnecessary danger.

In the years since the Vietnam vets came home, our country has fought more wars like this—wars in which we fought with honor only to have politicians give back everything we won. This is the most unfair thing a country can do to those who answered the call to duty and sacrificed.

When I wasn't sledding or building forts, my early life in Whitefish was about what it should have been. I fought with my siblings and played with the other kids in town, most of whom were from either railroad or timber-working families. But all that changed in the third grade when my parents divorced. It was a pretty acrimonious divorce, and the three of us kids often got caught in the middle of the fight.

I was lucky, though: Grandma and Grandpa Harlow lived just a few blocks from me, and I spent a lot of time either at their home or at the Chevrolet garage getting to know every tool in the shop. The garage was located on the best corner in town, where every parade would pass by the large display windows. Whitefish was and is home to one of the top-ranked winter festivals in the world—the Whitefish Winter Carnival. Among the featured attractions are the famous "yetis," folks dressed in white canvas overalls adorned with brown leather and fur masks and boots in an attempt to resemble an Abominable Snowman. During the parades they contribute to the merriment by kissing the girls and chasing kids. My friends and I used to go down the street to the local five-and-dime store and purchase a straw and a bag of peas for one of those dimes I got for delivering the bankroll. Back in the early '70s, smoking was common, and the yetis made it a habit to duck into the alley behind the garage before making their long walk down Central Avenue. Armed with a peashooter and an excellent firing position, I would open the bottom of one of the large garage bay doors a crack and take aim. The yetis would always have pillows tucked inside their overalls to add volume. They would take their masks off for a quick smoke and be subject to hearing the sound of peas hitting their puffy costumes. No head shots, just the somewhat muffled impacts. They never could figure out the source of the green projectiles, and the last drag on the Camel was more important than spending time in pursuit. Years later, when I became a yeti in the parade myself, I would always cast a glance down that alley and smile.

In addition to shooting peas outside of a garage, I would go to church every Sunday with my grandparents. I divided my time between the fire-and-brimstone faith of my Missionary Baptist grandfather and my grandmother's Missouri Synod Lutherans. From the Baptists, the joke was that the Missouri Synod Lutherans, who in some ways are even stricter than the Catholics, were so private that even the pastor didn't talk about religion.

I probably learned more from Grandma Harlow than from any other person I've known. And not because she talked a lot. As you may have gathered earlier, I wish she had! The things I could have learned about her life and experiences. But I learned all right. From her example. My grandmother was self-reliant, hardworking, innovative, frugal, and modest. She believed—and so do I, with all my soul—that charity should not be a role played by our government. She was heavily involved in charities but always anonymously; she wanted nothing to do with headlines or credit.

I owe my conservative values to her as well. Like my grandfather, she recycled and saved everything in the event that someday they might find a use for it. The barns were filled with scrap lumber and parts for cars that we no longer owned. If you travel across the plains of Montana, you will find that a lot of farms and ranches practice much of the same philosophy. Some call it hoarding; others call it storage. I owe a lot of my fiscal conservativism to the stories told by the children of the Great Depression like my grandparents.

All that said, while I choose to live my life as a social conservative, I'm very much a social Libertarian—not liberal but Libertarian. I believe that there is a role for government, but that role is limited, very limited. In general, unless it involves abuse of small children, the elderly, or the unfortunate, the government should stop at your mailbox. Unless you are causing harm to your neighbor, the government should not assume the role as the moral compass. The Constitution is the framework to keep the power of government from intruding on our God-given individual rights of life, liberty, and the pursuit of happiness. In the words of Thomas Jefferson, "In questions of powers, then, let no more be heard of confidence in man, but bind him down from mischief by the chains of the Constitution." The best form of charity is a charity that is supported and distributed by a local community and not some faceless bureaucrat in Washington. You should reach out and help your neighbor in order for your neighbor to become self-reliant and share in the opportunity to obtain the American Dream. Sure, there are communities worldwide, many of which I support, that need our help to have clean water, education, and basic human needs. But in my experience it is always better when a community is given the tools to rise up by itself. It doesn't matter what race, religion, political party, or background your neighbor has; when your neighbor is in need you give a hand. My grandfather used to say, "If your neighbor's barn is on fire, you don't ask why; you just put it out." It's just what you do.

If my grandmother taught me conservatism and self-reliance, she also taught me the virtue of giving assistance when it was needed—and when it could help someone stand on his or her own feet. In addition to Teddy, Grandma loved another Roosevelt: FDR. She didn't feel the programs in response to the Great Depression during his presidency morphed into entitlements. She just thought charity was something you had to do when people needed it and when they wanted a chance to work for themselves.

A lot of the government programs under FDR did just that—like the Works Progress Administration (WPA) under the New Deal. The president had an inspired vision of a work-relief program that ended up hiring nearly nine million people. Unlike far too many modern-day welfare recipients, WPA employees rebuilt our infrastructure. The infamous "Going to the Sun Road" in Glacier Park and the Fort Peck Dam Project in eastern Montana were examples of federal work projects. They raised bridges, erected buildings, constructed roads, built public parks, and gave us modern airports. They kept people employed, they gave people training that they could bring to private enterprise, and they kept our country together at a time when very real socialist and communist threats were promising rose gardens that would have destroyed us. I have toured Job Corps camps, today's version of the Civilian Conservation Corps (CCC) with a twist. They take young adults who went off the tracks and offer job-skill training and a fresh start. No one gives them much; they earn it. The program is making a difference but is not a charity; it is an opportunity.

Grandma didn't wait for the government, though. She believed in charity, and she taught me to believe in it too. She just felt it should come from the individual and the community. To her, charity was something that, as a member of society, you did. She gave to all the town charity organizations, such as the Lions Club, Kiwanis, and orphanages.

My grandmother taught me how to be kind. I learned how to be stupid all on my own. But then, boys are going to find ways of being stupid. This is pretty much a given. And when you're a young kid and are inquisitive, unafraid, and have access to things like train yards, gravel pits, and explosives, there are all sorts of ways to be stupid. Later on we'd add girls to the list of things we found age-old ways to be stupid about, but for now it was train yards, gravel pits, and explosives.

Stupid may be too strong a word, actually. I came through childhood with all of my fingers and toes and some really good times under my belt, so how dumb could I have been?

Whitefish was a railway town, so a lot of our fun focused on the railroad yards and the trains. In the winter we spent a lot of time "hooky bobbing." If you live in a major city, you've probably seen that harebrained activity: matching speeds with a vehicle, ducking low, grabbing the bumper, and hitching a ride. When the ground was icy, we'd grab on to a train's ladders or handrails or whatever else we could get ahold of as the train was leaving the yard. The idea was to stay on our feet, skating along the top of the ice as we were dragged by the train. If the ladders or rails we were holding on to were wet, our mittens would freeze to them, and when it came time to let go, we sometimes ended up with bare hands.

We weren't completely stupid: expert hooky bobbers knew to grab on to ladders near the front of each car so when we did let go—or if we got bumped off—we'd have enough time to scramble to safety before the wheels got us.

As I've moved around the country, I've heard this sort of grab-and-go activity called by a lot of different names: skitching, bizzing, and bumper-, ski-, or skate-hitching. Decades after I was young, boys are equally adventurous—or equally stupid—everywhere.

The thing about hooky bobbing is that you weren't supposed to actually go inside the boxcars; the goal was to hang on for a joyride on the outside ladder and try not to get thrown off. But one time a friend and I were going to hooky bob on a boxcar that was waiting in one of the yards. When we peeked inside, we discovered a couple of *Playboy* magazines on the floor. So we hoisted ourselves up into the car to have a look.

Of course, the train started moving. We were distracted, because . . . well, it was *Playboy*! By the time we were done with our periodical review, the train had left the yard and was going too fast for us to jump out.

We rode that train to Troy, Montana. That's a straight seventy miles if you're a bird. The route between Troy and Whitefish includes a couple of tunnels, one of which goes on for miles. We were two kids in a boxcar going through dark tunnels without any idea when and where the train was going to stop. I remember crying during the dark patches and thinking I was going to be in trouble in the light. Most of all, I was scared and wanted to go home. The total trip was about ninety miles by rail.

Hours later, but what seemed like two lifetimes, we arrived at the small timber town of Troy near the Idaho border. The train finally slowed, and we jumped off. We were lucky. About the time we jumped we saw a train going the other way, and we figured it had to at least pass through Whitefish, which was a significant switching point. So we climbed onto the back of a grain car—not where the grain was; these cars have a little alcove at the ends—and made it back to Whitefish in time for dinner. My mother did not find out until I was out of college.

The rail yard in Whitefish offered something that is at least as interesting to boys as trains, if not more so, and that's explosives. A quarter stick of TNT isn't enough to derail a train, but it does make a hell of a noise when a train runs over it. This was the point, actually: the rail workers would put three emergency compression charges on the rail to indicate to the engineer that there was an emergency up ahead. The trains would roll over them, and the resulting *bang! bang! bang!* would let the engineer know he needed to put on the emergency brake.

The rail yard used to store dynamite, caps, fuses, and percussion charges in an old caboose in the middle of the yard. The caboose was one of those old-time cars where the toilet was just a hole that went straight through to the tracks, the kind that couldn't be used while the train was in a station because it would stink up the entire terminal area. The practice was that riders simply did not use the toilet while the train was still in the yard.

Another digression: this reminds me of a true story I heard from a soldier who had been on a troop train during World War II. As in the war before it, a lot of kids were called up to fight. And countless stories, still very green in the memory of veterans, came from that war and from troop trains when the boys had the time to write home.

The old veteran was telling me about how the latrine was in the back of the car and he went to use it. He turned the knob several times, and when it didn't respond he figured it was in use and went back to his seat to wait. When the soldier came out, the other man went in, closed the door, and immediately flung it open and stepped out. He told me the odor was "positively obnoxious," and even holding his breath didn't help. He didn't know how he was going to stay in there for the time needed to do his business.

"I swore not to go into that shithouse even if I had to burst," he told me.

He drank as little as possible, ate sparingly, and did not go back inside, he says, for the two days and a night it took to make the journey.

Anyway, back to my train yard. We'd time our runs for when the railroad police had passed by our target—that caboose. The caboose didn't have any wheels, so it wasn't going anywhere, which meant—I hope—that the toilet was never used for its intended purpose. We used it for an unintended purpose though: some of us were just small enough to crawl underneath the car and climb up into the caboose through the hole.

Once in, we'd help ourselves to whatever we wanted along the rows of stacked crates of explosives. Then we'd make our escape over to the gravel pit and set off whatever we'd gotten with gasoline or whatever other fuse system we could devise. Aerosol cans wrapped in gasoline-soaked rags and black gunpowder were among our favorites.

I actually started my demolitions education in the gravel pits of Whitefish. For instance, early on, I learned that you need a long trail when using gasoline and never to add gas to the flame. And I was making Molotov cocktails long before I knew the name for them. It was around the second grade when I first started playing with explosives. (For those of you who led less volatile childhoods, a Molotov cocktail is a jar filled with a flammable liquid, a cloth wick dipped in that liquid and protruding from the neck of the bottle. Light the cloth, toss the bottle, wait for the *boom*. It is named for Vyacheslav Molotov, an acolyte of the tyrannical Joseph Stalin, who used a lot of them during his storied career.)

We weren't just destroying things, though. The railroad used to store wooden ties and posts for bridges in the yard, and there was a plywood plant where we could get a nearly unlimited supply of wood, so we would spend a lot of time building these great forts in the gravel pit. Some of them were huge, multistoried buildings that were pretty solid.

Of course, after we'd finished building them and playing around them, we usually blew them up.

When we blasted, only on rare occasions was it strong enough to give concern to the neighbors' windows (to this day, I can still hear the *"whumph"* of the blast and the crack, then tinkle of the glass), but we never got in trouble. The railway people always thought it was the lumber people clearing with explosives, and the lumber people thought it was the railway people doing demolition, so nobody gave a damn.

Did anyone ever get hurt? Not too seriously. A few kids got a little burned, but ultimately a quarter stick of dynamite is a lot more to a kid than it is to an adult, and we all made it through our childhood more or less unscathed.

In 2008 after I retired from the service, my wife and I established the Great Northern Veterans Peace Park in the same old gravel pit once used for demolition training and building forts. Together we created a children's sledding hill in a setting that recognizes the contributions of the railroad and the veterans to the community. After reshaping the hills, removing obstacles, and adding topsoil, the park offers a place for families and kids to enjoy playing together. The sledding hills are named after famous battles, and the kids' smiles as they speed down the slopes are a reminder of why we go off to war. We had a pretty clear idea what we wanted the park to represent. We looked at traditional military memorials honoring the sacrifice and remembrance of the fallen, but in this case we wanted the park to celebrate life—which is, after all, the reason why veterans fought the battles they did.

Unscathed physically in my youth by exploring the railway lines and learning demolitions, my otherwise happy childhood was challenged by my parents' separation and later divorce. And that divorce was pretty nasty. At times my parents would use us kids as bargaining chips and leverage against each other. It was right around this time that I started spending a greater amount of time outside and taking refuge with my grandma Harlow.

My parents' divorce was rough. Divorce is tough for any kid. Hell, it's tough for any adult. But I knew a lot more about the bitterness between my mother and my father than any kid should. There is no need for a child to know all the ugliness and pettiness that can go on between two people who used to love each other but don't anymore. I'm a bit at a loss to explain the mechanism that makes it happen. It's too simple to say "familiarity breeds contempt," though it can; some of us felt that in the military. Even a good officer with good soldiers can be a terrible "fit." In marriage, maybe the bonds of physical attraction go stale; having too little money while raising a family applies pressure; the challenges facing two-income families where the hours don't intersect, or one spouse has long, long hours on the job; physical or emotional liaisons with others are desired or formed; possibly a little of all of that. All I knew as a kid was that I loved both my parents and did not want to have to make a choice of loyalty and love between my mom and dad.

Incidentally, there is something inherent—I guess you'd say narcissistic—about telling your life story, about asking people to understand and embrace the kinds of feelings the author has for his or her family. That's part of my intention, but I also want to encourage everyone reading this to cherish *your* parents or children or grandparents, to go that extra mile to find the beauty and good in them. There's a part of me—and maybe that's one reason I love meeting my constituents—that would love to see those feelings in the eyes of everyone I meet when they look at their family. My God, what a gift . . . what blessings we have around us. Sometimes it doesn't take more than simply opening our eyes or pausing to take a breath to enjoy them.

My mother and father splitting wasn't the only way our family fortunes changed that year. Right around the time of my parents' divorce, grandpa Harlow had a stroke. It wasn't fatal, but he had to give up his Chevrolet dealership. Remember how my grandma Harlow couldn't keep her job as a teacher when she got married in 1929? In some ways things weren't much better for women in 1973. Chevrolet didn't allow women to take on dealerships. Simply because she was a woman, the heir apparent, my mother, was not allowed to take over the dealership our family had built. This was before GM and the other Big Three promoted minority ownerships. It was an actual policy of prohibition. That was after the women's liberation movement had begun, after the term "Ms." had been coined, after towering figures like Germaine Greer and Gloria Steinem had appeared on the world stage. Even now, I find it pretty inconceivable.

Before grandpa Harlow had his stroke, his son-in-law—my dad—had tried his hand at being a car salesman, but he really wasn't cut out for it. Even if he were, after the divorce grandpa Harlow wouldn't have turned the dealership over to my dad. And my brother and I certainly weren't going to take over the dealership—we were kids.

That pretty much exhausted the supply of Zinke/Harlow men who could have gotten the dealership transfer from General Motors. Grandpa ended up selling it for around $150,000. That was a lot of money in 1973, but there was a real and unexpected downside: since he no longer had a business, he and grandma lost businessman status in a small town. I don't know how much that truly mattered, though I'm sure it smarted. They were the same folks they'd been the day before they sold it, but, as any politician will tell you, real connections and authority come from interaction and pressing flesh and hearing what people have to say on a daily basis. Without that, you're a memory. And unlike sharply delineated events like love and war, many memories fade.

Grandpa's life wasn't over, though: not by a long shot. He recovered and was active again, primarily with his stable of fourteen Tennessee walking horses—a smooth-gaited breed he introduced to Montana. Throughout his time in Whitefish, he showed them, and other breeds, regularly at horse shows: he and his buddies in the Mountain Trails Saddle Club brought home their share (and then some) of ribbons too.

Grandpa Harlow was tough, and he lived to see me join the SEALs in the last years of his life. When not deployed or training, I would come home on leave. He was living in a manor and wanted me to take him home. I was gone more than 250 days a year, and my home was a parachute bag and a footlocker. By the time death caught up with him, though, he was a wreck, primarily from years of working hard and active living. He didn't smoke, except for the occasional cigar; it was just time, and probably his stroke from fourteen years earlier, catching up with him.

Grandma Harlow, the most important person in my world, had suffered a heart attack and died two years before at age eighty-two. I was deployed to the Philippines with the SEALs when that happened and did not know she had passed until after the funeral.

By the time of Grandpa Harlow's death, all he left for his only child—my mom—was his house, a small farm, and the remains of a ranch that had once been much larger. We didn't have any horses left at that point. As the saying goes, having a horse is a sure sign you have too much hay.

I wish I could have done more for him. Looking back on the lives of my grandparents, I am grateful for what they taught me and the values they instilled in me. It also makes me think how we can do better for our elderly and how important family really is.

There was something about growing up in Whitefish that softened the blow of my parents' divorce a bit: you probably knew most of the potential suitors when your folks separated. The Petersens and the Zinkes and all the other families hung out together. They were all part of the same social clubs or community organizations. There was one summer in which every family seemed to go through a divorce—and then got remarried to someone else everyone already knew. In this case, my mother married Doc.

His first name was John, but since he was a dentist everyone called him Doc—and he was a former marine. He was an enlisted man, an aviator who worked in transport during the Korean War. He was a radio operator and crewman. He was disciplined and, like most marines, never really left the service. I learned a lot from him, especially about how to love and appreciate the outdoors. That education is different when it comes man-to-boy instead of as part of a scout troop. You are mentored, not just shown how to do something or talked to. Doc also had three children, and the whole new family moved into the little house on the lake. Bedrooms were shared, and being outdoors was a welcome relief.

It was hard for my mother trying to raise two families. When you are raising six kids and later learning to be a single mom, you have to be fiercely independent and strong-willed. Mom could hold her own when she had to. She could also be very kind. For instance, when you live in a railroad town, you're going to have hoboes—people who ride the rails from town to town, looking to trade work for a meal. I don't know if that term is politically correct; all I know is that "hoboes" is what we called them. (I am not one for political correctness. More on that later on.)

The hoboes would usually come knocking at our door three or four times a week, and when they did Mom would try to find some sort of task for them, like chopping wood or raking the lawn.

Our house was known as a safe place for them to ask for work. Mom would make them a hearty meal of tomato soup and grilled cheese, which they'd take and very respectfully eat on the patio. We kids weren't supposed to talk to them, but we did notice the chalk marks around our property indicating to other hoboes that there would be at least some sort of welcome for them.

My mother had her hands full with raising kids and keeping the house running. Between the two families, it was a poor person's version of *The Brady Bunch*. But the two families living together under one roof is where any similarity to *The Brady Bunch* ended. On top of this, my grandparents' health was deteriorating, and much of their finances were being depleted by growing medical expenses and care. The marriage between Doc and my mother lasted only about five years, and they separated as friends when I was in the eighth grade. Doc ended up remarrying, and I remain close to him today. Why not? He was a marine!

Things got a little less cramped in the house after the divorce and when my older brother went to college and studied chemical engineering at Montana State University, followed by an MBA from the University of Chicago. Randy and I have had a love-hate relationship all of our lives. He had better natural athleticism and was one of the smartest guys I know. When my grandfather got sick, he was older and shouldered most of the burden of helping my grandfather with his Tennessee walking show horses. I think he felt more comfortable in the academic world and focused his attention on physics and constant care of the horses. Strange combination, but it worked for him. Things changed between us when I was a senior in high school and Randy came home one weekend. I had already accepted a full-ride football scholarship at Oregon and had skipped my senior year playing basketball to lift weights and prepare for Division I athletics. Our last fight in the little house on the lake did not last long as he slipped into the tub and could not get up with me over him. The war was over between us, and since then I have always admired his successful strings of being CEO and a turnaround specialist of small technology start-up companies.

My relationship with my little sister, Jamie, has always been unshakable. I was a few years older, and our parents divorce brought us closer. After my parents separated, we used to go to the local Orpheum Theater to see movies together. We spent most of our childhood either at Grandma's house or in Whitefish Lake practicing with the local swim team. Small note: The Whitefish Bullfrog swim team did not have a swimming pool and used the lake for practice instead. During the beginning of the season, there was typically snow in the mountains and lake temperatures could be in the high forties. The coach would line up the kids on the beach and throw balls out for us to swim around. Every lap required doing push-ups and jumping jacks on the beach. Thinking back on it, it was a lot like BUD/S training for kids, minus the underwater knife fighting, of course.

My first job as a protector of the innocent was fully "vetting" all of my sister's suitors to ensure they acted like gentlemen and knew the rules without exception. Later in college, Jamie and I would spend spring breaks or summer hikes together. When I was twenty-one and she was a senior in high school, I took her with me to spend spring break in California. A couple of other Oregon football players joined us. What I remember clearly of that entire week was having fun with Jamie at Disneyland and how nice it was to have such a great sister. We'd have fun together, but I could also keep an eye out for her.

Jamie went to the University of Montana and then transferred to the University of Arizona. She worked long summer hours waving construction signs for our father on road projects across Montana. She was beautiful and blonde, so I am sure her waving that sign turned a few heads of the many long-haul truckers who passed by. She was also smart and tough when she had to be. She graduated with a degree in accounting and is brilliant at managing companies and making sure the books are perfect. It's in her DNA, and I see the same traits my grandmother had in being independent and having the knack for running a business from the back room. Today, she and her husband own a fire and security firm in San Diego.

As I mentioned already, my father had become the youngest master plumber in the history of Montana. So after his separation from my mom, he went back to his roots and started a plumbing construction company. He became successful and started spending more time flying and finally taking some hard-earned vacations. Dad became so successful that he treated himself to a 1952 Beechcraft Bonanza 35. He loved to fly, and that plane represented a status symbol for him. It was the sort of plane owned by doctors and lawyers . . . and by my dad, the tradesman.

The Beechcraft Bonanza 35 was designed to be a high-performance aircraft. It had a low-wing design and a V-shaped tail that served as both rudders and elevators. It could hit speeds a lot faster than most personal planes could.

It also had a nickname: the Doctor Killer. The plane would shake at high speeds, and while it was a high-performance craft, it was also more difficult for pilots to fly. A number of those planes were involved in high-profile crashes. The plane that crashed and killed rock stars Buddy Holly, J. P. Richardson ("The Big Bopper"), and Ritchie Valens—the crash that inspired the song "American Pie" by Don McLean—was a Bonanza 35.

So was the plane that my father died in.

In 2004, Dad was a passenger in the plane, which was piloted by Steve Schuldheiss. By all accounts Steve was a conscientious pilot; he had just passed a BFR—a mandatory biennial flight review. After the instructor signed the pilot's log, he told Steve to check the fuel tanks.

They had fuel, but they didn't have a fuel-tank selector engaged on any of the tanks, so the plane couldn't draw fuel from them.

Steve and my dad went up for a cross-country flight, and as they were returning to the airport in Kalispell, the plane began to sputter and stall. We happened to be in Montana on leave from San Diego, and my son Wolf and I were going to take a flight with my father. If not for a promise I made to my wife to have a family day at the lake cabin, both of us would have perished as well. People who saw the crash said the plane went straight down, plunging into a nearby house that was empty except for a dog, which also died in the crash.

It was after my father's death that my mother admitted that divorcing him had been a mistake. They were young and brash. I knew they still loved each other but were too proud and hurt to admit it. She didn't have to live with her admission long: she died in 2005 after losing her battle with cancer. It was the only time she ever lost a fight.

FIVE

EARLY TEAMWORK

EVERY TEAM I'VE BEEN ON—AND THERE HAVE BEEN A lot of them—has trained hard. And I trained hard right alongside them and usually harder.

I've enjoyed incredible successes alongside teammates, as well as humiliating defeats. I've been on military teams where we got the job done—"mission accomplished," as we say, even though the winners and losers weren't always immediately clear. The SEALs could be like that. Congress is definitely like that. A military commitment or a political movement is a process with a lot of moving parts. Your team has control of only a small portion of the big picture.

The great thing about sports is that on any given day there's typically one clear winner and one clear loser. I happen to subscribe to that old saw, "Ties are like kissing your sister," which is an intentionally disturbing concept. Either you're in it to win or why else play? (Though there's always an exception to every rule, but I'll get to that in a bit.)

For now, I want to talk about some flat-out successes.

I was on the track team at Whitefish High School. I ran the 100-, 220-, and 440-yard dashes, which are, of course, nominally team activities; mostly, they're individual events. As I got stronger and heavier, the distance got shorter and my competitiveness at the top bracket lessened. I made it to the state finals by running the 100-yard dash in 10.2 seconds, which is pretty fast for a big Montana kid.

The determination I developed as a kid to always do better was great training. You do things as a kid instinctively before you understand what "ego" or "pride" are. For many of us, the first place we understand that is in physicality. I'm not an anthropologist, but I'll bet it has something to do with survival. Back in the early days of civilization, being able to hunt better was more important than remembering how many ribs a woolly mammoth had. Even today, kids learn to walk before they learn how to count. Physicality is in our genes.

I'm not saying that education is less important; it's not. My point here is that one follows the other naturally. Lifting weights, running track, being aware of yards to go for a first down—you learn to "learn" by *doing* things. Whatever a teacher tells you is reinforced, really burned into your brain, by execution. Consider broken field running in football: "Hey, that wasn't a shorter way to go. Oh, *that's* what the math teacher meant by square of the length of the hypotenuse being equal to the sum of the squares of the lengths of the other two sides . . ."

So I knew from an early age that if I wanted to play sports to the best of my ability and really make a contribution, I had to train harder than the guy next to me. The simple fact was that there were other kids who were more skilled than I was or who had more natural ability. I couldn't control that. But I could control whether or not I was the best-trained athlete *I* could be. I was the first kid in the gym on school mornings. When I was allowed to drive, I would get to the gym early in the morning—before the coach showed up. I would wait in the car or do calisthenics in the parking lot. It became so routine that the coach ended up giving me the keys. Fall mornings in Montana are beautiful, but the temperature is usually below freezing. Workouts are a great way to beat back the effects of the weather.

Later on, when my SEAL training included cold-weather endurance, I thought my background gave me a leg up. Between the glacier-fed waters around Whitefish and having to wait in my car for someone to open the gym, the cold wasn't my enemy but my ally! When you "embrace the beast," any beast, you control *it* instead of the other way around.

But my biggest successes came with our football team—the Bulldogs. I played guard on offense and strong safety on defense. I would have been a great tight end had I not had bricks for hands. What I did have was speed, strength, and desire.

The Bulldogs were undefeated in 1979, which was my senior year. And we beat a pretty tough team—Powell County High School in Deer Lodge—14–7 for the Class A state football championship. They were good, but our offensive line averaged 230 pounds, which was big for high school at the time. Our quarterback, Eric Smith, was six foot five and solid, with a great arm. He's now in management at Boeing.

That was the Bulldogs' first championship. We didn't earn our second one until 2015. That first championship year, 1979, was very special: we had Smith and some great receivers, like Frank Wright, and great coaching. Sometimes little cities and towns happen to have one or two years of phenomenal athletes and coaching. For me, that experience was the first solid link of winning and teamwork.

I got something else out of high school football: a chance to train under Bob Raeth. He was with Whitefish High for only three years, but he gave the school that first football championship season. He not only sharpened my game, *our* game, but he taught me the importance of leadership. A championship season is a combination of factors. Here's more math for you: great coaching, great talent, and the support of the people in the stands equals motivation. Motivation equals success. That's not just true in sports or in the military. It's true in every aspect of life.

And by the way, I cannot overemphasize the value of knowing that a town or population supports you. Back in the 1960s, the widespread and vocal public disapproval for the Vietnam War and the simultaneous ambivalence or downright dislike for the men who fought it helped to create disillusionment in the field and disenfranchisement when the warriors came home.

Contrast that with today and the omnipresent and heartfelt shirts and banners and bumper stickers declaring "I support our troops."

Americans have recognized that saluting our military men and women is not a partisan issue. It doesn't mean you are *for* war. It means that you do not take for granted the fact that one soldier (or one police officer or one firefighter, for that matter) is prepared to step into danger for you.

So, talent, motivation, support—all are needed, inseparably, for any successful endeavor. Bob Raeth understood that. He viewed his players as both students and athletes who could be shaped into a team. Being successful on the field also meant you had a responsibility to lead by example off the field. From Coach Raeth I learned about the importance of being a part of a team in order to accomplish greatness and the duty and obligation expected of every teammate.

The personal gain would have been enough, but I cannot overstate the importance of the public support I experienced when Whitefish High School named me to its Hall of Fame for athletics and leadership. By now you've probably guessed that, for me, high school wasn't all about athletics. I pulled nearly straight As and graduated with a 3.85 average, which was good enough for third in the class. I was class president my freshman, junior, and senior years. I missed out during my sophomore year because . . . well, it's not always about competency but also popular message and focus. I took the job for granted and got beat. I learned from that kick in the can that I didn't like losing. I would learn to like it even less when it mattered far, far more, but for now it was good to know how it tasted. I'm not telling you something you don't know; everyone who has ever lost—at work, at love, at cards, at anything—understands that you do not want that to happen again. Ever.

I was in the Boy Scouts of America, which I loved. I'd started in Troop 17, which was a big deal in Montana—it was one of the oldest troops in the state. It was established in 1919, just nine years after the Boy Scouts got started and three years after Congress formally chartered the organization. The Boy Scouts of America has gotten a lot of bad press over the years because of their now-abandoned stand on gay scoutmasters. I want to give them some good press here, one that is of particular importance to Montanans and, increasingly, to all Americans.

The BSA has always been at the forefront of environmental aware-ness: You put out fires you build. You leave a campsite cleaner and better than when you found it. You respect wildlife and habitat. This is in addi-tion to the cliché of helping elderly citizens cross a street—which isn't a bad quality either, this idea that we should slow down and help one another.

Scouting gave me an early taste of leadership. I attended the 1973 Boy Scout Jamboree in Idaho and could easily swim a mile. I had learned how to cook, camp, and use a compass. During our 1974 Scout-O-Rama in Flathead, Troop 17 built a rope-and-pole footbridge I'd designed from scratch in about six hours. That bridge would have supported a whole Scout troop wanting to cross a stream or chasm, and it was the first real sense of accomplishment that I remember. I was twelve when I had the opportunity to design it and lead our entire troop in constructing it. Not only did I earn merit badges in the Boy Scouts, but I learned a lot during my Eagle Scout service project. It was the first time I had ever looked at the environment with a critical eye. I had grown up on Whitefish River and never really thought of it as anything more than a place to swim, row the boat, or catch crayfish. The project I chose was to follow the banks of the river and look at the sources of any pollution or runoff that was coming into the river. I took pictures of the railroad's oil holding ponds and looked at how the ponds of oil would overflow into the river. I looked at the storm drains dumping into the river, took soil samples, and pro-posed solutions to the degree a young student could. When an old logger downstream was mowing his lawn and caused a spark which caused the river to catch on fire, I knew the source. The project promoted a lifetime of conservation values. I am not the only one that the Boy Scouts have had a positive influence on. Presidents and leaders from almost every aspect of American culture have been involved in scouting. Yet, despite all the good the Boy Scouts of America have done for millions of young adults, the organization is being assaulted and vilified for its intolerance.

Scouting also taught me about the conservation policies of one of our greatest presidents Teddy Roosevelt. It was Roosevelt and his sidekick,

Gifford Pinchot, who perhaps had the greatest influence in establishing the conservation ethic enjoyed by millions of Americans today. Pinchot advocated for planned use and renewal of natural resources, and Roosevelt took action by wrestling 230 million acres away from timber and railroad interests and placing the land under federal protection. It was Roosevelt who had the courage to look into the future and use his powers under the Antiquities Act to preserve and protect public lands for the benefit of generations to come. Both Roosevelt and Pinchot understood that public lands are best managed for multiple use, and natural resources are to be used for the benefit of greater public good, not just for a select group of special interests. The same president who established one hundred and fifty national forests, fifty-one bird reservations, five national parks, and eighteen monuments is also quoted as saying, "Conservation means development as much as it does protection."[1] Planned use did not mean "no use" but rather "managing use" of our resources based on scientific methodology and sound public policy. Roosevelt agreed that some public land deserved greater protections as advocated by preservationists such as John Muir—where man is an "observer," not a "manager." But the public lands and the vast resources they contain were to be managed for the benefit of everyone and not just the select few. As a result, the model of multiple use and planned natural resource management has been the bedrock of traditional and sustainable conservation public policy for more than one hundred years. Recently, however, multiple use has come under fire as special interest groups have misused policy to successfully block resource management, reduce public access, and even lock out local communities from being a part of the land use process. Lawsuits have stopped timber sales from removing dead trees, roads have been closed, and even bikes have been banned from public lands. Our elderly and disabled no longer are able to access lands, as paths and trails are only for those able to backpack in or ride on horseback. Catastrophic fires creating billions of dollars of damage in 2015 alone ravaged critical habitats, threatened watersheds, and placed communities at risk. By government figures, more than seventy-one million acres of US Forest Service land requires treatment to remove dead and dying timber.[2] Fire seasons are becoming longer, and the fires are so hot from excessive fuel loads that even the soil is being sterilized and depleted of valuable nutrients necessary for regrowth. In the words of Dale Bosworth, the former chief of the US Forest Service, "We do not have a fire problem on our nation's forests, we have a land management problem."[3] It is a tragedy that can only be solved by prioritizing collaboration and returning to policies that promote healthy forests and lands through management based on sound science and practical application.

It is ironic that it is the intolerance of both sides of an argument that often drives dissention and divides communities. It's not that the issue in question does not matter or isn't important; it's that one issue should not overshadow everything else. When it does—and, boy, is *this* a lesson for politics—you solidify the support among fellow believers but alienate those who are moderates or who may have valid reasons to disagree with you. You may win your argument, but the ill will and resentment you create will come back to bite you. Take it from a SEAL who did a lot of local-focused community-relations work: diplomacy, good diplomacy, strong diplomacy (which isn't the same as making a bad nuclear deal with Iran) is always preferable to out-and-out warfare.

The Republican Party better figure out this lesson too. You grow the party by recruiting others to your side, not by exclusionary tactics that create division and draw lines where there were none before. The Republican Party needs to rebuild the Grand Old Party that was once an inclusive coalition of American values of small government, individual liberty, and opportunity for all. Today's GOP must include conservatives, independents, and, yes, those Democrats who see their party of Jefferson and Jackson moving too far toward socialism or worse. Closing the door to new voters and supporting mechanisms that would allow elections to be determined by political insiders or elites only serve to create a permanent minority divested of the general voter loyalty. Elections are about winning ideas and not excluding others from participating. Political parties on both sides must place higher purpose over political

positioning and understand that a role of the minority is to offer con-
structive criticism and present a better solution, as well as to compliment
when the opposition fulfills its obligation of higher purpose. Similiarly,
the role of the majority is to include good ideas from the minority into
policy and accept honest criticism without retribution.

SIX

GO DUCKS

BY THE TIME I WAS READY FOR COLLEGE, I WAS RECRUITED by several schools, including the US Naval Academy, the University of Notre Dame, the University of Southern California, UCLA, and both the University of Montana and Montana State University. The only school I might have wanted to go to that didn't recruit me was the University of Washington, where Don James was head coach of the Huskies. Coach James died in 2013 at age eighty, but even in my day he was legendary. He was the winningest head coach in the team's 128-year history, with a staggering 153–57–2 record in over eighteen seasons. His teams had a reputation for being well disciplined and tough. They would hit you hard but fairly. Always to the whistle. Even off play, always to the whistle. You *know* that you don't come away empty-handed from working with a man like that!

I visited the University of Oregon as a prospective student on a beautiful January day. It was sixty-five degrees, and there wasn't a rain cloud in the sky. I'd left Montana during a blizzard, and the temperature was twenty below zero. The Oregon coaches told me everything I wanted to hear: they showed me a depth chart that had me competing for a starting job at strong safety. They took me skiing and to the ocean on the same weekend. My grades, my athletics, and my extracurricular activities earned me a full-ride scholarship offer from the University of Oregon.

I could do that math too. Come the fall of 1980, I was wearing the green and gold of the Oregon Ducks.

I played at Oregon before Phil Knight began writing his checks to the school, so instead of the elegant Nike-inspired uniform designs, I had Daffy Duck on the side of my helmet. I missed out on the wilder uniform designs, including the ever-changing logos on the helmets that have come in recent years.

I also played with a weak right ankle. You know that TV show the *Weakest Link*? Having an infirmity of any kind is actually an instructive life lesson, one that's valuable when learned very young. First, you lose that false, youthful sense of immortality and invulnerability that many kids have. The kind that, when you *are* injured, throws you into the shock of depression. Second, you learn to compensate. You can't put a lot of weight on that foot? Then use it more for balance as you shift the big, strong strides to your good side. You have to stop and pivot on it? You learn to use your toes instead of your entire sole.

You learn that in hand-to-hand combat too. It's not *just* hands you're using. We heard a story about a guy in Korea who lost two fingers off his left hand to a bayonet: index and third, just above the knuckles. The wounded soldier's hand continued on in, pinning the guy to a tree behind him with those knuckles while he stabbed him with his good hand. That's another truth about sports, combat, or even street fighting. Many people, even those with severe injuries, don't register that wound or blow until the adrenaline has dried up. That's why you learn never to count an adversary out.

Oh yeah, that's also true for politics, though I get ahead of myself.

Back to college athletics. I was constantly spraining my right ankle, as it had been injured several times. Right before games I'd get an injection, and at halftime I'd get a booster shot of Xylocaine to numb it. I never had the time—or the inclination—to slow down enough to let it heal properly. This particular football memento still bothers me from time to time, although I suspect the nine hundred parachute jumps I did while in the SEALs (many in darkness and/or HALO, or High Altitude Low Opening) did not help it heal either.

Nobody's going to be shocked to hear that football in what was then the Pacific-10 (PAC-10) Conference and is now the PAC-12—welcome aboard, University of Colorado and University of Utah—is a completely separate beast from high school football. First, the priorities are different. Early on in my time there, I was sitting in Head Coach Rich Brooks's office, and he was letting me know exactly where I should be putting my energy.

"Zinke, here at the University of Oregon football, academics is priority number one," he said while holding up two fingers, "and football is number two," he finished by pointing a single finger at me. "As long as that is crystal clear, you should have a very good career at the University of Oregon." To this day when I talk to Rich, I don't know whether he was kidding or not, but I got his point.

Second, the play is different too. I found that out from the get-go, my first afternoon. I'd been recruited as a strong safety. Tackling hadn't been a problem for me in high school, but since I couldn't run a forty-yard dash in 4.2 seconds, I wasn't going to make it in that position in college. My speed was nowhere near good enough to cover Division I wide receivers, so the position of strong safety was out. Oregon was known as a track team, and the first time I ever saw real speed was on the old grass Hayward practice fields. I thought I was fast in Montana, but after seeing fast, I readjusted my pursuit angles. But I was able to add a few more pounds of muscle, and I seemed to be a good linebacker prospect.

I went into the first scrimmage as an outside linebacker. At the time Oregon had a fullback named Vince Williams, who would later play with the San Francisco 49ers in the early '80s.

I'd bulked up in high school, adding fifty pounds of muscle in four years. But in that scrimmage I was supposed to tackle Williams, who at 245 pounds had 20 pounds on me and still could run a 40 in 4.4. We lined up across from each other. He got the ball, I stepped in the hole to defend, and then I lowered my shoulder to tackle him. I remember being in good position and then seeing his thigh come up and hit me in the helmet, which sent me flying backward. I found myself on my back looking up at Vince as he stepped on my chest and vaulted over me on his way to score. The offensive coaches replayed the film over and over at practice to show what a great running play it was. I was embarrassed but had to admit it was a hell of a run.

Welcome to the PAC-10, time to work harder.

When I started college, Oregon was a middle-of-the-road PAC-10 team. It was a tough league. Washington, USC, and UCLA were all powerhouses. Oregon was on the upswing, but it was not the juggernaut it is today. Case in point: When we first reported for gear issue, the equipment manager, Rap, handed me a helmet that was too big. It went down over my eyes. He immediately removed it from my head. I was impressed as I was expecting another helmet. Instead, he took a knee-pad off the shelf, dropped it into the oversize helmet, and placed it back on my head. "Next."

Rich Brooks was a phenomenal coach. He's credited with turning Oregon from a mid-level PAC-10 school into a national contender, and he deserves that credit. He taught a class—the History of Football 1 and 2, which went into great detail about the development of various offenses and how they were and weren't effective. Rich knew football.

Coach Brooks was incredibly demanding and even intimidating. For much of practice, he would observe from his perch high in the stadium bleachers, watching like a hawk. When he swooped on the field, it generally was not good. The coaches and players instinctively picked up the intensity. I don't remember a time he was so elated with my play that he descended to the field to say, "Hey, Zinke. Great block. Great job. You're having a really good practice."

I later became a SEAL commander who took part in more than three hundred combat missions, but to this day my palms still sweat when I see Coach Brooks. As I got older, my respect for him has only grown. He would have made a great SEAL commander.

Thing is, even though Brooks didn't dole out compliments or pats on the back, he also wasn't passing blame. If his team lost, he took responsibility for the loss, whether it was due to a bad play by an individual or a bad call by a coach.

A football head coach is like a commanding general in that you can't blame failure on anyone else. Whether a success or a failure, an operation's result is always the commanding general's responsibility. I liked that, respected it, and learned from it.

Part of taking responsibility for an operation's success or failure is knowing what's available to you in terms of resources or abilities. In my sophomore year, I transitioned from an outside linebacker to center. It was more of an emergency move, actually; we had a number of injuries on the offensive line. Even though I was the largest outside linebacker on the team, we were flush with talent at that position. I remember being called into the football office during the week we were preparing for UCLA. Coach Brooks and the rest of the offensive coaches were seated at the table. They asked me to sit down across from them and asked me what I thought about finishing the season on the offensive line. Before I could answer, they took a moment to share all the advantages the move would bring to me. It would make me a better athlete, give me an opportunity to start, etc. The pitch sounded vaguely familiar. I said yes, and Coach Neil Zoumboukos, aka Zoomer, drew the offensive line playbook from his lap and the deal was done. I weighed about 225 pounds and became the smallest starting center in the PAC-10 and probably in all of Division 1. But I was happy to step in where needed. I played center for two years and was a four-year letterman.

Center turned out to be a good position for me. It requires a lot of in-game awareness and quick strategic thinking. Size-wise, it was less of an ideal position—I used to wear double sweats to make myself look bigger—but I liked the challenge of blocking noseguards or cutting off linebackers, of having to be aware of the right and left side, and of calling line positions. And, of course, figuring which angle to take on my defender.

I had a few memorable encounters with players who ended up in the NFL, including Scott Garnett, a defensive lineman for the Denver Broncos, San Francisco 49ers, San Diego Chargers, and Buffalo Bills. Impressive guy; you just had a feeling that, if he wanted it, the pros were his. When I went up against Garnett, he was playing for the University of Washington. Washington, remember, was the only school I was interested in that didn't recruit me.

We were on offense. I was an inch taller than Garnett, but he had about eighty pounds on me, and that day he was playing taller than me. NFL-quality players can do that. Garnett had tree trunks for arms, and I think he had "Boss" carved on his bicep. He was Samoan and more locomotive than human.

The play was a draw. My job was to shotgun snap the ball, stand Garnett up, give him his choice as to which way he wanted to go, and ride him when he started moving. Our running back was supposed to read off my block. Simple enough.

The ball was snapped, and Garnett was facing me straight up and looked over me. He started left, and I got into a perfect blocking position. Garnett then saw that it was a draw and reached under my pads and picked me up off the turf. My feet left the ground. He tossed me aside and tackled our running back for a five-yard loss. It was going to be a very long day.

Even though Washington didn't recruit me, on that day that school—and Scott Garnett—contributed to my education. I learned that: (a) I wasn't going to the NFL, and (b) physics applied to football too.

But I was still playing for Oregon, and one of the other players I went up against was Ronnie Lott—a future Pro Football Hall of Famer who played for the San Francisco 49ers, Los Angeles Raiders, New York Jets, and Kansas City Chiefs.

Lott was with the University of Southern California (USC) Trojans when my Oregon Ducks played a game at their home stadium—the Los Angeles Memorial Coliseum. Lott was part of the team's legendary defense—a near–pro-quality line that, right before a play, would stand up and go back down as a single unit. The USC line was so large that when they stood up they literally blocked the sun, and it seemed like for an instant the sky would go dark.

When we played USC, Lott was a strong safety. He took out our team's entire offensive core in about five shots—four guys, five hits. He went to his third helmet during the game. That's how hard the guy hit. The game was a rout.

So I clearly couldn't get the better of an NFL-quality player through physical ability, but I was once able to do so by using tactical deception. The Ducks were playing the Arizona Wildcats, and I was lined up across from Joe Drake, also known as JoJo, who later played for the Philadelphia Eagles and the San Francisco 49ers. JoJo was built like a fireplug and as strong as a bull. His neck was so big that his helmet looked small. There was little chance that I would be successful in moving him anywhere, so Zoomer, the line coach, devised a plan. The plan was divided into three phases. The first was to get JoJo riled up by calling him names before the snap. When I snapped the ball I would let him bull over me and grab his jersey while rolling back and hang on for dear life. The second phase was more devious. After the play I would walk over to the referee and tell him that JoJo was throwing punches. In the PAC-10, all of the referees knew who I was and watched in amazement how a guy my size could survive sixty minutes of play. It was fair to say they gave me the benefit of the doubt. The final phase was to repeat phase one and hope that JoJo would actually start hitting me as I had falsely claimed after the previous play, giving the referee reason to flag JoJo for unsportsmanlike conduct and toss him out of the game. As planned, phases one and two were executed perfectly, and during phase three JoJo started punching. The first blow nearly knocked my helmet off, and a yellow flag was thrown just in time to save my life. Zoomer taught me a very important lesson that I would use over and over as a SEAL commander. When you can't win going toe to toe, change your tactics to your advantage. SEALs call it Unconventional Warfare; football coaches call it drawing a penalty.

I wasn't the best player on the Duck football team, but there were some great ones who played next to me. Gary Zimmerman played right guard and was drafted by the United States Football League's Los Angeles Express before moving into the National Football League with the Minnesota Vikings and the Denver Broncos. Gary was part of the 1997 Super Bowl XXXII champion Broncos, and he's now in the Pro Football Hall of Fame. Gary was the only person I ever saw throw a beer keg over a roof. True, the building was single story and the keg bounced and rolled over the peak, but it counted just the same. He was a force to be reckoned with and feared by every defense in the league. Playing next to him probably saved me from permanent injury.

But I was working hard to be the best player I could be. My drive probably isn't much different from that of other folks; it comes from a desire to succeed (or why bother?), but it also comes from fear of failure. No, *fear* isn't the best word. That's what you have when you ask a girl on a date. It's more a matter of shame. Like bringing your folks a report card where you knew you could've done better or letting your teammates down in any endeavor. I never want to fail, and in athletics I was always looking over my shoulder. Let's call it a soul-deep detestation of failing, of not doing my duty. That is an enormous driver. It has defined me.

Whatever you want to call that quality, it works. In college I benched just under four hundred pounds and squatted more than six hundred pounds. I held the squat record at Oregon for many years.

So while I might not have been the top man on the Ducks, I was good enough at center to be named All-Conference and awarded the Pacific Ten Conference Medal for Athletics and Leadership. And in 1984 Oregon's athletic department and the *Daily Emerald*, the university's newspaper, awarded me the prestigious Emerald Athletic Trophy for outstanding achievement in athletics, scholarship, and citizenship. It's the highest honor a student athlete can receive at Oregon.

I said earlier that sometimes there isn't a winner or loser. That was true in one of the ugliest college football games in history—the November 19, 1983, game between the University of Oregon and Oregon

State. It was my last time in a Duck uniform, and it should have been a nondescript game between two pretty bad teams. The Ducks' record was 4–6, and we were the favorite by two touchdowns. The Oregon State Beavers came in with a 2–8 record. Neither team would be mistaken for the cream of the PAC-10 that year.

When I was a prospective freshman looking at schools, I visited Oregon on a beautiful clear January day. That day was four years in the past. My senior year, the 1983–84 academic year, was one of the wettest in Oregon's history, and this day was doing everything it could to help set the record. There was wind, there was horizontal rain, and there was about an inch of water on the field. The weather was part of the reason that game was eventually nicknamed the Toilet Bowl. It has been referred to as one of the worst college games ever played. The horrible weather wasn't the only reason for the poor level of play in that game, however. Earlier in the season the Ducks lost our quarterback Mike Jorgensen and two linemen to injury. By the time we reached the Ducks-Beavers game, the coaches had decided that 1983 was going to be a rebuilding year. They chose to redshirt the better players, taking them out of play for the season so they'd have an extra year of eligibility.

For this game we had a freshman quarterback by the name of Chris Miller. After college, Chris ended up playing for the Atlanta Falcons, the Los Angeles and St. Louis Rams, and the Denver Broncos. He even was selected to the NFL Pro Bowl in 1991.

On that day, awful play was a team effort. I was not one of the guys who got redshirted, so I had been out there taking hits for the team all season. Miller wasn't showing off his Pro Bowl form. He tossed two interceptions, including one that looked more like a punt than a pass and wasn't anywhere near a player with a Duck jersey.

Actually, awful play was a two-team effort. The Ducks and the Beavers managed to combine for five interceptions, eleven fumbles—including five that were recovered by the other team—and four missed field goals, including two that were from under thirty yards. Basically, we were slopping the ball all over the field, and neither team was scoring.

If the puddles on the field had gotten any deeper, I would have been able to breaststroke into the end zone.

We went into the final two minutes of the game with the score tied 0–0. Miller was out of the game at this point. I hiked the ball, and our new quarterback, Mike Owens, passed—successfully—to kick returner Lew Barnes, who lateraled the ball to Ladaria Johnson.

Ladaria Johnson had made his mark with me earlier in the year at the school's kickoff banquet. Ladaria was from Los Angeles and built to be a running back. He was fast, strong, and athletic. At the start of every season, Oregon Alumni Association sponsors the annual Duck Football Kickoff Banquet where the team would meet the legends and enjoy a free meal. During the event, the players would stand up and introduce themselves. "I'm Ryan Zinke, Whitefish, Montana, center, number 66, senior, major in geology."

Ladaria got up and said, "Ladaria Johnson, running back, Compton High School, senior, majoring in electronics," and sat down. The coaches were all nodding in approval and commenting, "Electronics, that's great." I broke out laughing. Oregon didn't offer electronics as a major. Ladaria just got up and decided electronics sounded cool. I thought it was hilarious. Not only was electronics a vocational trade not offered at Oregon, but none of the coaches caught it. Remember, at Oregon, academics was "number one."

So there was Ladaria with the ball, running through the muck and the puddles until he was finally forced out of bounds. Time ran out, and that's how the game ended, with the score tied 0–0. Game over. The people in the stands started rioting. They'd been sitting through this awful weather watching sloppy play, there was no resolution, and they didn't know who to be pissed at, so they took it out on everybody. They were throwing stuff onto the field at the players and the coaches. And so my college football career ended on a scoreless and rainy afternoon being hit by garbage.

Nobody likes an uncertain ending, and that's true in football and in war. That's why when you do go to war, you make sure that you have the right training, the right equipment, and the right rules of engagement to win decisively on the field of battle, because our troops deserve it.

Incidentally, the National Collegiate Athletic Association changed the rules in 1996 to allow overtime, meaning that there would be no more scoreless tie games in college football. The Toilet Bowl was the last one. I'm not sure if that's a win or a loss.

One last football story. A few years later I was at The In & Out, a distinguished military club in London with dark wood-paneled rooms. I was there having a drink with a few of the officers and our wives from the Naval Headquarters Plans and Policy Branch when I saw a man standing at the bar wearing a Navy Cross pin, which is the second-highest honor awarded by the US Navy, behind only the Medal of Honor. The Navy Cross is awarded for extraordinary heroism in combat, and the bar is pretty high since many of the presentation ceremonies coincide with their funerals.

Turned out he was a retired marine who served in Vietnam. When I introduced myself, he said, "I know exactly who you are. You played for the Ducks. My wife and I were season ticket holders and are huge fans."

I was flattered as I thought he remembered me as the guy who persevered through adversity. The guy who went to the whistle. I was smaller than most of the other players, but I never gave up. I worked harder and played harder, and surely that ethic must have been etched into his memory.

He turned and said in a serious tone, "You were a lot smaller than the guys around you, and my wife always thought you had the best ass in the PAC-10." That's how he remembered me.

Not knowing what to say, I just said, "Thank you," and invited him back to the table. Lola and the rest of the wives thought it was hysterical, but I just sat speechless in the club's high leather chair drinking a fine bitter beer and enjoying a Cuban cigar.

I went to college on a full-ride football scholarship. Even with it, though, every summer I'd come home to Montana to work with my father in construction. Being my father's son, I did not get many breaks. One of my first assignments of the job was to pump out septic systems. These were the big ones, the ones that would have ladders and large grinder pumps at the bottom. I would don coveralls, pump the sewage out, and descend to the bottom of the tank to clear the grinder of debris. Typically, it was a wedged pair of women's panties or a towel that was the culprit. It was a time where little concern was placed on contagious viruses or diseases, and the only precaution was a well-earned shower at the end of the day. I was well respected by the rest of the men, but only a few would eat lunch with me.

When I was in school, though, the scholarship took care of my tuition, books, room, and board, but with three kids and a single mother in my family, there wasn't a lot left for incidentals. And even though Oregon had held its minimum drinking age steady at twenty-one when a lot of other states were lowering them during the 1970s, I still managed to generate a few additional noncollege expenses.

I'm not going to pretend that kids in college don't drink. They do. We did. I'm not going to pretend it's a good thing. It isn't. I cannot say it's a wise thing. It surely isn't that either.

What it is, though, is part of cutting the cord. It's like that other stupid thing most of us try: smoking. It's ironic how destructive the things are that we do to prove to ourselves and others that we're all grown up. I'd include in that learning to drive and then a week later acting like we're in a *Fast & Furious* film. Or premarital sex. A bunch of years back, there was a copy of the *I Ching* in a rec area on a base, and I picked it up. The ancient Chinese had a way of putting down philosophy that was wise yet so accessible, and this stuck with me: "On average, an infant laughs nearly two hundred times a day; an adult, only twelve. Maybe they are laughing so much because they are looking at us."[1]

We *do* do stupid things. Maybe members of the armed forces

understand this better than anyone else; you enjoy life while you can, while it's yours.

Back to drinking. The trick—dumb luck might be a better description—is making sure that whatever you end up doing while you're drinking doesn't do much damage, either to yourself or anyone else.

There are a lot of things people shouldn't attempt when they've been drinking, and one of them is cutting their hair. But one night, aided by a bottle of cheap tequila, that's exactly what I decided to do with two of my closer friends from college, Hud and Bock.

I went first. I wanted z's carved into my head on both sides and connected in the back with lightning bolts. Painting them the school colors of green and gold would be an option for later. Hud's girlfriend, V, short for Vanessa, managed to get them shaved in; my hair was pretty short, but you could tell they were there. Then we drank more tequila, and it was Hud's turn.

I started in on him with an electric razor that had an attachment for mustache trimming. It seemed like a really good idea at the time. A mustache trimmer and a pair of scissors—just like a real barber, right? What could be so difficult? But Hud's hair was a lot longer than mine, and halfway through the haircut the trimmer broke. Let's just say the effect was less than professional. His reaction was less than human. It was weeks before he looked normal again.

But that didn't stop us from working together. That was the night I broke the Oregon track record for the 440-yard dash at Hayward Field. Actually, Hud and I broke it together, and nobody else knew about it until the release of this book.

You see, after we finished cutting Hud's hair—or, at least, after the mustache trimmer gave up on us—we decided to go get something to eat at a local all-night diner. So Hud and I piled into my Chevy Blazer, a tough four-wheel drive with an open top.

On the way to the diner, we made a small detour onto Hayward Field. Hayward is where the university track team trains. It's where Steve

Prefontaine, the great Oregon track star from the early '70s who ran in the 1972 Munich Olympics, mesmerized track fans. His big event was the 5,000-meter run. He set the American record in the 1972 Olympic trials. It didn't matter what event he ran in; he dominated almost all of them. I think he lost maybe four races during his entire college track career.

Prefontaine would have lost that night, though. There wasn't a sprinter alive then or today who would have beaten Hud and me. Of course, we were sitting in my Chevy Blazer, which we pushed to around sixty miles per hour on that running track's straights. I remember actually passing a few late-night joggers on the final turn.

Somehow we didn't get caught. Although today, with the increased security, we wouldn't have even made it onto the field.

After our unofficial record-setting run, Hud and I headed to Hoots, the all-night diner I mentioned, for a little grease to soak up all that tequila. We walked in, and they took one look at our new haircuts and called the police. I kid you not. Hud and I both had white T-shirts on, and we looked as though we might have escaped from the local mental institution. We managed to talk our way out of that. Hud was extremely bright, and both of us were smart enough not to mention our athletic achievement from earlier in the night.

As smart as Hud was, he was also a hell-raiser. We'd go to parties, and if I went to the bathroom or stepped outside for a few minutes, I always asked if anything had happened while I was away. If anything had, Hud was usually right in the middle of it.

There was a house party near campus one night. I showed up late, and the place was packed. Hud was already there. When I looked into this wall-to-wall mass of people, I saw a washing machine coming through the party, just mowing people down as it moved through the crowd.

That washing machine was on Hud's shoulders. Hud had seen a car outside that needed a wash, and then he saw the washing machine, and something just added up right in his head. So he pulled the washing machine out of the wall, carried it through the house, and threw it onto the car. Problem solved.

Somehow it made sense at the time.

Look, we were football players. Not all of us were Tim Tebow. The Ducks needed talent that could play now, and the coaching staff was under a lot of pressure to win. So a lot of the players on the football team had been recruited from junior colleges in California. As I said earlier, this was in the days before Oregon was a household name and had the ability to recruit and sign top-quality players. Recruiting players on the basis of athletic talent alone, as the coaches in my time had no other choice but to do, sometimes comes at a higher risk.

Oregon used to have a team book with photos and stats, which the Oregon police used for mug shots. Whenever there was a crime on campus, they'd pull out their copy of the book, put it in front of the victim, and ask, "Which one of these guys did it?"

They could have used fraternity pictures too. The Delta house there was something else, and the Beta house was infamous too. It's no coincidence that *National Lampoon* filmed the movie *Animal House* at Oregon.

Despite the six or more hours a day I would spend either at practice or in training, I knew my football days were limited, so I paid attention to academics as much as I did athletics. I studied geology as a result of closing my eyes and randomly pointing to a major from the academic catalog, and I never looked back. I am just glad I did not find electronics. Late-night studying earned me the nickname "The Professor" among my teammates, but I was never sure whether they were referring to my being crazy or brilliant. Nevertheless, I was awarded the Sahlstrom Award for Outstanding Academic Achievement and Attitude at Oregon my senior year.

SEVEN

THE ENERGY PLAY

GEOLOGY TURNED OUT TO BE A GOOD FIT FOR SOMEONE with a passion for the outdoors and the acquired interest in earth sciences. I've drawn a fair amount on my geology background when I've considered America's energy policy. My studies helped me put some science behind my thoughts on energy independence, which I consider an economic, diplomatic, and environmental imperative. And we can achieve it through the natural resources we have. In the mid-1980s, the common belief among geologists was that North America would run out of accessible domestic oil and gas by around 2005. The world would be depleted a few decades after. But thanks to the advent of horizontal drilling technology and refined hydraulic fracturing techniques, America's vast shale deposits can be tapped. The shale formations of the Marcellus on the East Coast, the Bakken in North Dakota, the Eagle Ford in Texas, and the Monterey in California alone can produce enough energy in the form of natural gas and crude oil to power America for generations. Moving from thinking that North America has nearly depleted our reserves to realizing that the region has more energy potential than any other region on the planet is remarkable. And that's before we factor in the Keystone Pipeline System, which we share with Canada and that links American and Canadian crude oil reserves. The Keystone exists today along with over fifty pipelines between the United States and Canada. The controversy was the Keystone XL extension, which by any measure was the safest, most well-designed pipeline in the history of mankind. Even an exhaustive US State Department study concluded it was both safe and did not present any significant environmental damage. There can be even less debate about the risk of using rail as an alternative. The controversy was not about an extension of an existing pipeline; it was more about the central argument about the use of fossil fuels.

Since President Jimmy Carter was in office, the policy of the United States has been for America to be energy independent. In fact, the Department of Energy was created to move America in that direction. That direction includes the triad of energy policies to promote greater efficiency and conservation, promote alternate fuels and sources, and develop and improve the use of known reserves of energy—primarily coal, oil, and gas. Gaining greater efficiency by improving the national grid system promoting the transition to energy efficient systems and equipment across the United States is prudent policy. Investing in research and development to create alternative forms of energy to include nuclear, wind, and solar is also a wise investment. Technology improvements in wind and solar technology, especially on the small, residential scale, have made alternative energy viable. Improvements in battery storage technology will accelerate the trend.

The last leg of energy independence is where the greatest change has occurred. The North American oil and gas revolution has changed everything in regard to energy. To some on the left side of the political aisle, it has evoked fear that past gains in efficiency and alternative energy will be overshadowed by the boom in fossil fuels. To others, it offers a clear alternative to foreign sources of energy. The truth is we should continue to emphasize all three parts of the energy strategy. A concentrated focus on one element while ignoring or, in the case of the Obama administration's war on fossil fuels, trying to inhibit advances threatens to keep America from achieving energy independence and becoming economically strong. It is indisputable that America has the ability to extract and refine fossil fuels, including coal, oil, and gas, in a responsible manner under reasonable environmental and safety regulations. In fact, the United

States follows the most stringent regulations in the world. The alternative is to continue to be held hostage to foreign oil- and gas-producing countries that not only don't have enforceable environmental standards, but are frequently our enemies or global competitors. Whether one accepts climate change or not, the promotion of domestically produced energy under reasonable regulation is far better than foreign-produced energy under no regulation at all. Can we produce energy cleaner? Absolutely. But reliable, abundant, and cost-effective energy is more important to the American economy than the single adoption of highly expensive zero-emission energy. Inexpensive, zero-emission energy would be preferred, but more research and development is needed, and we are years away from any meaningful transition. Given that alternative energy is largely not cost competitive, some have argued that we should ignore the economic cost of energy and instead focus on the social cost of carbon: calculate the cost of going to war in the Middle East, calculate the cost of losing American jobs and families without a future, calculate the cost of human suffering from hunger.

Why are the economics of low-cost energy more important? The answer is simple. Without low-cost energy America cannot manufacture or produce goods and services at a globally competitive price. Unless we are competitive, the American economy will fail and there won't be any jobs or food production. Without jobs and food production, there will be no government revenue and prices for commodities will rise and people will go hungry. The government won't be able to afford to enforce reasonable environmental regulations or provide the critical conservation protections we enjoy. If you want to look at what happens when a government or an economy cannot provide adequate enforcement or environmental protections, I would invite you to take a look at the devastation in Africa. New pipelines are built and immediately tapped by tribes for convenient fuel or barter. After the tribes take their bounty, the holes are often left unplugged to release millions of gallons into the environment. In Iraq, there is no longer any potable surface water in the country, and there hasn't been since well before the first Gulf War.

Trash is taken to vacant lots and burned, and industrial waste is flushed into the rivers. In China, visibility is often measured in meters. How can continuing to support oil production and manufacturing under those conditions be in our best interest?

If the United States was energy independent today, it is doubtful that we would give the amount of attention and American blood to the oil-rich Middle East that we do today. With the exception of Israel and a handful of our allies, we would have far more flexibility and leverage to intervene economically and militarily under conditions of our choosing rather than being dictated a set of terms by OPEC or others. For some, it's hard to believe that there are people and regimes that simply are evil and subscribe to an ideology of hatred. These people also believe that if we just talk to these regimes, we can all be happy and live in harmony. I am not one of those people, as I have been there and seen hatred up close. Anyone who puts a pilot in a cage and sets it on fire, crucifies entire villages, and cuts the heads off children can't be reasoned with. Same goes with those who launch intercontinental ballistic missiles (ICBMs) with "death to Israel" written in Hebrew on the side of them. The reality is there are true threats in the world, and obtaining energy independence and increasing our role as a global energy supplier makes sense economically, militarily, and environmentally. It's simply good domestic and foreign policy.

Getting back to the Keystone Pipeline—a few additional comments. As a Montanan, the proposed Phase 4 Keystone XL initiative would have affected me directly; it would have linked the Hardisty reserves in Alberta, Canada, with the Baker reserves in my home state before running lines to refineries in Illinois and Texas.

I've already written about the Montana outdoors. I've played in it, trained in it, and taken my kids through it. I love it and actively support policies that protect it. But I also love my country, and I'll tell you this about what President Obama's ill-advised quashing of Keystone XL has done: his rejection has made oil and gas transport operations in our country more vulnerable to everything from infrastructure failure to acts of terror.

Currently, synthetic crude and diluted bitumen from Hardisty is carried in a pipeline—the Phase 1 pipeline—that runs parallel to the Canadian border before turning down into North Dakota toward Steele City, Nebraska. That section runs almost 1,200 miles, with more than 750 miles of it in Canada.

The Phase 4 pipeline—Keystone XL—would have run 327 miles of pipeline through Canada. There were several different proposals for the US portion of the pipeline floating around, but under most of them the total pipeline length, including both the United States and Canada, would have been under 900 miles. That's 300 fewer miles of pipeline to defend against potential sabotage.

Keystone XL would also have featured a pipeline with a larger diameter than the one used in Phase 1, which would have resulted in more oil reaching refineries in less time. It also would give the United States a backup option if Keystone 1 was damaged: the flow of crude from Hardisty would be slowed but not stopped.

That's something else the people who opposed Keystone XL don't seem to realize: The Keystone pipeline is up and running. Phase 1 has been operating since 2010. Nor is it the only pipeline between Canada and the United States. There are more than fifty pipelines, and the newest was built while Keystone XL was being debated. When President Obama rejected Keystone XL, he didn't stop oil pipeline transportation from Canada into the United States. He merely obliged us to continue relying on a less-efficient, more-vulnerable system that doesn't have another backup.

Of course, we do have other sources of domestic energy. We have reserves that can be tapped by using horizontal drilling to create wells within seams in shale and injecting liquids into the area. Current methods call for a sort of soapy sand-and-water mixture to serve as the injection fluids: previously, drillers used benzene and diesel. The current mixture used by explorers is potable: people have, in fact, drunk it.

As a driller injects the soapy solution, sand, and water into the well, the mixture creates incredible pressure in the shale. That pressure causes fracturing and forces a release of oil and gas, which can be captured once the water is removed from the well. Here's the beauty of the process: the sand remains behind, essentially building a dam as you build up the pressure.

This method is effective, and if you use a casing (a lining for the drill hole that protects nearby groundwater and aquifers, by allowing drillers, using fiber optics, to immediately identify potential areas for bleed offs before they occur), monitoring devices, a geology report, and best practices in the technology realm, it's clean.

It's also what is known as hydraulic fracking, and like so many other situations people opposed to it haven't done their homework. Most of the allegations about minor cases of fluid pools are unclear as to whether the fluids are from surface spills or earlier drilling efforts that didn't have the right type of casing. The industry is well past earlier techniques of injecting benzene and diesel fuel into a well without adequate groundwater monitoring.

One of the key safety features of fracking is one no explorer would be without—the geology report. There's no sense in drilling a $10 million well without first conducting a $150,000 geologic study. Fuel explorers are guided by scientists, and scientists don't leave things up to chance.

Take concerns about groundwater. In the Bakken Formation, which is under parts of Manitoba and Saskatchewan in Canada and North Dakota and, yes, Montana in the United States, fracking activity is separated from groundwater by thousands of feet of solid rock. And Bakken is a significant source of desirable low-sulfur, light, sweet crude oil.

When an explorer understands the geology, doesn't drill in a fault zone, uses seismic monitoring to measure shifts and other geologic events, and handles the fluids properly, fracking is safe and effective. Even a hostile Department of the Interior (DOI) and the Environmental Protection Agency (EPA) said as much.[1]

Extracting gas makes economic sense as well. European gas prices are usually three to five times higher than prices Americans pay. We could fund the infrastructure needed to extract this light, sweet crude based off the premium prices we could charge Europe without raising prices in the United States, much in the way Saudi Arabia provides cheap gas for its citizens.

Here's another argument, focused solely on economics. Through exploration and extraction, California could hasten its current financial recovery without drawing even more heavily on personal income tax receipts than it already does. It could more adequately fund its pensions and boost education spending all by opening up the Monterey Formation to drilling and adapting existing technology to take advantage of salt-water injection fluid. We don't yet have the technology to use salt water as injection fluid, but there are a lot of good jobs—and good resource yields—ready to be realized if we go ahead with this exploration.

We would gain more than just energy independence through these activities. We'd have surpluses, and being able to export fuel would yield global political benefits. Currently, Russia is emboldened by knowing US allies in Europe are beholden to Russia for its natural gas. If we were able to extract and export liquefied natural gas—we have the gas, but we don't have the infrastructure yet—we'd be able to counter Russia's aggression while reassuring our allies that their fuel needs would continue to be met.

There'd be benefits at home too. The reason the United States is losing manufacturing jobs is the high cost of doing business. Yes, labor is usually the number one cost, and we're not going to be able to compete on labor costs. But we can compete on energy costs. Solar and wind sources don't have the economies of scale yet to deliver cost-efficient energy the way coal can.

If we have an abundance of energy, and we can reduce the cost to turn on machines and keep them running on domestic soil, businesses will be better able to absorb higher labor costs, and for the most part they'll be getting a better educated and trained labor force than they would overseas. If nothing else, corporations won't face the language barriers a lot of consumers find frustrating! We'd also free up military resources. A lot of people in government do not consider ramifications like that when they have knee-jerk reactions to a single pet issue (especially when that issue is unsupported by good and objective science, like the presumed environmental impact of Keystone or fracking). Right now, the US Navy is responsible for maintaining safe sea-lanes in the Persian Gulf. We police them and enforce the rules of the sea on a daily basis, which is something no other nation's navy—or coalition forces—could do. There's no greater peacemaker than a US aircraft carrier. Our presence in these waters helps stave off piracy and national conflicts; we are the peacekeepers on the high seas.

Now imagine that the naval resources used to protect those sea-lanes could be pulled away because we were self-reliant. The next time we need to impose sanctions against Iran, we'd be able to back up our resolve with a blockade. The last time we imposed sanctions, they were porous and Iran was still able to sell around a million barrels of oil a day. The next time, they wouldn't.

I'll admit that I have a personal stake in this. My son-in-law—Jennifer's husband—is a Navy SEAL too. I'd rather not see him sent overseas for the purpose of defending foreign oil when we have untapped energy resources here. His training and talents could be put to better use defending other American interests.

I've moved away from my thoughts on studying geology to global politics. I'd like to get back to my original story here, because once I get started on the destructive power of partisan—especially anti-American—politics, let's just say I could go on for quite some time.

At Oregon I took the usual requirements for the major and some elective courses as well. But one geology professor and class really made an impression on me, if only because in theory I wasn't supposed to be in it at all.

During my sophomore year, I was in the gym signing up for classes. The guy behind the geology desk was the infamous Professor Gordon G. Goles, the head of the department. Goles was a top cosmochemist; he specialized in extraterrestrial geology. Yep, that was a field, even then. Goles was one of the few people selected to examine the lunar rocks brought back from the *Apollo 11* spaceflight—the first moon landing. At the University of Oregon and among aspiring geologists like me, Goles was revered.

As I was signing up for classes, Goles turned to me and said, "Ryan, there's a course I'd like you to take: geochemistry. It's a graduate-level course, but I know you can handle it, and I'd really like it if you took this course."

There were a number of prerequisites that I hadn't taken yet, but Goles assured me that I could get in—after all he was teaching it. I was shocked and honored to be personally asked to take his class, so I said yes and signed my name on the dotted line. He smiled and left the desk to a graduate assistant.

On the first day of class I went to the geology department and looked for the room that the schedule listed. The room I found had mostly graduate assistants and even a couple of younger geology professors in it. "That's not it," I said to myself and searched the rest of the building for the right class. Eventually, I made my way back to the first room that was listed on the schedule, and there was Gordon G. Goles standing in front of the class. He looked at me through his black plastic glasses, smiled, and said, "Ryan, come on in and have a seat."

Goles began the lecture, and . . . well, he may as well have been speaking Greek. I had no idea what he was talking about.

The class ended, and I went up to him and told him I didn't understand anything he had said. He told me not to worry, that he would help me through the class, and that not only would I pass, but that I would enjoy the course as well. Confused, I stayed in and began to learn "the Greek."

It turned out the reason he wanted me in the class was that when he had previously taught it all of the students in his class were getting high grades. He was concerned that the pace may be too slow and the subject matter too easy. He worked with me and—well, my old friend the *I Ching* probably explains it the most appropriately: "Before a brilliant person begins something great, they must look foolish in the crowd."[2]

I was the perfect guinea pig. He would give me the exams a day before the test and coach me so I'd understand what the questions were asking. I didn't have a way of solving the questions, but understanding what was being asked was an important step forward. I found him to be a delightful man with a passion for scientific discovery. His conclusions were based on hard evidence that could be reproduced, not on conjecture or theory. When he had an opinion, he stated so and was careful to separate the facts from his thoughts or best guess. In short, he was a true man of science.

He ended up giving me a B for the class, and I did take away some knowledge other sophomores who were studying geology didn't have. Based on working with me, he concluded that the course was tough enough. His students, including me, knew that he was an extremely talented teacher.

Why anyone would be *that* enthusiastic about geochemistry, I don't know. The *I Ching* didn't help me there.

Okay, even if I wasn't going to be a geochemist, I liked geology and stuck with it as my major. I graduated in May 1984 with a bachelor of science degree. I knew I wasn't going into the NFL, my college girlfriend had dumped me for someone who was, and I decided to drown my sorrows. Literally. I was going to combine love for swimming and my degree in geology by enrolling in a diving school in the hopes of surveying the region's subsurface geological activity.

EIGHT

SO YOU WANT TO
BE A FROGMAN

BEFORE I WENT TO THE COMMERCIAL DIVING SCHOOL IN Seattle, I thought it would be a good idea to enroll in a PADI Dive course to learn the basics, especially since it was worth two credit hours and the final checkout dive involved diving for crabs and spearfishing. We took a morning drive from Eugene, Oregon, to Hood Canal, Washington, for my instruction. Oddly enough, the man I was assigned to dive with was a former SEAL. He had enlisted for five years and decided to leave the service and go to school. He didn't talk a lot about it, and I hadn't even heard of the SEALs at that point; the group had only been around officially since 1962, when the navy was staking its claim within the Special Operations Forces. When he did talk about being a frogman, he talked about how he had logged so many hours diving underwater and that diving in the "teams" was hard work and long hours. He had been assigned to a SEAL Delivery Vehicle (SDV) team on the West Coast and spent most of his time in a small open-water submarine in near-freezing water temperatures. He hated being cold, and I could not help but notice his SEAL-issued wet suit looked much better than mine.

The first two SEAL teams were picked largely from the navy's Underwater Demolition Team (UDT) and trained to serve as guerrilla and counterguerrilla units that could operate from sea, air, or land. Their predecessors were the Naval Demolition Units (NDU) who landed on

Omaha Beach during the D-day invasion. They did not swim in under the cover of darkness; they rode the first wave of landing craft to the beach. They landed in waist-deep water during low tide with basically only a pistol, a knife, and a sack of demolition charges. Their mission was to blow up the Nazi obstacles on the beach so that the next waves of landing craft could make it in as the tide rose.

A story told by one of the first frogmen is that the landing craft he and his teammates were in took heavy fire on the way into the beach. Only a few managed to make it to the first obstacle of concrete and steel. They set the charges but were quick to realize that the only cover on the beach was the very obstacles they were to destroy. When he waved to his teammate placing a charge on a nearby obstacle to hold off on igniting the fuse, his right arm was shot off by enemy fire. His buddy was also hit. He lay bleeding on the beach until a corpsman came by and gave him a tourniquet and a wave good-bye. His wounded buddy managed to link up with him, and there they were, two wounded Naval Demolition Unit frogmen left on the beach, braced against the concrete and steel.

As the battle moved inland, a few German soldiers were captured and sent down the line. A sergeant asked if the wounded frogmen could watch them. The frog with the one arm drew his pistol with his only arm and set about his newly assigned guard duty. As more Germans were captured, they were sent once again down the line to the newly desig-nated POW holding area. By the end of the day's battle, the two frogs were guarding one hundred POWs, or so the story goes.

As I mentioned earlier, when I was stationed in London, I worked under Admiral Jeremy Boorda, who was the first sailor to rise through the ranks from seaman to become the chief of naval operations. I was there during the fiftieth anniversary of the D-day landing, and Boorda brought over those two sailors who had been with the NDU during D-day. At the ceremony on Omaha Beach, Boorda presented them both with the Navy Commendation Medal, the highest honor he could give without going through the bureaucracy.

I shook hands with one of them. Though he must have been in his seventies at the time, he still had a handshake like a vise grip. I asked him if he was a SEAL, and he said, "Nah, I'm just a wannabe." But this was only because he was in the NDU before the SEAL Trident was even a thought. That Navy Commendation Medal was the only award they got, and it took the navy fifty years to get it to them. And he didn't feel comfortable calling himself a SEAL.

But all this was later. I didn't know any of the SEAL history right after I graduated college. All I knew was that I needed to get certified as a diver. We had some good times while my trainer was checking out my diving chops; once, we decided to mix diving with a little spearfishing. He lent me his speargun, and as I was looking for targets of opportunity, I saw a pair of eyes sticking up out of the mud. I lined up a shot right between the eyes, let the spear go, and hit the thing hard and square.

I was not prepared for what happened next. All of a sudden the bottom erupted, and whatever that thing was began to drag me down into the deeper channel of the Hood Canal. I'm not exactly sure how deep it was—I wasn't interested in looking at my depth gauge—but I knew I was heading for Davy Jones's locker. The speargun was attached to my wrist, and I was desperately trying to remove it. Fortunately, I was able to separate from the speargun and fish assembly at about ninety feet. The speargun vanished into the deep waters, along with the king of the halibuts. We didn't have halibut in Whitefish Lake.

I felt bad about losing the speargun on my first hunt underwater. It was like telling your coach that you just lost the ball. I bought my trainer another speargun, and he was cooler than I was about the whole thing. Despite my losing the gun, he signed off on my certification and went night diving for halibut.

But, psychologically at least, that experience prepared me for my first official introduction to the SEALs. That came from an Oregon alumnus, John H. Dick. Dick was an All-American player for the Oregon Ducks basketball team; the annual award for the team's best defender is named for him.

He was also a navy man to the core. He enlisted shortly after the attack on Pearl Harbor and eventually rose to the rank of two-star rear admiral. He was the captain of the USS *Saratoga*, a Forrestal-class aircraft carrier, from 1967 to 1969.

I met Admiral Dick at an Oregon football game. I'd come back from being certified to dive and had decided to check in on the football team. Admiral Dick was speaking to the team as he did often before the games, and we got to talking. He was incredibly charismatic, articulate, and engaging, and he walked the walk. He didn't just recruit for the navy; he believed in the navy.

I told him about my plans, which at that point were to go to a commercial diving school in Seattle, learn how to deep-sea dive, and pursue a career in underwater geology.

Admiral Dick had another idea. He told me that if I liked diving I should consider the navy. There was a special program for divers called the SEALs, and he thought I would fit in well with the group. The program was entirely on a volunteer basis: I would go to Officer Candidate School, and from there I would go to Basic Underwater Demolition/SEAL (BUD/S) training in Coronado, California. Even better, I'd get paid during all this, and I could leave at any time. The navy was being downsized, and it wasn't holding recruits to obligations if they quit.

Admiral Dick was hard to say no to. He called the recruiter, I took a physical and written exam, and then I sat through a half-hour film on the SEALs called *Men with Green Faces*. You can see it on YouTube. It's still watchable, even nearly fifty years after it was made.

I can see how the navy would use that film to prescreen people. It doesn't glorify the SEALs. It focuses on the gritty aspects of physical training, unit cohesion, and the personal satisfaction of accomplishing the hardest tasks. It says right up front that people who are in the military for medals and ribbons are not going to be happy in the SEALs; recognition for your efforts is going to come from your fellow team members.

The film also emphasizes the mental aspects of being a SEAL. It shows how SEAL activities support intelligence-gathering operations and stresses having or gaining the ability to keep cool in adverse situations.

The film doesn't sugarcoat anything. Again and again, viewers are told that SEALs are going to be called on to do the toughest jobs, and that actions that would get most combatants medals are considered routine for team members and therefore usually go unrecognized by the brass.

There was something else that struck me about it when I saw it in 1984, and that aspect has stuck with me: there are no names in the film. SEALs and SEAL trainees who speak in the voice-overs aren't identified, and there are no names or titles superimposed. The only speaker who is identified is the narrator, who isn't named until the end of the film.

The one thing the film doesn't linger on is the dive work or the cold-weather maneuvers SEALs do. In this, it's a product of its times: the film was made during the Vietnam War, and it focuses on jungle combat in Southeast Asia. SEAL duties, I was to learn, encompassed more. A lot more.

I'd had a vacation scheduled, and I went on it after I had my meeting with the recruiter. But the film and the possibilities the SEALs offered were in the back of my mind as I ran on the sandy beaches. I realized that I was doing a lot more thinking about SEAL activities—or what I thought SEAL activities would be—than I was about geological exploration and surveying.

After the short vacation, I came back to Eugene, Oregon, for the annual alumni football game. It was a time when the varsity would play the alumni in an exhibition match during the final practice of spring training. I'll tell you this much: there's a reason why athletes train every day. After not playing for nearly a year, being back on the field was brutal. My play had not improved with absence, and the day's only saving grace was a keg of beer on our sideline. Oregon has wisely discontinued the game; having its alumni pushed up and down the field offered better training for the medical trainers than it did the varsity team.

But I was there for the game, and so was Admiral Dick. I met him on the sidelines, right next to a keg the alumni had set up.

He came right over to me and said, "I have a set of orders for you. The first set is for you to report to Officer Candidate School in Newport, Rhode Island. I also have a set of follow-on orders for you for Basic

Underwater Demolition/SEAL (BUD/S) in Coronado, California. These orders are voluntary, but I would urge you to accept them." He stuck out his hand. "What do you say?"

I knew what I was getting into—or, at least, I thought I did. I had gone through double practice days and triple practice days as a football player for Oregon, and I figured I could handle the BUD/S—the basic SEAL training—regimen.

So I shook his hand, and he gave me the oath. And then, after sixteen weeks of Officer Candidate School, I learned what real physical training was.

NINE

DROP AND GIVE ME 50

LET ME BACK UP A BIT, BECAUSE IT'S IMPORTANT HERE TO talk a little about how SEAL training works. In martial arts—which was part of said training—they have a saying: "A black belt is a white belt who didn't give up." Put another way, I once heard a fellow SEAL describe it as having a million-dollar dream that you achieve with a minimum-wage work ethic. Both are very true. It's a long, hard haul . . . and worth every challenging second.

SEAL candidates have to start off with the ability to swim five hundred yards using either combat side or breast stroke, perform at least forty-two push-ups and fifty sit-ups in less than two minutes for each set of exercises, complete at least six pull-ups from a dead hang (not with your hands curled toward you, the easy way), and run one and a half miles in boots in less than ten and a half minutes. Until you've had those boots turn from urethane and rubber to iron, drawing protests from every muscle between your ankles and your hips (rubbing your skin raw and bloody at some point of contact if the laces aren't tied exactly right), until your lungs have had to wheeze and fight for every breath, until your brain is forced to act as the tough drill instructor against its own self-interest—until that happens, you cannot know the meaning of a true aerobic, cardiovascular workout. And until you add, "Your life and the life of your buddies depends on this," you cannot know what it's like to be a SEAL.

That's why anyone who wants to join the SEALs is tested regarding whether they can meet these initial standards. We weren't allowed to take breaks during the tests themselves; although, there are short standing breaks after each set of drills. I never knew that relief could be had on my feet, fully geared, until I received those respites. More than four in ten candidates drop out during this stage of training.

To make matters worse, each of these tests is performed one after the other. When I did them, officers stood over each one of us, making sure every rep was done precisely to navy standards. The navy wanted a high level of baseline fitness before it even considered whether or not to whip us into the shape needed to become a SEAL. When I would later become a SEAL instructor, I discovered that the screening test is designed to indicate whether you are qualified to even go to SEAL training and is not a measure of being a SEAL at all. It is simply a test to find out whether you will have a good chance of making it through the first day without getting hurt.

I've used the phrase "embrace the beast" to describe my approach to these physical ordeals. You learn not only to endure the burn but to like it, to look forward to it, to know that it is building you into something greater, making you a piece of something truly formidable—the best of the best. That's a helluva motivation! You know, when people look at a mosaic, they see a carefully calculated organized design; they probably don't consider—should *not* consider—all the forces that went into the painstaking creation of each tile.

I have to laugh. People have suggested, politely, that an individual has to have a touch of masochism to put themselves through extreme physical training. I respond, politely, that it isn't true. Your body is but a conduit to boosting the mind and soul. That's where the real boost, the real strength resides. You've seen those little desktop toys, "Newton's Cradle," the suspended metal balls that pass kinetic energy from one to the other? It's like that. The body takes the "hit" to elevate every piece of you. And remember, it's not *just* about you. It's about you *and* your team. Your growth helps support and motivate the others, and their experiences boost you. You become attuned to that kind of exchange. Today, on the campaign stump or on the House floor, that's one of the qualities that allows me to plug into people instantly, to relate to them, to hear them, to care about them.

Those of us who satisfied those foundational training requirements, as well as those who passed the written tests and the interviews, were accepted into the program. The one benefit—if you can call it that—to SEAL training over most other specialized combat unit training is that you eat. A lot. SEAL trainees get four meals a day, because it's not possible to endure the level of physical strain the program requires without calories fueling your efforts. The colder the water, the more calories you burn.

Food plays a different role in SEAL training than, say, the Army Rangers. The Ranger training program is shorter—about two months in total—and it focuses on endurance with *less* food. The training reflects the missions Rangers undertake: short bursts under low-supply conditions. It's not a perfect analogy, but it'll do: if you're a sports fan, it's the difference between scoring a touchdown off a kickoff in football and playing a quarter of full-court basketball. Each requires a specific set of skills. The Rangers score the TDs. The SEALs play hoop. Both play for keeps.

In the SEALs, there's a focus on building strength—both mental and physical. Rangers tend to lose weight during training. SEALs tend to gain muscle mass in training becuase they get to eat as much as they want. The only way SEALs lose weight during training is if they start out heavy—and chances are if they're that heavy, they're going to have a lot of trouble passing the above-mentioned basic requirements.

While there was a big jump in physical intensity upon my joining the SEALs, I had at least a little experience with increased calorie intake. During summers when I was in high school, I had a job washing dishes. When I figured out that I could have a future playing college football, I focused on training hard and gaining weight. When I first went on dishwashing duty, I would grab a gallon of milk from the fridge and finish it along with leftover steak and crab. A gallon of milk alone is twenty-five hundred calories, and the steak and crab depended on how much the customers left on their plates. Even back then I was used to eating four meals a day, and sometimes I'd grab a sandwich in between. My goal was to consume ten thousand calories a day. That's about eight thousand calories more than the average, sedentary male teen.

While we're on the subject of other Special Forces units, in addition to the SEALs, the army's Special Forces and elite counterpart is as good as they come. The selection courses are very different from that of the physical demands of SEAL training, but the outcome produces the right type of warrior for their missions. Those who don't like the water and the waves best go army. A difference in selection is that the elite SEAL Team draws only from other SEAL teams, whereas any soldier in the army can request a chance at selection in the army's most elite force; a Ranger, Special Forces, a cook—are all allowed to apply. The training is shorter, and there's no high-intensity, high-stress week designed to weed people out at the start of it like in the SEALs. At the end of the army's elite training, a group of senior operators reviews your performance and determines whether you're in or not. It's completely subjective but proven effective over time.

You could get bounced and never know why. The SEALs? If you don't make the grade, you know why. You know as it's happening. I can't say which selection program is better or if better really matters. I have operated with both units and respect their capabilities and commitment to excellence. I do know the SEAL selection produces the results required to win.

Are there exceptions to the normal screening process? Rarely, but they can happen. SEAL selection to BUD/S is based on an interview, and there's a little bit of good-old-boy network involved in getting orders to BUD/S during the summer months instead of during the winter when the water is colder. I will talk about Hell Week later, but suffice it to say that warm pain is better than cold pain. A son-of-a-SEAL will go to the front of the line, as will Naval Academy graduates. But if you're a team player who passed all the tests and have competitive scores, chances are you will get orders to Coronado, California, for training. The folks running the show are patriots charged with defending this nation. In the end, the deciding factor is your own ability and your own toughness, not where you are from or who you know.

Officers and enlisted men go through the same SEAL training program, but don't think for a moment that the officers have things easier due to their rank. If anything, officers face a lot more scrutiny as they go through training . . . and then some. Officers and enlisted start out having to know the same skills. As they move up through the ranks, officers begin to focus more on becoming experts in planning, coordinating, and resourcing. Enlisted become experts in the arts of combat, such as explosives, sniping, and door kicking. I've always thought an officer's duty is to ensure that the men have the right equipment, the right training, the right leadership, and the right rules of engagement to win decisively on the field of battle. Period. If an officer has to fire his weapon or kick the doors in, either he is not doing his job or the team is in a world of hurt.

Officers tend to complete the course with only a 20-percent attrition rate, as opposed to the 80- to 90-percent washout rate for enlisted men. Some of the difference may be attributed to the increased competitiveness for the fewer number of available officer slots or their educational and life experience, but the fact is that expectations are higher for officers. They are expected to have leadership abilities and to demonstrate them by graduating from BUD/S training.

The navy's taken some positive steps to attract quality officers to the SEALs. When I joined, a SEAL wasn't going to rise to admiral rank. Commander was about as high as you could expect to climb. Since then, the emphasis on special operations has allowed SEALs to become admirals. In fact, two SEALs, William H. McRaven and Eric T. Olsen, not only rose to four-star rank but also were both commanders of the US Special Operations Command, which is in charge of all Army, Navy, Air Force, and Marine Special Operations Forces.

But all of this assumes the officers can make it through the training. And that's a huge "if." In BUD/S they're treated like any other trainee, with only slight differences: when you tell an officer to drop down and do push-ups, you say, "Drop down, *sir.*" As you may imagine, other words are usually used to describe a BUD/S student before the "sir."

From the moment a candidate raises his hand to take the oath to defend the US Constitution to the time a SEAL is sent to combat may take about three and a half years of training and more than 1.5 million dollars. After a student is sent to the Navy's Basic Boot Camp or Officer Candidate School, the next step is a short pre-BUD/S course in Coronado, followed by the infamous six-month BUD/S training program. All SEALs go through the same program in numbered classes, with BUD/S Class 1 starting in World War II. In 1985, I was assigned to BUD/S Class 136. Those of us who finished pre-BUD/S successfully could do at least sixty push-ups, sixty sit-ups, and ten pull-ups in less than two minutes. We were able to run a four-mile course in boots and pants in just over half an hour. And each of us could complete a thousand-yard swim with fins in less than twenty minutes.

There is no room for error. Any recruit who fails to meet even one of these standards sees his opportunity to start SEAL training come to an end.

I passed; although, at times that was not a foregone conclusion. As a football player, I had trained for short bursts of power with a rest between plays. My workouts were structured to give me explosiveness for about five seconds. As part of a SEAL team, there were times when I had to have quick, explosive power, such as when I loaded gear into a helicopter, or put someone over my shoulder and carried him out of harm's way, or assaulted a building using a grapnel and line, or climbed a ladder at night . . . with full gear.

SEALs also drill endlessly for long-haul activities that require not only strength but also endurance. One of the reasons even the most finely tuned athletes sometimes fail SEAL training is that they aren't used to having a fully rounded, diverse workout routine. They get injured pushing themselves in ways they hadn't before. As I said earlier, about the difference between football and basketball: unless you're a Bo Jackson, you can't simply switch from one discipline to another. The physical part of a SEAL is more a jack of all trades and a master of none.

A brief digression here: I intimated previously that, as a politician, I have the honor of getting a peek into others' lives. I learn about their work, their challenges, and their needs. When I meet firefighters, I am impressed by the fact that their training includes a lot of what I went through as a SEAL. We don't necessarily think of that when we walk past our local firehouses, but maybe we should. Firefighters (and police officers) have a challenge most SEALs never face: they have to interact with the public. Each man and woman represents the entire department. Again, as a politician, I have learned how challenging and rewarding that job can be. But to have to do that while on alert for an emergency, to give directions to tourists—listening to them while keeping an ear glued to your radio—and remember every departmental regulation and update is not an easy task. And to do it with good humor? I think of the missions I was on or oversaw. If, in their execution, the people I was trying to help or protect were calling me names or refusing direct orders, I'm not sure I would have been so pleasant while going about my duties.

In 2001, a friend who lives in New York was in an apartment fire on the ninth floor of 666 Greenwich Street. Yes, 666. Brown smoke filled the hall after someone's DVD player shorted, melted a plastic stand, fell on a rug, and set the place on fire. My buddy made sure the front desk had called it in, then made the choice to head for the fireproof stairwell down the hall. As he descended, he encountered a lone firefighter coming up the stairs—a young guy in his slicker and helmet carrying oxygen, axe, the works. The firefighter had already climbed eight floors and, looking at my friend, said, "Good afternoon, sir," then continued on his way.

A couple of weeks later, those responders—FDNY Squad 18—lost seven men in the North Tower of the World Trade Center attacks. That vital young man was one of them.

I salute all the individuals who wear a uniform in the service of their communities. Supporting them, making sure they are represented in Washington, is one of my most heartfelt agendas.

Class 136 began BUD/S training with 138 students and celebrated completion of pre-BUD/S with the tradition of shaving our heads in preparation for the first day of training. It isn't really much of a celebration—just a chance to catch your breath, like reaching a camp on your way up Mount Everest. There's still a whole lot of mountain to go.

In BUD/S, your objective is to survive the day. Each day was filled with classroom and physical training exercises called evolutions. Our job was to get familiar with the obstacle course, swim, run, learn small-boat operations, and come together as a team. Physical endurance tests were conducted as a team but graded as individuals. Academic tests were given on tactics and procedures and even on dive physics and demolition. You were allowed to have three deficiency "chits" before you were brought before a board of Trident-wearing instructors to determine your fate. The usual determination was to pack your bags. The instructors' job was to make reliable teammates, not friends.

On one occasion, I found that out the hard way. Our class had just run the two miles to breakfast and back when our class leader discovered that he had left the class patrol leader's notebook at the chow hall. Fearing unpleasant repercussions, I volunteered to run back quickly to retrieve it. We had a class in five minutes, and there was not enough time to run to the chow hall and back, so we devised a hasty plan of attack. I would run and get the notebook, the class would report all present, I would stay in the locker room until the break, and then I would slip back into the class with the notebook undetected. The plan was executed brilliantly until the instructors decided to count, and my absence was recorded. Unaware of being "busted," I hid in a locker as the instructors did a quick search of the compound for me. When the class came into the locker room at break, I was informed that the instructors had recorded me as absent with leave.

On our class schedule the next evolution was Physical Training (PT) Calisthenics in the center of the BUD/S compound called the "The Grinder." It was called the Grinder for a reason. It was an asphalt parking lot surrounded by pull-up and dip bars. The hot California sun would bake the Grinder to the point where the heat would blister the palms of your hands as you did push-ups. It was a place where students were ground into SEALs or quit. I felt like a Christian in the Colosseum about to be fed to the lions. The instructors had positioned a truck with the tailgate down so they could get next to my "spot" on the Grinder. They ingeniously fashioned a long cord extending from the bell across the Grinder to my position so it would be always within my reach. (A trainee can ring the bell three times to signal that he wants to quit the program.) The ninety minutes of PT began and ended with me doing eight-count body-builder exercises under the personal supervision of two instructors who had a bet on how many I could do before I quit. I am not sure who came closer to the number, but I did well over eight hundred before the time expired. They had me sign the deficiency chit and then promptly tossed it into the garbage. I was lucky they liked me.

We also went through cold water "conditioning" or, as we called it, "surf torture." We were commanded to enter the Pacific Ocean. One might think the ocean in California is warm. Even though I was from Montana and thought I knew cold water, there is no colder environment than the water in Coronado. The instructors were masters at keeping us wet and cold, and when your teeth are shaking and your body is shivering, the last thing you want to do is go back into the water and get colder. Cold water is the great separation between being a SEAL and all others. The standard procedure was to don lifejackets, line up the class at the water's edge, interlock arms, and walk into the ocean to your waist. The instructors, using a bullhorn, would direct the class to turn around and "take seats" on the sandy bottom as the waves crashed against their backs. Of the myriad of demanding physical-training evolutions at BUD/S, the simple command spoken by the instructors to "take seats" prompted the most trainees to ring the bell three times.

Because SEALs are a maritime force, basic conditioning also focuses on water-based operations, with a huge focus on swimming and being comfortable in the water. Again, this is not only about building physical strength, but mental strength as well. It's one thing to be an excellent swimmer, and another entirely to not panic when your hands are tied behind your back, your feet are tied together, and you're thrown into a pool to retrieve a mask at the bottom with your mouth. All the swim laps in the world aren't going to teach you to do that while keeping your cool. Almost seven in ten candidates who enter BUD/S don't make it through the first phase, or Basic Conditioning Phase, with the majority deciding to drop out during the fifth week—or, as it's known, "Hell Week."

Hell Week was a lot more entertaining for me as an instructor than as a student. I enjoyed the former and simply survived the latter. In one sense, Hell Week is a misleading term. It's under a week—five and a half days, to be exact. But it is, without question, hell. We exercised for twenty-plus hours a day, and we slept maybe four hours total during the entire "week." You're driven to beyond what you believe are your limits.

When you're in training, you know Hell Week is coming. You don't know the exact time, but you know it's going to start at some point. You might be in a tent on the beach, or you might be in the barracks. Like a storm on the horizon, you know it's coming and that the consequences are inevitable. The one thing that's certain is that you are not going to be able to stop it any more than you can stop the waves crashing over you in the Pacific Ocean.

Hell Week starts with "breakout"—a noise-and-smoke assault on the senses sprung on the recruits using fog machines, M60 blank ammunition, and M80 explosives. It starts with a firestorm of activity designed to create confusion and stress. When it happened to me, my classmates and I stumbled out of our tent cots and were immediately ordered into the surf. Just as we were starting to go into hypothermia, we were ordered out onto the beach to low crawl while M60 machine guns blazed above us. We ran as seven-man boat crews, carrying rubber boats called Inflatable Boat Small (IBS) on our heads and paddled through the surf and back to the beach. The officer would act as the coxswain, steeing and giving commands at the rear, and the enlisted would paddle and count rhythm. We were sandy and wet, and would remain so for the week. Our legs and bodies were rubbed raw from the wet sand. We had to keep moving to avoid stiffening up . . . and the more we moved, the more we chafed.

Then Hell Week got serious.

The first night we carried IBSs to the other side of the Naval Amphibious Base to the steel piers designed to bring supplies from ship to shore. The evolution was simple: Conduct drown proofing in the cold water by having your feet and hands tied behind your back. When exhausted, lie naked on the cold steel pier shivering until it was time to go back into the water. I remember the BUD/S physician draped in a wool blanket asking if anyone was too cold and wanted to quit. I hated him more than I wanted to quit. Hell Week isn't about learning SEAL skills. Most of the time, we were too exhausted to learn anything complex. Hell Week is about mental toughness to keep going, pure and simple. Navy commanders needed to know whether our minds and bodies were strong enough to withstand what the toughest combat missions could throw at us . . . because dropping out in mid-mission is never an option.

Because of this, instructors provide every opportunity for those who do not have the will to stay to ring the bell three times and quit. Admiral Dick's words were true, "It is a volunteer program; you can leave anytime you want." Instructors using bullhorns promote changing vocations for the benefit of your fellow classmates to create doubt in your head. They'll remind you of the discomfort, if not the flat-out pain, you're in. They'll tell you about the coffee and doughnuts waiting for you if you just give up and ring the bell. And trainees do drop out and ring that bell. They simply stop, even though their bodies are still more or less intact. Their spirits break. They ring the bell, and, for them, the ordeal is over.

Those remaining in mighty Class 136, after drown-proofing at the piers, spent the rest of the night running with boats on our heads and paddling in and out of the surf. Standing in the surf zone and watching the sunrise meant three things: breakfast was soon, you survived another day, and a new shift of fresh instructors was coming on duty.

As the Basic Conditioning Phase Officer, the challenges of training during Hell Week were much more than determining who had "the never quit" attitude. It was also about making sure the training was safe and that you neither killed nor injured a student. The most intense evolutions came early in Hell Week. There were two reasons for this. The first was that if someone was going to drop out, he would usually do it within the first few days. And the second was that after days of pushing students to their limits and not letting them sleep, the chances of them getting hurt jumped exponentially. The objective of the evolutions and Hell Week was to push men to their limits and give them confidence that they can go beyond what was ever before thought possible. BUD/S was designed to test the student, not to injure or maim those who failed. Hypothermia tables were followed strictly and the intensity of the evolutions were monitored carefully. As a student sitting in the surf zone freezing, it's hard to feel warm just because some table says the cold is not going to be fatal. Guys drop out during Hell Week for a lot of reasons. Sure, some of them can't take the exhaustion. But others simply can't complete the training. This isn't their fault, but they also can't be allowed to proceed without the navy knowing whether they can withstand all that being a SEAL requires. SEAL duty could easily mean heading out to kill Osama bin Laden without sleeping for days.

Sometimes trainees are strong enough, emotionally and physically, and are completing all the activities demanded of them . . . and then they break a bone, or develop severe tendonitis, and can't go on. There are no excuses, and no reasons: there is only being able to get through it, or not. There is also no chance of hiding from the scrutiny of the instructors or gaming the system. I once had a fellow student tell me that the way around surf-conditioning was to warm yourself by peeing in the water. I think he was kidding, but if he thought it helped, go for it. At any rate, for the amount of time they were in the water, even racehorses don't have bladders that big. He quit early.

But his comment reminded me of a phrase I hate: "If you're not cheating, you're not trying." I once caught a student who filled a hiking backpack with pillows to give it the appearance of bulk. I found that out only because I sent his squad team through a river and, damn, did those pillows get heavy, fast. And they dripped too. The SEALs don't need people who are able to do great things alone. The SEALs need individuals who are willing to work as a team and who understand that bringing the team to bear will bring success to a mission, while being an individual will put the team at risk.

The physical training is not always about being the best or the fastest. In fact, many of the exercises are about developing mental and physical toughness—endurance, with the expectation that higher performance will come later. Of course, there are minimum standards, and we do bounce trainees who can't meet those expectations. That's the reason I didn't cut the guy with the pillows in his backpack; that added water weight made the job tougher, and the drip down his pants made it uncomfortable too.

But we also try to determine which roles each trainee might best fill. Say you've got a big guy who's maybe not the fastest in the bunch, but he's strong with the never-quit attitude. Well, somebody is going to have to carry an assault team's communication equipment. If you've got an ox, load him up. And don't kid yourself; he may have finished in the bottom half of his group, but he can still cut it, and, at some point, his team is going to be very grateful they have all that communication gear. That is what leadership does: look at potential and set the conditions to succeed. This doesn't mean that individuals shouldn't perform brilliantly on their individual tasks. What it means is that they acknowledge their tasks support a greater team effort. If a team's radio man is carrying a lot of weight in radios, it's okay to relieve him of some of that weight. SEALs should chip in and lighten the load of the guy carrying the M60 and the hundreds of rounds of ammunition it takes, because if that 60 doesn't rock when you need it to, the team is going to pay.

This may seem basic, but a cowboy on a SEAL team isn't going to necessarily understand that while there's no extra glory in carrying a couple of bandoliers with one hundred rounds of linked ammo on them, it's absolutely essential . . . for the team.

It is possible for people who drop out of the program, or are forced out due to injury or illness, to go through the full training program again: Garry J. Bonelli broke his collarbone during an obstacle course accident during SEAL training. He got rolled back to the next BUD/S class, showed up in even better shape than he had the first time, and completed his training . . . including going through Hell Week a second time, which had to be even worse than the first go-round, because he knew exactly what was coming. I think the record is an enlisted SEAL who completed three Hell Weeks. That is the definition of "never quit"!

Bonelli ended up having a long and distinguished navy career that included a stint as commander of SEAL Team Five. When he retired in 2013, he was a rear admiral.

Tuesday night of our Hell Week was spent on a desolate part of Silver Strand Beach on the southern tip of Coronado. The site had mudflats where we crawled through the thick mud as a boat crew. We had been without sleep for fifty hours, and simple commands were harder to process. The misery of the mudflats transitioned into more surf torture and eating a box dinner in the water. It was cold, and our bodies were tired. The cold piece of chicken and a piece of bread was less than I had hoped for. As the sun went down, and its warmth went with it, the physiological effect of the cold night before us caused a run on the bell. Entire boat crews quit together, and a line formed just to ring out. A strange feeling came over me as I sat in the surf zone removing the lumps of sand from my wet bread and watching others quit. Perhaps it should have been a feeling of remorse for those classmates who tried and failed. Some of them had been my friends. Instead, I felt a sense of accomplishment that I was still in the class when others quit. I was happy for a moment, chewing on my sandwich and spitting out the small pieces of rock I had missed. Toward the end of the night, while paddling back to the BUD/S compound in the early morning fog, I saw the outline of a German U-boat appear in the distance. I knew I was seeing an illusion from not sleeping for a couple of days, but the U-boat seemed to keep pace just the same. I asked the rest of my boat crew if they were seeing the same thing I was. It wasn't hard to convince most of them that the U-boat was out there. I guess at that point in Hell Week, we could have convinced ourselves of almost anything.

Toward the end of Hell Week, the intensity of the evolutions began to lessen and the confidence of myself and my fellow classmates who remained increased. The instructors and the students both knew that no one else was going to quit after all the hours of wet and cold spent getting here. We still did a lot of physical training, but the instructors started mixing in basic problem-solving exercises, treasure hunts, long paddle boat drills, and other evolutions designed to keep us moving. The idea was to have us do anything that stopped us from sleeping.

During the final night of Hell Week, my knee injury flared up. I remember running while carrying the IBS up above our heads and awkwardly tripping on a curb. While we all were tall, we weren't fast, and we were shambling along, which didn't help my knee any. Then my knee swelled up like a beach ball. I had injured it the first time during a football game against the Washington State Cougars. At halftime, I had it drained but lasted only a few minutes in the third quarter before being unable to even walk, and I spent the rest of the game on the bench. It was excruciatingly painful both then and now during Hell Week. After four days of suffering, no way I was going to either quit or repeat Hell Week, and my brain said to my body, "Too bad. Deal." (That still isn't masochism, by the way. My mind was simply asking, *Are you or are you not a quitter?*)

The evolution was called "Round the World," which meant paddling and running the boat around Coronado Island. It was a race, and it always paid to be a winner during Hell Week. Whether the reward was being able to eat first or catch a few minutes of sleep away from the instructors' attention, it was a prize worth winning. We got to our destination first, and we basically threw down the boat, turned it over, and crawled under the protection of the rubber shell to get a few minutes of shut-eye while waiting for the other boats to arrive. It was a cold, windy night, and I tried to doze, but I woke up shivering and embarrassed that I was so cold while everyone else was sound asleep. I started to wonder whether I was fit enough to get through the training and thought about quitting. I think everyone goes through these moments during BUD/S, and mine came toward the end of Hell Week.

I'll confess something here. When another student quit, I felt better about myself because I was succeeding under the same conditions some-one else wasn't. As bad as that sounds, in the middle of the training, the thought that you could push through when other guys—guys you knew were tough, guys who had guts—were ringing the bell and quitting gave a sense of victory. You do *not* want to be one of those people. Teamwork is important; winning is everything. When someone drops out—well, it's a little like politics. You don't spend time on the poll numbers of the can-didate below you. You look at the people who might be running stronger and figure out what you can learn from them. That's the lingering benefit of SEAL training: life lessons. Barrels of them.

We used to do a "Hoo-yah!" when someone quit. Some leaders admonish their units for doing that, or try to do away with it, but I think there's value to it. Surviving gives a certain level of confidence that, if nobody quit, would change the personality of resulting SEAL teams for the worse. Again, it's like politics in the sense that as the field narrows, as the places at the debate podium go from ten to six to two, the dynam-ics change. Your personal game is enhanced. Your relationship with the survivors becomes much more seriously focused. I am still friends with some who quit our class and don't hold it against them. The SEALs is not for everyone, just those who don't ring out.

Besides physical trials, the navy also used Hell Week to put us through psychological exercises designed to confuse and strengthen resolve. One that sticks out in my mind is called "Creative Writing," which happened during the final few hours of Hell Week.

I'll be honest: I was pretty fried by that point. I was moving on auto-pilot, but I was moving. Moving was good. The instructors knew that, and that's why, for Creative Writing, they brought us into a classroom and sat us down at individual desks.

I remember that the heat was set on high, and the lights in the class-room seemed dimmer than normal. It was really the first time I felt dry and warm all week. We were given pens and paper and told to write an essay about the Constitution—how as a SEAL you could fulfill your oath to support and defend it.

A YOUNG BOY SCOUT FROM TROOP 17 AT THE
BOY SCOUT NATIONAL JAMBOREE IN 1973.

COMMANDER ZINKE RETIRES
AFTER SERVING TWENTY-THREE
YEARS AS A U.S. NAVY SEAL.

LT ZINKE LEADING EARLY MORNING SEAL PT ON THE DECK OF THE *USS ANCHORAGE*.

SEAL TEAM ONE ALPHA PLATOON, DECK OF *USS ANCHORAGE*.

LTJG HANS WALSH AND THE OTHER MEMBERS OF SEAL TEAM ONE BRAVO PLATOON
CELEBRATING THE PROMOTION OF THEIR PLATOON COMMANDER,
LT ZINKE.

SEAL TEAM
ONE ALPHA
PLATOON DURING
DEMOLITION
TRAINING AT
GREEN BEACH,
SUBIC BAY,
PHILIPPINES.

WATCHING THE PHILIPPINE VILLAGE DISASSEMBLE TARGET VEHICLES BEFORE COMMENCING DEMOLITION TRAINING.

PARACHUTING FROM OV-10 AT SUBIC BASE. A LAST-MINUTE

DEMONSTRATING DEMOLITION EXPERTISE, OR PERPHAPS JUST LUCKY.

VIEW FROM INSIDE
A HMMWV WHILE
ON PATROL..

OUT ON PATROL.
TAKING ROUTE
ALABAMA ON THE
WAY TO FALLUJAH.

ON PATROL HUNTING
FOR SADR IN A
SANDSTORM.

SPECIAL FORCES FOB HILLAH COMPOUND. A SIMILAR COMPOUND IN BENGHAZI IS WHERE TWO FORMER SEALS WERE KILLED BY A MORTAR ATTACK AFTER A HEROIC THIRTEEN-HOUR DEFENSE.

GUN POSITION ON THE ROOF AT SPECIAL FORCES FORWARD OPERATIONS BASE (FOB) HILLAH.

CDR ZINKE AT CAMP VICTORY HQ, BIAP

FEELING LIKE A KING. SITTING ON SADDAM'S THRONE AT CAMP VICTORY, BIAP.

ANIMAL CAGES WHERE SADDAM'S SONS WOULD REPORTEDLY FEED YOUNG GIRLS TO THE LIONS FOR ENTERTAINMENT.

INCOMING AND OUTGOING SEAL TEAM COMMANDERS WITH CDR ZINKE.

COL MIKE REPASS, COMMANDER, CJSOTF-AP; CDR ZINKE; AND BG GARY HARRELL, COMMANDING GENERAL, SPECIAL OPERATIONS COMMAND, CENTRAL COMMAND.

SEAL TEAM ONE SEAL BASIC TRAINING (SBT) GRADUATING CLASS. AFTER GRADUATION AND SUCCESSFUL OUTCOME OF AN ORAL BOARD DRILLING BY VIETNAM-ERA MASTER CHIEFS, THE FAMED SEAL TRIDENT WOULD BE AWARDED.

LOLA, KONRAD,
AND WOLF IN A
HAYFIELD ON A TRIP
RETURNING TO THE
FLATHEAD VALLEY.

A NAVY FAMILY. NAVY DIVER JENNIFER, KONRAD,
WOLF, LOLA, AND SEAL CDR ZINKE.

The instructors put on some soft music to "help us relax," and, better yet, they stepped out so that we were left alone to write. My eyes shut, and I caught myself nodding off. I started writing just so I could focus on something other than how tired I was. After a few minutes, I heard heads hit the desks. I don't remember how many or who they were, but I wanted to join them. After not sleeping for five days, I am not sure I was actually writing or just going through the motions.

After a while the instructors came back and began to tap individuals on the shoulder and point to the door. They repeated the process until they left one lucky student alone who was sleeping alone in the classroom. We heard what they did later. The student's essay—what little of it he had written—was quietly replaced on his desk with a disenrollment form. Then they woke him up.

One of the instructors stood over him and drummed his fingers on the form in front of him. "Sign it again!" the instructor said. The trainee signed it automatically. In that condition, you're not thinking. You're just following whatever commands are given to you.

"Now read it!" the instructor barked, and the recruit read over "his" paper, only to realize that he'd just signed a request to drop out of the program. Of course, he had no memory of doing so. And he was alone, isolated, and stressed.

I don't know how that trainee reacted—the instructors didn't tell us that part—but after a minute or two he was told what had happened. The instructors tore up the quit sheet, and the trainee was still in the program. A life lesson learned.

Later, when I was the officer in charge of Hell Week, I carried on the fine tradition of this drill. On occasion the trainees would break down and cry, shrug, and accept that they'd signed it, and I even had a few recruits call foul play and admit nothing. They were exhausted and confused. All of them returned to training stronger from the experience. A teaching point of the exercise was to inoculate against this form of psychological stress. A SEAL might be captured and have a similar experience at the hands of an enemy. A captured SEAL might be presented with a confession that had a real signature—his signature. When you're exhausted, your judgment may be off, and it is better to take an extra second to think before you act. The trick is to keep your conviction intact and not be fooled.

The training has to be objective, fair, and safe. The instructor's objective is to train and mentor, not injure. I also had the latitude to create exercises based on what a SEAL might face in combat. In other cases, the exercise may be simply to observe how a student acts under stress or if he has the fortitude not to quit.

Let me give you an example. Extraction is a Hell Week exercise geared toward getting the men to focus on remembering basic commands and procedures. I'd have the BUD/S class line up with interlocking arms in the cold water while wearing life jackets and facing the shore. I'd bring the person on the left flank out and give him an extraction frequency. The first would be easy—it would be a VHF signal, which only has four digits. Something like 38.75.

The rules of Extraction were that the man with the extraction frequency had to go back into the water, and the class had to pass it quietly from man to man to the end. The class would be given two minutes to complete the task. And, of course, I'd be on the shore with a megaphone, giving instructions and trying to distract them by shouting out numbers of other frequencies.

At the end of two minutes, the two men remaining would be directed out of the water to face each other. If the man on the far end was able to correctly state the frequency given to the first man, they could be "extracted" out of the cold water. They rarely did. And once they screwed it up—which they almost always did, and the reason we call it "training"—I sent them "deeper into enemy territory," which, in this case, meant waist-deep water. And the next frequency code was a UHF, which adds digits and complexity. At this point, some of them might have to get the code out past chattering teeth, which again wasn't supposed to be heard by the instructors.

There was one other benefit to an exercise like this: it usually came early enough in training that it built class camaraderie—or destroyed it, albeit temporarily. It's hard to feel solidarity with your brother when he's just screwed up a code for the second time, and, as a result, your testicles are climbing up into your stomach to escape frigid water. Eventually, they would be up to their necks, and they would pass one digit at a time. The radio was loaded with the right frequency, the extraction call was made, and they moved to the relative warmth of the sandy beach.

So why did I have my men standing in cold water, focusing on quietly and correctly passing frequency down the line? Sure, that particular situation may not occur, but one in which a SEAL must check another team member's gear and maintain enough attention to detail under high-stress situations to make sure he doesn't miss a check inevitably will. And you want your brother focused.

That's Hell Week. Once it's complete, there are still twenty more weeks of BUD/S training to go. Yep. Twenty weeks left, to include Land Warfare Phase and Diving Phase. That's a long time. I should note something about Hell Week: When trainees begin, they're wearing white T-shirts. If they finish Hell Week successfully, they wear green T-shirts. That's it. No medals, no ribbons. Just a different T-shirt. But those T-shirts mean they made it through the toughest part of SEAL training. When you see people wearing those T-shirts, they've got an aura of confidence about them other trainees don't have. And they should—about 90 percent of the men who make it to the green T-shirt phase complete the rest of SEAL training.

Actually, training got a lot easier after that. In fact, our class, after Hell Week, was pretty cocky. We started with 138 and were down to fewer than a couple dozen original members. We were young and stupid. We would get hammered every day by the instructors and earned a reputation of being undisciplined but tough. They had it right. A BUD/S class did not have to be undisciplined; it just happened to be our fate.

That changed with the very next class. Pete Van Hooser, one of the toughest men to wear the Trident, came in as the next class officer, and he had that group marching in formation. His class, Class 137, has been held up as a prime example of what a disciplined SEAL class should look like. Pete was a former marine officer in his mid-thirties. Our class marveled at watching him line up his class and teach them basic marching drills. We were amazed at his organization but quickly dismissed the notion that we could do the same. Our die had been cast; we had made it through Hell Week, and, at that point, even marching like marines would not change our lot. Pete graduated and was assigned to SEAL Team Three before getting promoted and losing a leg in a parachute accident. Never one to quit, he later commanded SEAL Team Four and was the only former marine to command the navy's most elite SEAL Team.

My class may have been rough around the edges, but we were learning. Once our basic conditioning was finished, we moved on to two months of land warfare training, which included basic weapons marksmanship, fire and movement drills, land navigation and patrol, and training in land and underwater demolitions. It also included a seven-mile night swim off the coast of San Clemente Island. San Clemente Island is the breeding grounds of the great white shark, and the instructors would make us watch *Jaws* before the swim. The difference between the animal seal and a SEAL trainee in the water is that a SEAL trainee is an easier lunch. Seven miles is a long way, especially when every shadow in the dark water could be an eighteen-foot shark. We were motivated to make record-breaking swim times.

The last phase of BUD/S was combat diving, which included basic aquatic combat and open- and closed-circuit diving. The difference is whether, when you exhale, your breath is released or circulated back into your tank so the carbon dioxide can be removed—it's easier to be stealthy underwater if you're not releasing a trail of bubbles. Even though it was January, and the water temperatures were in the low fifties, conducting dives and ship attacks allowed a greater degree of autonomy away from an instructor's wrath.

Dive Phase also brought to light the story of Min and Tin, two foreign officers from Burma assigned by their country and the US Navy to conduct BUD/S training. It was not unusual to have foreign students in SEAL training, but it was the first time two officers from Burma were enrolled. Min and Tin arrived in Coronado, having gone through a short two-week course in English. Physically, they failed almost every evolution, but the standards for foreign students were different. A foreign student who was sent home in disgrace could face severe personal repercussions as well, as there were larger diplomatic considerations. Because the standard for foreign students was different, the instructors would look the other way when it came to performance. The water temperature was the same for everyone, and they still suffered, but the punishment for failure to keep up on a run or swim was lessened. And so Min and Tin suffered being cold, wet, and sandy through the first phase like the rest of us without the benefit of understanding much of the language. Almost every day they would ask about "diving," and instructors and their classmates would respond, "Third phase." At one point I even showed them on a calendar when Dive Phase would start. They seemed to be only partially satisfied with the answer. Not until we entered Dive Phase did their plea for "diving, diving, diving" change to "welding, welding, welding," and they became quite insistent. Their English had improved and so had their physical conditioning. Min and Tin became obsessed with welding, and a visit by the Burmese consulate was scheduled. As it turns out, Min and Tin were actually two engineers who should have been enrolled in the navy's Underwater Diving and Welding school rather than Basic Underwater Demolition SEAL training. Someone in Washington made a mistake and enrolled them in the wrong course. No wonder during Hell Week they talked about diving!

After their meeting with the consulate, Min and Tin were less than enthusiastic. "Very bad," I remember Min saying. Burma was going through a civil war, and when their government found out they had two officers about to become the first Burmese officers to ever complete SEAL training, they were immediately reassigned from the engineer corps to leading Special Operations troops at the front line. Their life had changed forever over a mistake in course titles.

BUD/S graduation was highlighted by our giving a hammer we had purchased from the local hardware store that morning for the traditional class gift to the Command. Like everything we did in Class 136, we were late in ordering the plaque and had to mount it later. I was ready to move on to the Army's Airborne School ("Jump School") at Fort Benning, Georgia, for basic static line parachute training. I qualified as a navy/marine corps parachutist and a free-fall parachutist within a month.

At this point, attrition rates among potential SEALs drop to nearly nil; once you've gone through Hell Week and graduated BUD/S, you've developed the core steel needed to be a SEAL. Now it was time to learn the trade, stay out of trouble, and prepare for battle.

For me, the next half year of training—SEAL Basic Indoctrination (now SEAL Qualification Training)—included advanced learning in counterguerrilla warfare, close-quarters combat, cold-weather training, demolitions, direct action missions, evasive and escape operations, intelligence collection, land navigation, maritime operations, medical training, small unit tactics, training and advising friendly military and paramilitary forces, and unarmed combat techniques. At the time, SEAL Basic Indoc (SBI) was conducted as a SEAL team; today, it is a separate course completed at the Naval Special Warfare Center before you are assigned to a team.

During my time in the SEALs, I was issued more than a dozen knives: the KA-BAR, Bowie knives, even a Buckmaster, which has a sawtooth edge, grappling hooks, and a hollow core used for small-item storage. I still keep them all at my office. It's ironic that the first knife I was issued is nearly identical to the last knife twenty-three years later.

And there's the lesson. It's fine to strive for improving tools, whether actual physical tools or legislation. That said, not everything that is modified represents an improvement. Sometimes, modifications just represent someone getting his hands on something he shouldn't and changing it for the sake of change—and that's as true of regulations as it is of tool design. At times, returning to classic wisdom or tactics is the wisest choice.

TEN

THE TEAMS

BY AUGUST 1986 I HAD MY TRIDENT AND WAS ASSIGNED to SEAL Team One. My first day at SEAL Team One was memorable. I showed up over the weekend and was told by the Quarterdeck Watch that the team was jumping on Monday after PT. Officer's call was 0730. "Don't be late." I showed up Monday ready to go. After an hour of PT that was led by a master chief who started with three hundred flutter kicks, we were told to go to the parachute loft, grab a chute, and get on the bus. I waited in line like the others, grabbed my chute, and got on the bus. On the way to the airfield, I opened my parachute bag and noticed an altimeter mounted on an unfamiliar emergency chute. In fact, everything in the bag was unfamiliar. I had just completed the army's basic static line parachute course, and in the bag was a parachute commander (PC) free-fall rig. The chief and petty officer next to me noticed the expression on my face. "Dude, are you free-fall qualified?" the petty officer asked. I responded with a negative. "It's okay, just hang with us!" That was the beginning of my instruction in free-fall that lasted until the bus pulled up to the waiting C-130. In fairness, they stayed with me all the way until I exited the ramp at twelve thousand feet. I never saw them in the air, but when I landed they said I did a great job, and I owed them a case of beer for my first jump.

Once assigned to SEAL Team One, I made the most of my time in Coronado. I continued my education and received training in evasion and escape operations, intelligence gathering, training and advising friendly military forces, and a variety of clandestine functions in a variety of environments. I made my first six-month deployment as an assistant SEAL platoon commander and spent most of the deployment on board an older navy landing ship dock named the USS *Anchorage*. We conducted cold-weather operations in the Aleutian Islands and battled fifty-foot swells in the North Sea. At one point, the seas were so high that the navy's flat-bottom Navy Landing Ship (LST) took such a heavy roll that her attached deck crane tore off and tumbled into the depths. The ship's unfortunate navigator had a heart attack, died, and ended up spending the rest of the storm in the cooler until we pulled into Japan. We also visited Australia and Thailand, which was my first real introduction to jungle warfare.

Jungle warfare was not what I expected. When I first checked into SEAL Team One, most of the senior enlisteds and officers had fought in Vietnam and knew the ropes on fighting in the jungle. Training in the desert in Niland, California, and growing up in the thick forests of the Northwest did not prepare me for survival in the jungle. True jungle is so thick you have to hack your way in. Paths are preferred but can be booby-trapped. Everything bites or stings, and many things are poisonous. In this environment, my first SEAL squad was tasked to conduct a combined patrol with our Thailand counterparts in a region called the "devil's triangle," an isolated part of the world where Thailand, Cambodia, and Laos share a common border notorious for trafficking of all kinds: drugs, human, contraband, and anything that could be bought and sold. Our mission was to take a helicopter into a village north of the Cambodian border, meet our counterparts, conduct a long-range reconnaissance patrol, and report any observed activity. We were loaded for "bear." Within the nine-man patrol, we went heavy and carried two M60 machine guns, four M-14s, and three M-16s with M203 40mm launchers. Plus, I was carrying an additional M79 40mm launcher just for fun. If there was going to be trouble in the jungle, we were going to come out on top.

The mission called for an easy fifteen-kilometer day patrol though a mixture of swamps and dense jungle, an overnight lay up on a hillside, and a similar day patrol on back to a designed landing zone where we would be extracted by a helicopter and taken back to our ship. The insertion went off without a hitch, and we found ourselves slow-going in the dense jungle. Walking trails were nearly nonexistent, and even small game trails were few and far between. Using any dirt road was a sure way to be spotted, so that was out. Instead, we spent the morning hours wading through swamps and watching for snakes. About noon, we found a dry high spot and decided to take a small water and food break. The patrol set security in pairs, and the men pushed out in different directions but within sight of myself and the radioman in the middle. Other than being slower than expected, the patrol was proceeding as planned. I decided to adjust my socks, and as I pulled up my pants, I was struck by the color of my leg. My calf was nearly black from being covered by leeches. I quickly released my H-Harness and unbuttoned my shirt. An inspection determined the same. My body was covered with leeches feasting on fresh blood. Not thinking, I created a little stir as I began to shed my clothes and rip off the little demons. The rest of the squad thought it was funny and laughed at my misfortune. Then the laughter turned to a distinct moment of silence and stark realization. *If Zinke is covered with leeches, then I might be too!* The stealthy SEAL patrol turned into a frenzy of clothes and leeches flying, ambushed by thumb-sized blood suckers! After removing the leeches and reassembling our clothing and composure, the patrol continued its march with pant legs tucked in and periodic stops to remove the new hitchhikers. Never did thirty kilometers seem so long. To this day, every time I look at a swamp, I think about what creatures may be hidden in the mud.

We made it back to the *USS Anchorage* and participated in training exercises in South Korea and the Philippines. The daily routine on board was PT, eat, PT, eat, PT, watch a movie, and repeat. By the time it was all over, I could do 140 push-ups and do flutter kicks for forty minutes.

During all this time, however, I wanted more. I knew the administrative and training work I was doing was contributing, but in my heart I was a warrior, and—it is a young man's prerogative—I wanted to go to war for my country. In the back of your head, you think of the giants—John Paul Jones, Robert E. Lee, George S. Patton—and you want to uphold their traditions.

The Greeks had Alexander, the Romans had Julius Caesar, and the Russians had Prince Alexander Nevsky—but those heroes are quite removed in the rearview mirror of history. Us? We are a rough, pioneering people just a short handful of generations removed from our legendary heroes, from the famed to the anonymous, the everyday folk who packed their families into wagons and, with rifles and Bibles in hand, crossed uncharted plains for an unknown future. For a young man to want to be like one of those titans is not only aspirational or due to simple testosterone, it is damn near genetic. I do not want war. No one but an Armageddon-bent group like ISIS does. But when it was forced upon us, I wanted desperately to be a part of that bold and singular tradition.

In 1988, I got a little closer. I shipped out to the Philippines for the second of two deployments I'd ultimately have there. I was a lieutenant and platoon commander. I had fifteen SEALs and a small boat detachment and felt I was on top of the world flying to the Philippines.

The Philippines is where the SEALs had a base that fed into operations in and around Korea and, of course, our "friends" in what was then still called the Soviet Union. Between the Philippines and, potentially, Russia, the all-terrain training SEALs went through came in very useful. We reviewed surveillance technology from cutting-edge early-warning devices and did a lot of recon work.

Even beyond our proximity to the Russians and the North Koreans, the Philippines at the time weren't exactly hospitable. During part of my time there, James N. Rowe, a Vietnam-era army officer, was serving as chief of the army portion of the Joint US Military Advisory Group stationed there. Rowe actually had a direct impact on my training: he was one of the few prisoners of war during Vietnam who escaped successfully. He developed the Survival, Evasion, Resistance, and Escape (SERE) tactics that are at the basis of most elite US military forces' SERE programs.

He wasn't so fortunate in the Philippines, though. He'd been called back to active duty to design the SERE program—the compound at Camp Mackall in North Carolina where it's taught is named for him—in 1981, and by 1987 he was in the Philippines, providing counterinsurgency leadership against the Communist-led New People's Army.

In April 1989, Rowe was killed by members of the Sparrow Unit, the hit squad under the control of the New People's Army. He was ambushed in his car while driving through Quezon City, which is part of the metro Manila area. The assassination wasn't that far from us. It seems our enemies knew then what it has taken us so bloody long to embrace: attack the leadership to strike at the body.

We were operating against this hostile, ugly backdrop in the Philippines. We staged some combined operations with the Philippine marines and specialized units. We helped identify and hunt down the Sparrow squads throughout the islands, especially on Mindanao, where they had their base. We gathered intelligence on them and other forces hostile to the United States and Philippine governments' interests.

Our primary mission, though, was to protect the US embassy in Manila. This contingency operation was called Silver Bullet—as in, we were the shiny, magic bullet that would be called on to reinforce embassy personnel if the embassy was compromised. The embassy overlooked Manila Bay, and it had a huge park next to it. Every once in a while, there would be a protest or a rally of upward of a million people in that park, and it wasn't hard to imagine a scenario in which a protest went bad and folks started coming over our fence. We were there after President Ferdinand Marcos' government fell, and a few coup attempts had already been aimed at his successor, Corazon Aquino.

Under Silver Bullet, in the event of a disturbance, a designated SEAL platoon was to come by helicopter from Subic Bay and provide additional security. We spent a lot of time conducting security assessments, identifying and fixing shortfalls, making plans for securing the roof and the perimeter, and going back to our Underwater Demolition Team (UDT) roots to make sure Manila Bay in front of the embassy was free from obstacles should we have to evacuate by sea.

Manila Bay is notoriously polluted. As part of our mission, we performed the classic UDT mission of conducting a hydrographic survey to determine the depth of the water and the location of obstacles that could snare a small boat. Millions of people live in Manila, and I could see where the sewers spilled in. The survey was completed and every obstacle was recorded to include a few dead animals and a submerged barge. How the barge got there was anybody's guess, but it was deep enough that it wasn't an issue. Swimming in a sewer was not at the top of my bucket list, but we donned fins and facemasks and completed the mission in time to down a few San Miguel beers for medicinal purposes.

Despite all this, the Philippines had a certain charm. US-Philippine relations have been pretty strong for a long time: Americans and Filipinos fought side by side during the Spanish-American War, which resulted in Philippine independence after more than three centuries of Spanish rule. When President Theodore Roosevelt sent the Great White Fleet around the world in a show of force, one of the highlights was demonstrating that the United States was prepared to protect its interests in the Philippines. And Filipino and American soldiers died side by side during World War II's Bataan Death March, when the Imperial Japanese Army starved, beat, bayoneted, and tortured them during a sixty-mile prisoner movement.

Marching, fighting, and, sadly, dying weren't the only things Americans and Filipinos did side by side. Many of the West Coast SEALs married local Filipino gals. In fact, the platoon responsible for Silver Bullet before I got there—part of SEAL Team Three—was headed by a guy who had married a Filipino woman.

He and I were supposed to do a turnover of target folders and intelligence updates, a process that usually includes some ground recon and briefings that last two or three days. But the C5 aircraft that was supposed to fly in my guys and me from Seal Team One was delayed, and by the time I got to the Philippines, we only had a few hours, as the same C5 was to turn around and bring them back.

Another digression, if I may. All military personnel have found ways to do a fast-unwind, whether it's reading a Marvel comic book, playing a video game—or having a party like my contact in the Philippines. To each his own, right? Where *I* draw the line is when the participants don't or can't draw a line—as in the unfortunate matter of the fifty-six-year-old rear admiral who, late in 2015, was removed from his post as director of Strategy, Policy, Capabilities, and Logistics at US Transportation Command after the thirty-year navy man got so drunk during a conference that he could not stand and had to be helped back to his room—and, later, was found staggering naked through the hotel. Military service is tough and that goes beyond the obvious threat of physical injury; there's deployment in unfamiliar places and the absence of family. Whatever branch of the armed forces, members need each other for support. You want to recognize and help someone in crisis before they get to that level of distress.

Anyway, my contact in the Bachelor Officer's Quarters (BOQ) room didn't bother to put on any clothes. He just went over to his dresser, opened a drawer, and took out a double handful of Silver Bullet files labeled SECRET: the target folders, communication plans, and reports on everything he had done during the past six months. He handed all this to me and said, "Good luck. I'm leaving in an hour. You're in charge now." I grabbed the files and left him to get dressed, which I suspect required only three minutes of that last hour.

The executive officer of the SEAL unit in the Philippines at the time was a Vietnam Mustang SEAL officer named Edward C. Bowen, a tough, quiet warrior who had managed to amass three combat tours in Vietnam while earning Silver and Bronze Stars. He was one of the early Military Assistance Advising Group (MAAG) advisors and liked both the people and the mission. He was one of the few to deploy as both SEAL Team One and Two. Usually, once you did two deployments on a team, SEAL command said, "That's it. You're done. You've got to do shore duty or instructor duty."

Bowen thought differently. He got out of the service with SEAL Team Two, drove across the coast, reenlisted, and was deployed again with SEAL Team One. He wanted to be in the jungle.

His men respected that. Having that many deployments was unusual back then. Nowadays, most SEALs have double or triple that if they're in the same amount of time he was.

Bowen wasn't the only notable officer there. The commanding officer was a guy named Wally Merrick, and, because of him, we called Unit-1 "Wally's World." Well, not so much because of him, but because of the little oddities he foisted on the headquarters. He used to make pencil marks around his flagpole on the quarterdeck to make sure that whoever was responsible for cleaning moved the flag and dusted around it. He'd put pennies around his office and surroundings to do the same thing. I'm not certain if that was to make sure people cleaned; maybe he just liked being surrounded by brass and zinc. One thing for certain, it kept us off the quarterdeck.

We also had a command master chief named Louis MacIntosh. Nobody called him that, though; we all affectionately called him Screwy Louis, because he had a sense of humor that could make anyone laugh. He was also a Vietnam vet who came up through the ranks. All these guys had seen combat and enjoyed giving the younger "tadpoles" a hard time. The first time I saw him, I was walking by Merrick's office and Screwy Louis was on top of his desk while Merrick was reading some report. I didn't know why and I didn't want to find out, as spending more time in the gunsights could not have gone well for me.

I was there for other business, but I ended up having a pretty good time in Subic. Once you got off the naval base, life was sort of the way it was in Vietnam, I'm told; there was an "anything for money" attitude among the local residents, and you didn't need much money to participate. For instance, a fifty-cent beer on base would be forty-five cents in a nearby barrio, and maybe thirty cents if you took a bus out to the more rural area.

Something else would happen as you got further from the base: the region's rules, which were marginal at best, would vanish. Let's just say the term "liberty" was folly applied.

So were the threats from local thugs. People in this part of the world weren't—still aren't—rich, and in-country military personnel usually have a bunch of cash on them . . . and often drink. Manila was worse. If you wandered off the main beat, chances were pretty good you'd be surrounded and rolled—at best. At worst, you could be knifed and killed. After all, these streets, the doorways, the shadows, were known to the locals and not to us. When I think back on those years, it's amazing most of us came home in one piece.

With few rules holding us back, we were more than willing to take advantage of any opportunities for distraction that presented themselves. I remember one New Year's Eve. The tradition was to set off fireworks. But these weren't sparklers. They were more like giant bottle rockets with M80s that would come up to your hip. On this particular New Year's Eve, we'd purchased several of those rockets, and one of my friends from the base wanted to set one off.

We'd been having a couple of San Miguel beers on a bar balcony—a cheap balcony structure, because Subic had zero in the way of building codes. If you had some nails and boards, you had a home. Or a bar. Or a balcony. At least, you did until the next big storm came through (or *partly* because those big storms came through, as they knocked down even well-built structures).

So we were on the rickety balcony overlooking the street, and my friend decided that the correct launching position would be to hang over the balcony rail upside down and ignite the fuse while holding the rocket in a beer bottle. The fuse flashed in a cloud of smoke, and the ignition nearly burned him alive. The sizzling rocket bounced off the middle of the road and shot straight through the door of a bar across the street. The bar was poorly lit inside.

A collective, "*Oh, shiiiiit!*" passed from our lips.

A second later there was a huge flash of light, a boom, then finally smoke billowing out of the bar's door before a few marines who had been drinking in the bar exited.

Nobody got killed—or even seriously hurt—but the marines wanted revenge, so they went over to the cart where we'd bought our rockets, got themselves a double handful, and shot them at us on our balcony. Of course, we had to defend ourselves.

It was a terrific fight, but I can't say definitively who won because soon enough the mayor of Subic came out and put a stop to things. In a world of no rules, we finally found the first one. He was polite enough, but he was pretty firm that our fun was over. There weren't many rules in Subic, but burning the place down was clearly over the line.

I ended up shuttling to the Philippines quite often during the next six months. We actually had a chance to put the Silver Bullet contingency plans to a real test during that time: there was a coup attempt against Aquino's government, or what looked like a coup attempt to the naked eye. But when we did our post-event analysis, we found that even though there had been hours of firefights, nobody had been killed or even seriously wounded.

We realized that despite the different factions, the people were Filipinos first, so they really didn't want to battle each other, and they didn't want to hurt any civilians. The fights were little more than various political factions flexing their muscles—more for show and control of power than military maneuvers. So they would warn each other when they would come around corners and fire their weapons knowing they weren't going to hit anyone. They'd launch mortar rounds, but the rounds would be carefully targeted for minimal damage. The Filipinos are by and large a gentle people, and, unlike the factionalism of the tribes in Iraq, ultimately, they are one nation that more or less wants to live together.

The Philippine marines' commander ended up putting down the coup and "saving" Aquino, and she rewarded him by making him her minister of defense, thus elevating the status of the Philippine marines.

This turn of events ended up working in our favor. We had a pretty good relationship with the marine commander, which ensured we would have little trouble as the Philippine government was run by connections, and those relationships were usually made on a local level. If your connections were solid, you could get what you wanted without a problem. If you were out of the circle, then you were generally out of luck.

I'm only going to be half-serious here, but I do have a story about how locally negotiated deals resulted in win-win situations. We did a lot of Special Operations training around Subic. For explosives and small training, we used an area called White Beach. In the small fishing villages, the Filipinos have a matriarchal society: females ran things, and when you wanted something, you had to negotiate with the head lady called the mama-san.

Most of the time, the trade was simple. We had Meals Ready to Eat (MRE), target material, and ammunition brass. She had chicken, rice, and beer.

So we'd go in and say, "We have three jeeps we brought over here for target practice that we're going to blow up. You can't have the vehicles, but you can take everything out of them that you can get, including the engines."

If they agreed, we'd tow in the vehicles. When we did, you'd see a swarm of kids—maybe fifty or so, all with screwdrivers and pliers. They'd descend on those vehicles and in forty-five minutes the engines would be lifted out, put on wooden planks, and taken back to their village. The villagers used those engines to power their traditional banca boats or generators. Getting our engines into their banca boats was important: without them, the villagers couldn't make a living or go and get the beer!

In return, the platoon would eat well for three or four days.

In addition to the good food, these negotiations made being in these areas a lot easier. We'd make a point to throw in a little money to sweeten the deal. What was a few bucks to us was a pretty big deal to the mama-sans, and we wanted them to be happy. If you made sure a mama-san made money, she'd look out for you.

The mama-sans also learned to negotiate for the brass from our bullet casings. In most cases, we had to guarantee them a certain amount of brass—usually around six thousand or so casings, which they would collect, melt, and turn into knives or belt buckles. I still have a belt buckle from the Philippines with a Trident on it.

Only when those local relationships were broken, and authority was moved from the front line to the command in the rear, did the supply system became clogged; at that point, you had bureaucracy trying to manage remotely what had been customized to local conditions. The bureaucrats were trying to impose one-size-fits-all systems on their operations, and, quite frankly, the whole machine became much less responsive.

The Mark 48 Torpedo has been a mainstay in the US Navy's arsenal since 1972. It's carried in every class of American submarine and is also used by several other countries. It's about as blue chip a piece of armament as there is.

Despite this, every time there's a minor modification to the Mark 48, the Department of Defense (DoD) insists on testing it as if it has never before been fired. The modifications and the tests have to be signed off on by dozens of bureaucrats. The excessive testing costs money, time, and resources, and does nothing.

This creates an environment in which there is absolutely no incentive to incur any risk. Nobody wants his signature on the order that pushes something into action if there's any risk of error. Because of this, the navy is slow to deploy modified torpedoes—torpedoes that are vitally necessary to help our armed forces further their mission of defending us. It's not that tests aren't necessary; they most certainly are. It's that there's no reward, only risk, for saying yes and getting needed modifications, changes that would help us retain our edge, into the field. So someone looking for security over innovation has a huge incentive to say no.

Consider the Chinese. They steal blueprints, sure, but they're able to go from design to fielding of their major weapons systems in just three to five years. It takes us between seventeen and nineteen years for a similar launch, which means that supposedly cutting-edge technology is outdated before the first unit is deployed. The F-35 fighter plane is a perfect example of this: it's been in development since 1996. The marines took delivery of their first plane in 2015. The navy isn't getting its fighters until 2018. Yes, it will be a good aircraft, but if we were truly concerned with maintaining our air superiority, we would be at the third generation of F-35s by now.

In the meantime, China's J-31, which has more than a coincidental resemblance to the F-35, is already rolling off the production line, despite China not starting work on its planes until late in the last decade. By the time our F-35 is being delivered en masse, it likely won't deliver the tactical air supremacy that decisive victory demands. Technological innovation is moving faster than our acquisition process. We've become process oriented, not results driven.

This problem goes beyond technology. The military's priorities have gotten totally out of balance between fighting forces and the bureaucracy. Active-duty forces have been cut in favor of more desk roles. The budget lines year after year may be similar, but there's been a shift from active-duty personnel to bureaucrats. There are currently more than eight hundred thousand DoD employees. That's far more than the number of active US Army military personnel, and not too far behind the combined number of active army and navy military personnel. And the DoD figure doesn't include contractors. I wish I could tell you how many contractors the military is currently using, but even SOCOM—the United States Special Operations Command—hasn't been able to give an accurate count to Congress. We've asked. The best we can say is somewhere between 1.2 and 1.6 million.

What can we do about all this? A good starting point would be to push acquisition and much of the decision-making back to service chiefs and streamline the DoD process to assist rather than resist. Ideally, the same person responsible for setting requirements would be responsible for the outcome. We are too top-heavy across the board and there are too many bureaucrats whose job is nothing more than to say no. The way government spending is currently set up, the acquisition process is such a labyrinth of desks and processes that there is nobody one can point a finger at and say, "This is your fault. This is your success."

Other measures include demanding a simple audit. Literally thousands of programs are not approved or authorized by Congress or even have the necessary oversight to determine value. A hiring freeze and the authority for commanders to reorganize as civilians retire would at least change the growth trajectory of overweight bureaucracy. Lastly, the entitlement and benefits side of the DoD needs to be reviewed and reformed; otherwise, our Defense Department will become a health care and disability system that also happens to fight wars.

I mentioned DoD spending as one instance where this happens, but it's hardly the only one. This phenomenon occurs across all government agencies. Take the regulations that inhibit small businesses. The amount of paperwork and oversight small companies face is stifling innovation, hiring, and new product releases. Two small banks fail every day as a result of not being able to adhere to arbitrary regulations and government rules. Without access to local capital, small businesses struggle to expand.

Want another example that will almost certainly hit close to home? Sooner or later, everyone is going to interact with the medical field. In general, American medical devices are tops at advancing quality of life. But medical products, such as devices and pharmaceuticals, are taxed and heavily regulated by nonelected government entities. Any guess as to what happens to innovation when potential products have artificial costs built in due to taxes and regulations? Right. There's no money left over to spend on innovation and advances.

Decentralization could actually work well in health care. As I suggested already, Obamacare has been a disaster: structurally it's not viable, as only a dozen or so states operate their own exchanges. If the goal is to offer access to good affordable health care, several options work, such as individual health-care accounts and low-cost and cost-sharing clinics, where physicians provide basic preventive care. These clinics may not have an MRI—there are a lot of things they don't have—but they do offer basic care and preventatives.

Community health clinics provide a better bang for the buck than the labyrinth of insurance, co-pays, and billing with which the medical community is currently struggling. Ask medical professionals these days how they like their jobs. Many of them are dissuading their kids from becoming physicians, because the amount of paperwork they deal with every day prevents them from practicing medicine. Doctors practice by checking off codes on their iPads, and patients have become little more than a billing entity.

States are in a better position than Washington, DC, to examine their needs and devise plans that can be better executed, and that are more relevant to their populations. Look at the amount of money the government spends and the number of people it covers; it would be better to buy everyone a premium plan and write a check for it. We're spending an enormous amount and getting very little in the way of results. Under Obamacare, health care is more expensive and access to physicians has been reduced. Hospital parking lots are full; unfortunately, they are filled with compliance and billing specialists rather than patients and service providers.

If you've applied for a loan, you've probably encountered the Consumer Financial Protection Bureau, an independent government agency whose directors never had to face the voting public or even answer to Congress. These folks restrict how banks make loans by making their processes and disclosures subject to government oversight. This means if you're an established figure in your community, but you don't meet a Washington bureaucrat's rigid standards, you've probably been denied that loan.

Consider a farmer or a rancher subject to the rise and fall of commodity prices. His long-term income is going to be steady—he's a prosperous farmer or rancher—but because some bureaucrat wanted to see two years' worth of income statements, he'll be turned down for that loan because his income is inconsistent . . . and some inflexible set of regulations says there can't be any additional considerations. But a local banker would know his situation, because it was common to the region, and would be able to comfortably make that loan.

That scenario is frustrating when the money would be used for a personal expenditure, but it makes no sense when it could be used to bolster a business, create jobs, and otherwise benefit the country. Who does that legislation, which is supposed to be consumer-friendly, benefit?

We've run across this in Montana. I've said it before (a lot) and will say it again (also a lot): I'm a son of the state, and, like my hero, President Theodore Roosevelt, I love the outdoors and consider myself a traditional conservationist.

I also have special knowledge of Montana, unlike many DC bureaucrats who have publicly stated that oil and gas exploration is responsible for the decline of the sage grouse population in Montana.

Here's the thing: at the time there was only one active oil derrick in the state of Montana. One. What Montana does have are ravens and crows and hawks, all of which are natural predators of the sage grouse. I know that because I've seen them. I also know that West Nile virus, coyotes and hawks, and wildfires are far more detrimental to sage grouse than a pump jack. What I don't know is what a healthy population of sage grouse is, or how it's changed, and I'm pretty sure the Bureau of Land Management (BLM) in Washington doesn't either. What the BLM does knows is that false tears for the sage grouse offer a very real way to arbitrarily restrict energy exploration activities. If we were serious about the sage grouse, a start would be to determine what a healthy population would look like and develop a plan to maintain it. The BLM does not seem to be interested in the number of birds; they seem to be interested only in the number of acres they can control.

Conservatives in Washington try to rein in the excesses of regulatory entities, especially nonelected regulatory bodies. We've shrunk the BLM's budget in hopes of reducing its reach, but there are pitfalls. Once we do so, bureaucrats counterpunch by listing a variety of wildlife on the endangered species list, which automatically causes a new set of restrictions to come into play.

Still think this is for the common good? Consider the number of wildlife organizations that use these causes to raise money, despite no wildlife census to back up their claims. Oil companies face thousands of dollars in fines for the alleged death of a handful of ducks, while wind farms are given a pass for killing thousands of birds, including endangered eagles. Look at the organizations that promote so-called alternative energy sources. Many of them have a personal pocketbook interest in stopping oil and gas exploration. Do they love the environment, or do they love their investors?

That is why moving decisions down to people who have relevant, ground-level data and experience makes sense. It's entirely possible that there are man-made reasons for the sage grouse's population drop—if there has been a population drop at all, of course. But the people most likely to have that data and experience are those who live and work where the sage grouse are, not those who go to work on the Interstate 395 in DC. The view from the Potomac is a lot different than the view from Yellowstone or the Missouri, so why does Washington think they are the same? It goes back to the same theme: Washington bureaucrats think they know how to manage nearly every aspect of our lives better than we do. But whether it's our health-care system, our banking system, our water, or even a little bird on a prairie, Washington has it all wrong.

I sit on the House Natural Resources committee. I can draw on my studies in geology and my experience in the outdoors. I can ask the right questions, and I can make some informed inquiries, but, ultimately, there are people in forty-nine other states—and yes, Montana too—who are a lot more informed than I am about on-the-ground conservation issues. I'd like at least an opportunity to listen to them, rather than dictate to them.

For national concerns, such as the economy or criminal activity, federal lawmakers need to take local concerns into account. Yes, people in Congress represent their locales, but, ultimately, individual representatives and senators only have the bandwidth to monitor and review issues on a broad sense.

What happens is that they end up relying on their staffs, which are generally made up of the young and unpaid. And those individuals often move from office to office, or from committee to committee. Every time there's noise about congressional term limits, I want to raise the point of limiting staff tenures too. Entrenched congressional staffers can wield as much or more influence than the congressman they "work for." Few people know who they are, and nobody voted for them. They and their agency counterparts end up being the powerful fourth arm of government.

It's not that I'm automatically opposed to centralized government functions. Our Constitution calls for national unity in a common defense, a monetary system, and commerce. There are some places where centralized government is necessary. Take cyber security, for instance. Twenty years ago it wasn't an issue. Now it's a major concern with international threats cropping up every day. The connected nature of the web means that there have to be nationwide standards for domestic security. Thing is, cyber security concerns are the sort of government issues that can produce concrete results—better protections. And those protections have to be universal: compromised systems due to patchwork security regulations can affect people across the country in a matter of seconds. The most sensitive systems also need to be isolated as they will always be vulnerable to new hacking techniques. The more integrated the system is, the more vulnerable the system is to attack. The drive toward centralization for convenience has to be weighed against risk.

But there's a big difference between a common terrain like the web and America's range of environments. So I say, keep the centralized oversight for concerns that are truly nationwide, but allow for greater flexibility for issues that are better managed by the states or at the local level. If the Washington bureaucrats would listen, they might even discover that the answers to better management are not found within the beltway.

Shift back to the Philippines. It may sound as if life in the Philippines was all fun and games. Yes, we had fun being SEALs overseas, but there were plenty of serious moments and training was rarely easy. One training exercise sticks in my mind because it provided a valuable learning experience at my expense.

I was a young lieutenant assigned as a SEAL team platoon commander on my second six-month deployment to the Republic of the Philippines. At the time, the US Navy maintained a base in Subic Bay and the SEALs maintained a forward deployed unit on the installation. The role of the SEAL unit was to provide logistics and command and control in support of fleet and Pacific theater operations. Since the Vietnam War the West Coast SEAL teams maintained a rotation of SEAL platoons to the unit that was highly trained in jungle warfare and other unconventional warfare skills. Eager to impress my new unit commander, I decided to conduct a combat swimmer operation that simulated an attack on the aircraft carrier *USS Midway* which was in port. The operation was divided into several phases and involved a night parachute jump, a small boat transit, a closed-circuit dive to the ship, the placement of a simulated explosive charge, and then a return to the waiting small craft at sea. My Underwater Demolition Team (UDT) ancestors would have been proud of the classic frogman operation. We had completed similar training missions in San Diego and the platoon felt comfortable that the task was well within our capability. Each phase of the operations was briefed to the unit commander and his staff for their comment and approval. By my calculations, the whole operation could easily be completed in the course of six hours. We could be done and all the equipment washed up and put away by midnight—perfect for those who wanted to celebrate our victory with a well-deserved beer out in town. The afternoon before the exercise was spent preparing equipment, studying charts, and conducting rehearsals. It was going to be a full moon; the water temperature was toasty warm, so there was no need for full wet suits. In fact, the decision was to go light and swim with just a thin polyester suit and minimal equipment. The simulated explosives were already heavy and six hours was easy. A few hours before we commenced the exercise, a final-five paragraph operations brief was delivered and approved by the senior officer at the unit. True to his nature, Commander Bowen sat quietly in the back of the room and took a few notes but made no comment as I went through the different sections.

That night the operation went flawlessly. The full moon made the parachute jump easy, the small boat navigation was spot on, and the dive to the ship and back out to the rendezvous point was routine. Even the tides were right as it made the swim relatively painless. As the swimmer pairs gathered at the rendezvous point in anticipation to the small boat pickup, I looked at my watch and wondered why the small boats were late. My answer came soon enough. From the bow of a small patrol boat speeding toward us, I saw Bowen. He was shouting, and as the boat drew closer, the words, "You have been compromised, Lieutenant—go on E&E" echoed across the water. As we floated and bobbed up and down in utter amazement, we pondered for a moment the significance of what E&E—Escape and Evasion—meant. I then remembered the outrageous E&E plan I had briefed him just a few hours before, and the slight smile on Bowen's face as he took notes. My heart sank for I knew that the exercise that seemingly went so well was about to change for the worse. He was throwing us a curveball, and a quick inventory of our situation suggested that I would not make last call.

Up to this point, the exercise had been going just the way I had briefed it to the men. Like most exercises, my briefing was also observed by the unit headquarters—in this case, Bowen, who, true to his nature, sat quietly through it as I ran through the standard five-paragraph briefing format: Situation, Mission, Execution, Administration/Logistics, and Command and Signal. Each step was briefed and contingencies identified. After we covered those, we went through the final escape and evasion plan should we be compromised and have to evade enemy capture. The whole thing took about ninety minutes, which was standard.

We had hit the ship and placed the limpets exactly as we had briefed. We dove back out undetected and surfaced well away from any danger from being spotted. Now came the easy part: paddle along on the surface and let the falling tide do the work. I was feeling more than a little smug at how well the mission had gone. The water was pretty nice too; it was around seventy degrees, which made for a good, comfortable swim. We weren't wearing full wetsuits: we'd put on thin black polyurethane suits that were almost like triathlon suits. The suits had hoods, so when we came to the surface there wouldn't be white faces above the waves. Except for the Drägers, we were swimming light.

But when we got to the rendezvous point, the rubber boats that were supposed to take us to the mothership were nowhere to be seen. We waited, floating in the dark, for almost an hour before a little patrol boat showed up with Bowen standing on the bow. He was yelling, "E&E!" as the boat circled. The boat slowly pulled up close to the cluster of swimmers, and he looked down at me and said, "E&E. Your mission has been compromised, Lieutenant." My heart sank, because what he was telling us was that he was throwing us a curve ball, and we were far from done.

E&E means Escape and Evasion. In short, Bowen was telling us that we had done everything correctly: we'd swum out to where the boat was supposed to pick us up, but he wasn't going to let us come aboard. The idea was that we had to act as if the boat hadn't shown up and go to our E&E plan. And the reason Bowen was doing this was because he had sat in on my briefing, and he knew I hadn't spent a lot of time on that portion of the plan. He was making a point.

The so-called E&E plan that was briefed was one I simply made up in my mind. If compromised, we were going to swim all the way across Subic Bay, which was about five miles, and then hike over the peninsula to the next beach. Of course, in between these two beaches was a mountain range with a dormant volcano and jungle.

The equipment list did not include anything that would remotely prepare us for what we now faced. All of us were wearing booties suitable for short walks but not for hiking across volcanic rock and jungle. We had anticipated a swim into the bay, where we were going to get picked up, right?

We also didn't have food, water, or any equipment other than a mask, fins, a knife, and a pistol. What we did have was all of our dive equipment, which was pretty heavy on land. Under the rules of the exercise, we weren't allowed to leave anything behind.

So the E&E part of the exercise began. By the time we made it across the bay and onto the first beach, the sun was coming up. It was time that I took a little initiative, so I found the mama-san. With a little hard negotiation and some promissory notes, we were able to obtain sandals. We certainly weren't going to walk in our fins, and the little rubber booties with the eighth-of-an-inch soles were next to useless on land. I wear a size twelve shoe: the biggest sandal in that village was about half the size of my foot, but I did the best I could.

We ended up trading fins, face masks, and a few IOUs for flip-flops, food and water, and even a couple of porters to help us haul the gear. Mama-san definitely got the better of that negotiation, but at least we didn't have to carry those damned Drägers.

But I—and my team—got some valuable experience out of the exercise. When we made our action report and lessons-learned presentation to Bowen, we stressed a few important findings: Don't do a combat swimmer operation without being prepared for the worst. Swim in cammies, because if you have to get out of the water, a wet suit isn't going to be your friend as you're walking. Carry weapons, which was a new way of thinking for us, more in line with the German view of combat swimming. When you get out of the water, you have to be prepared to fight.

Most of all, though, was to have a QRF—a Quick Reaction Force—set up and on-call if your main extraction plan went belly up. Bowen knew exactly what he was doing when he listened to my briefing; he zeroed in on the weakest aspect of it and quietly changed the exercise—without telling us, of course—to stress that aspect.

At the time it was enormously painful, but Bowen, like many of the frogmen who served in Vietnam, was a hard man, and he drilled into us an important lesson: don't blow off any part of the brief, and make sure the elements within it are sound.

I learned a lot from instructors who had been battle-hardened in Vietnam. I had a commanding officer of SEAL Team One who once observed a desert training exercise my platoon was conducting. He'd been a platoon commander in Vietnam, and I was briefing a plan to conduct a coordinated ground assault of a well-fortified enemy position. I had a strategy for every enemy action and about nine different options to hit the enemy hard no matter what.

He looked at my approaches and offered a simple, but wise, assessment.

"Ryan," he said, "your plan is great, but sometimes it's better to step back and take the fight to tomorrow, unless there's an absolutely compelling reason, such as not hitting that target today, resulting in a catastrophic loss. As a commander, you have to evaluate risk and return. If it's not right, it's better to live to fight tomorrow than to die fighting for nothing today."

He was right. I was a young SEAL at the time, and I was gung ho to move on the target. Since that quiet lesson, I've always taken a step back, at least in evaluating the reality of a situation against my enthusiasm for an immediate solution.

I combined that with Bowen's lesson—that when I brief I should consider every situation as though there is not just a possibility but a probability that something will go wrong. After that I took to heart my rule of threes: always have a list of the three most likely screw-ups at every step, and have in place plans for how to address those screw-ups.

I did love it all, even with the hard lessons learned. I spent a couple of years in the Philippines, on and off, and even though I was away from home more than I might have liked, I really enjoyed my time there.

I mentioned my Trident belt buckle before—the one I got from the Philippine craftsmen who were repurposing our brass casings. In addition, there was another souvenir from my days in the Philippines I wish I still had, but to tell you about it I have to mention something else: during Officer Candidate School, I got married. I met her at Oregon; she was fun, and we were young.

She played sports at Oregon, and we had a lot of mutual friends. We seemed to have similar interests, and we both were comfortable taking risks. So one night we had a beer or two more than we should have, and we decided to elope.

We were married in Newport, Rhode Island, on Easter weekend, and after I graduated OCS, we both went to Coronado. She went to work as a waitress; I went to BUD/S. We were married for five years, and I was deployed for more than three of those five years. Not exactly the makings for a successful relationship. Some estimate that the failure rate for a SEAL's first marriage is well over 90 percent. Although I don't have official stats on this, I knew my marriage was on the rocks and would not last.

During my last deployment in the Philippines, I had measured an L88 airplane pallet and commissioned a local craftsman to build a bar that could fit on the pallet. It was teak and mahogany, and it had three charts representing the three locations where the SEALs trained. The bar was beautifully carved. The Filipino craftsmen could carve a Trident overnight, so you can imagine the work they can do in six months. The bar was carefully brought back to the small house on base that I rarely saw. After a deployment, I came home to the house and opened the door. All the furniture was gone. I stepped back and checked that the address on the door matched the checkbook in my pocket. It did. Standing just inside the door of the empty house, I remember that my first thoughts were not about losing a wife. They were about losing the bar. God, I miss that bar. The marriage was over. I wished her the best.

ELEVEN
_____

THE LOVE OF MY LIFE

LOLA HAND AND I MET IN 1990, WHICH MEANT WE MET
the old-fashioned, pre-Internet way: at a bar. At the time, I was a BUD/S
instructor at Coronado, where I was biding my time until I could get to
the most elite SEAL Team.

McP's Irish Pub & Grill is a SEAL bar about a ten-minute drive from
the Naval Amphibious Base in Coronado. The pub is owned by a Vietnam
SEAL and has long been a SEAL hangout, especially on Thursday nights.

McP's, incidentally, is where Chris Kyle, the Navy SEAL portrayed
in *American Sniper*, once allegedly decked former Minnesota governor
Jessie Ventura. The story goes that Ventura—a navy guy himself who
was in the Underwater Demolition Teams (UDT) before the UDT and
SEAL teams combined—had allegedly been disrespectful toward both
the SEALs and President George W. Bush, so Kyle flattened him. It's not
a solution I advocate, though I can tell you we'd probably get a helluva lot
more done in Washington if we employed it!

Lola was originally a Santa Barbara girl, but she was attending law
school in San Diego. She was at McP's with a girlfriend. The two of them
had been helping their girlfriend's mother move, and then after dinner
they decided to stop for a quick drink on the way home. It was really a
coin toss; both ladies were tired, but they didn't want to stay home. On
such random decisions are future lives often built!

They were in McP's more or less by accident. They'd been driving down Orange Avenue and noticed a bar with a bunch of good-looking guys standing out front, so they decided to go in.

Lola and her friend didn't have any cash, so they were going to have to use a credit card if they wanted to drink. The minimum for a credit card purchase was ten dollars, and the drinks were pretty cheap then. (Remember, this was a SEAL bar; it made its profit on volume.) Actually, they were surprised they had to buy drinks at all. Usually, when two good-looking women go into a bar, guys will come over to them and they don't have to take their purses out for anything other than lipstick.

But at McP's the men, many of whom at the time had mustaches and almost all of whom were in really good shape, were more or less keeping to themselves. Lola and her friend quickly and naturally assumed they had stumbled into a gay bar.

I was at McP's with my roommate and we were double dating. I'd gone as a favor to my roommate, and the evening wasn't going well.

One of my buddies took pity on me. He'd seen Lola at the bar, so he went up to her and said, "Do you want to meet a friend of mine?" Her look told him, "*Not really*," so he added, "He's going through a divorce and he needs a date." Well, Lola saw that I was sitting and talking with another woman, so she revisited her first reaction, which came out as, "Absolutely not."

But my friend was persuasive, and he told her, "You really need to meet this guy. He's the nicest guy in the world, and I promise you won't regret it."

So Lola agreed to at least be introduced to me and bought a round of drinks to help meet the ten-dollar requirement on her tab. It was love at first sight. It may sound corny, but I knew when I saw her that she was the one. I still remember the color of her skirt and her black cowboy boots.

I don't know what happened to the girl I had gone to McP's with, other than that she made it home okay, according to my friend. But Lola and I ended up talking for the rest of the evening. I didn't get her number, but when she closed her tab I saw her name on her credit card. I knew what law school she was going to, but when I called its information line they told me her number was unlisted.

I responded with a four-letter word that wasn't "darn."

I was trained never to quit, so the next day I began to hunt. I called the Office of the Register at her school and was able to finesse my way to get her schedule. Today, my approach would probably be considered stalking. I was smitten and sent flowers. She decided to skip class that day and the flowers went undelivered. But the very next weekend, I saw her and her girlfriend on the beach. This time, I didn't let her get away without giving me a number . . . and a promise to let me take her to a friend's barbecue that weekend.

That was it. Hamburgers and destiny.

I had moved from base housing to a small house in Imperial Beach, just south of Coronado. Lola and her daughter, Jennifer, were living in downtown San Diego. Back then, San Diego wasn't what it is today: Lola got mugged while she was there, and after that, she and Jennifer moved into a team house with me, because we all agreed it would be safer for them.

Even before she moved in, Lola had a sense of what she was in for as a military would-be wife. But she also knew the hazards of dating a SEAL, and as we got serious, she let me know her expectations. If she was going to sink time, energy, and money into our relationship, she wanted to be assured that I was as serious as she was. She'd already loved and lost once: her former husband, a JAG officer, died in a car accident in southern Turkey near Incirlik Air Base.

She didn't have to worry. Lola was the love of my life, and I know when I have someone special near me, whether that person is toting an MP5 or a basket filled with laundry. I'd told Lola of my plans to apply to the secrective SEAL Team that would ultimately take me across the country. In turn, she wanted a commitment: if she was going to go with me, she needed to know that I'd be worth the trip. I know I've said this elsewhere, but I'll say it again: Lola is the rock of our family, a military family, where being a rock is a tough assignment and not for everyone.

At one point in 2004, I was in Iraq. Our daughter Jennifer was providing medical support for our forward deployed SEAL unit. She was at Unit 2 in Bahrain, where she was a Diving Medical Technician who made sure SEAL divers were ready for action, whether that meant being physically fit or having the requisite shots. And Jennifer's future husband, who at that time was in the SEALs, was also deployed to the sandbox.

In short, Lola had me, our daughter, and our future son-in-law deployed overseas while she had two small children at home. Yes, they were in a controlled environment—by this point we were living on-base in Virginia—but that control ended more or less as you walked in the front door of our house.

Jennifer left the navy in 2008, after she'd made it to Petty Officer Second Class. She'd signed up after the tragic events of 9/11, despite my misgivings. I had told her to go to college and not join the navy or marry a Navy SEAL. She joined the navy, was honor man of her diving class, and married a Navy SEAL.

Jennifer completed her six-year contract right around the time her daughter—my granddaughter—was born. She had to make a tough decision whether to continue her service or end her enlistment and become the backbone of her own military family. She decided to move on with her life. I'm proud of her service, and I'm proud of her decision. Who knows? Maybe my granddaughter will be a SEAL someday . . . she certainly has the tradition in her family.

TWELVE

INTO THE FIRE

PLAYING SPORTS FOR MOST OF MY LIFE GAVE ME A unique perspective going into the SEALs program. It wasn't long into my training when I realized something that helped me understand how what I was doing *now* was a continuation of what I had done *then*.

In baseball, for example, if you are a millisecond late, you miss a fastball that's going by at one hundred miles per hour. With the "athletes" in the SEAL teams, the decision to "swing"—in this case, pull the trigger—has a far different result. But if can imagine this, when you are in that moment, as Hank Aaron or as Ryan Zinke, there is no game, there is no war. It's only you and an incredibly quick decision to make. No, scratch that. It isn't actually a decision, as the brain plays almost no part: it's a reaction. Once that call is made, the action must be perfectly, and I mean *perfectly*, fluid and precise. And this is exactly what the SEAL teams are taught.

SEALs are actually the most highly trained, underpaid professional athletes on earth. Their level of physical fitness would rival any professional decathlete, their hand-to-hand fighting skills are the equal of any steel cage professional fighter, and their shooting ability is on par with any Olympic marksman. Each and every one of them. All of these are required skill sets for survival. Flub any part of it and you don't make the grade.

Can you imagine a baseball team comprised of nothing but multi-threat superstars?

However, the quality that separates a SEAL—an "operator," as he is known—from a professional athlete is that a SEAL must be a superstar every time he goes to bat. Babe Ruth could afford to strike out twice as often as he homered. A SEAL cannot.

Yet with all of that said, even among superstar operators was a best-of-the-best. Men who are—I kid you not—a thousandth of a second faster than the others. The SEALs have developed a secretive "all-star" team among themselves, a SEAL Team that even the navy does not officially confirm its existence.

Some people in professional sports call it muscle memory; others call it motor learning. The bottom line is that when a task is repeated so many times, it eventually is performed without conscious effort. The process decreases the need for attention and creates maximum efficiency within the motor and memory systems. Examples of muscle memory are seen every day in riding a bicycle, typing on a keyboard, or playing a piano or guitar. The operator no longer has to consciously tell the body what to do; it just does it.

So, too, is the key to refining the athlete at the SEALs, except his task is arguably a little more dangerous than the average baseball player trying to hit a fastball. Once the threat is identified, he must shoot faster than the opposing player, or die. The stakes are higher.

In addition, not only must you make the play quicker than the bad guy, you must be certain that the bad guy is a "bad guy" and not throwing you a "curve ball" in the form of an unarmed decoy or other obfuscation (vest-wearing suicide bomber).

A mistake could land you in Leavenworth, or you and/or your teammates could be dead. All the while, you are making less per hour than McDonald's workers have been lobbying for nationwide. Seem a little out of whack? Sure does to me, but I thank God we have the men willing to take on the task.

You may know that the existence of an elite SEAL Team itself is sensitive, especially among the SEALs themselves. There are a couple of reasons for that. The first is, officially, there no longer *is* such a team. I'm not being secretive here: the team was officially disbanded in 1987, and most operators refer to those assigned to it as the "Jedis." Its public mission is to test and evaluate equipment used by the various Naval Special Warfare forces.

When I use the word "execute" I use it in connection with undertaking a mission. I want to talk a little about its other meaning, which has to do with taking out enemies of our nation.

In the closing days of 2015, under intense pressure, Barack Hussein Obama—with reluctance—finally authorized special ops teams to stop operating from behind barbed wire and go after the leaders of ISIS. Despite the fact that Special Operations Forces demonstrated great capability and phenomenal success taking out the terror group's chief financial officer, Abu Sayyaf, in May, it took the president another *half year* to authorize this as military policy. I should also remind you that the raid snagged Sayyaf's wife, who was running a slave ring for ISIS. Women were being held against their will and trafficked. How did bringing them justice not fit in with the president's alleged pro-women positions?

Reportedly, the commander in chief was dragged to this position by the fact that ISIS controlled so much territory and was so well organized that it could only be stopped by putting a significant force on the ground for several years . . . or by tactical decapitations. He chose the latter. And even then, only after blood was spilled in the streets of Paris.

One of the problems with putting boots on the ground in Syria and Iraq is not just tactical, not just cost in lives and tax dollars—but, to put it crassly, perception. A massive, uninvited US force in both nations would turn us into invaders. Becoming such an invading force would allow ISIS and other Islamic fighters to position themselves as a defending army. That would literally rally moderate Arabs against the "infidels" to a group they would normally not support. It's the old saying, "The enemy of my enemy is my friend." American troops on the ground must be accompanied by a larger force of our Muslim allies. An American military force must be viewed as an invited force within a greater coalition of the Muslim world. The fact of the matter is, without American leadership and military might, defeating ISIS is impossible. Also a fact is that without our Muslim allies joining in the fight, ISIS will simply go underground and metastasize into another brand of evil. The fight against ISIS or any radical Islamic organization is a struggle with Islam as much as it is between the ideas of Eastern and Western cultures. Defeating radical Islamic terrorism, whether in the form of ISIS, Al-Qaeda, or Boko Haram, will take unity of effort. We saw that kind of unity, then schism, in our own history when the colonies banded together to expel the British. When that was accomplished, the former colonies, now states, grew increasingly disenchanted with one another until the Civil War erupted. Of course, the difference with our revolution and subsequent War Between the States is that in all cases we were fighting for freedom, religious and otherwise, not the vile, enslaving madness of ISIS.

I will not, at this point, get too deeply into the question that remained largely unresolved by our Civil War, that of states' rights. However, this is as good a place as any to say that under Barack Obama and the extreme left—on matters as wide-ranging as the establishment of health care exchanges under the misbegotten "Obamacare" and the Syrian refugee relocation program—the precious and necessary quality of self-governance, of tailoring leadership to our inherently and wonderfully unique populations, has been crushed and discarded in a way that threatens a new revolt. When known felons and potentially soon-to-be mass killers are welcomed to these shores—as were Juan Francisco Lopez-Sanchez who murdered young Kate Steinle in San Francisco, or the radicalized Tashfeen Malik of the San Bernardino killings—voters must decide locally whether these inherently dangerous policies are something they want. California's allowance of sanctuary cities aided in the death of Ms. Steinle: Why is the opposite, non-sanctuary cities, not allowed? Isn't that kind of choice the very essence of our democracy? The statement on sound immigration policy from my favorite American, Theodore Roosevelt, is worth quoting:

> In the first place, we should insist that if the immigrant who comes here in good faith becomes an American and assimilates himself to us, he shall be treated on an exact equality with everyone else, for it is an outrage to discriminate against any such man because of creed, or birthplace, or origin. But this is predicated upon the man's becoming in every facet an American, and nothing but an American. . . . There can be no divided allegiance here. Any man who says he is an American, but something else also, isn't an American at all. We have room for but one flag . . . We have room for but one language here, and that is the English language. . . . And we have room for but one sole loyalty to the American people.[1]

In a few words, that is one of the reasons I have devoted myself to politics, to help restore the values, traditions, and spirit that made America great. The number one loyalty of any elected official must be to the American people and the Constitution upon which our freedoms and pursuit of happiness were founded.

Getting back to ISIS. Even without the perception risk, cutting off the hydra heads of the terrorists achieves the same thing that taking out Saddam Hussein did in Iraq: it removes the strongman (in this case, strongmen) who use cash, ingenuity, prison, slavery, and broad dogma to keep disparate groups and ideologies fighting in the same direction. With those leaders gone, their underlings would turn on one another to win those vacant positions. The losers in those struggles would take their factions and go off on their own. The cancerous mass that is ISIS would fall apart, in the same way that Saddam Hussein's nation crumbled when his fearful methods of maintaining unity (hangings, rape, and chemical warfare) were removed.

In both of its definitions, "execution" is a delicate, careful business in which a single misstep will result in the capture and/or death of a number of American heroes.

Lastly, with our enemies using everything from drones to electronic eavesdropping, keeping the training location under wraps is a wise policy. Since the killing of bin Laden and other high-profile raids, the existence of the team is now public knowledge, but who they are and specifics about how they do their mission should remain dark, period.

What is discussed openly is that there are East Coast SEALs and West Coast SEALs, and while nobody likes to admit it, internal jealousies and tensions exist between the teams located on the two coasts. (As I said above, factions—even when they have the same general goals—tend to butt heads, or worse. I don't think I need to remind everyone about the hostility between many Democrats and their GOP colleagues.)

Still, the rivalry between East Coast SEALs and West Coast SEALs is odd, because everyone goes through BUD/S training in Coronado, and SEALs aren't assigned to one coast or the other until after they graduate.

I suppose I should be used to this sort of regional rivalry; heck, I saw it in eastern and western Montana while I was growing up, and that was true in football, schools, and general attitudes of in-staters from one side or the other. But being used to something doesn't mean I like or condone it.

East Coast SEALs tend to think of the West Coasters as having bought into the Hollywood mentality. Now, it's true that Hollywood is just up the coast from Coronado, and many BUD/S instructors end up being extras in movies, including *Top Gun*, *Rocky*, and *Uncommon Valor*. There are other opportunities available to West Coast SEALs, too, and, as a result, many of them end up doing their own things individually. The East Coast guys tend to do more as a team; they tend to think that, because of the Hollywood connection and other distractions like surf and sunshine, the West Coast guys don't work as hard, and that's absolutely untrue.

There is an underlying competitive theme among SEALs. The pecking order among the different groups within the SEAL family goes something like this: You were just Underwater Demolition Team (UDT), you were just a SEAL Delivery Vehicle (SDV), you were just a regular team guy, you were just a Jedi assault team guy, you were just a Special Projects guy all the way to "you are just not me." All SEALs, whether UDT or a member of a special unit, are type A, competitive, self-centered, and, most of all, have earned the right to wear the Trident upon their chest.

I'll tell you what was true, though: when I was first assigned to SEAL Team One, the perception was that the first to go into combat would be those from the elite SEAL Team—and combat is where I wanted to be. At the time I joined SEAL Team One in 1986, it had last seen battle in Vietnam. In the meantime, the guys from the elite Team had been in Grenada in 1983 as part of Operation Urgent Fury, when members did beach recon, an extrication mission of Grenada's governor-general, and destroyed the country's only radio tower; and in Panama, as part of Operation Just Cause in 1989, when, among other missions, they knocked out President Manuel Noriega's escape routes.

If I wanted to go to war—and I did—I thought that going to the elite Team was where I should be. I wanted to fight for my country and lead the best into battle. Call it ego or patriotism, I had a calling. Back then, the SEALs trained hard but were sent into conflicts intermittently. These days, if you are a SEAL, chances are you will spend your entire career at war. Many of them have never experienced not being at war.

I made it to the elite Team in the early '90s, while the first Gulf War was still in swing. Ironically, though, other than a few boats, the only team that wasn't called to go over was us: we were "on standby," which isn't like being on the bench in football, when you tend to be an observer and, barring a field injury or collapse, are not going to play. As a member, part of you is on constant high alert. The reality is there are no time-outs.

You probably won't have time to gear up before a mission falls in your lap. No, scratch that: falls on your head. They tend to be that big and bad. You have to be *ready*, to sleep with both eyes open.

When I was on standby, I was never more than forty-five minutes from the compound, as you never know when a situation will call for a rapid deployment. Back then we had beepers, and if you were a SEAL on standby, you had your beeper with you at all times. It's important to note that it wasn't just the member who was on the "beeper," it was your whole family. Every aspect of your life was organized around being able to respond to the "010101" code that sounded the alarm.

Of course, that's only true part of the year. As a SEAL, sometimes you're on standby and basically glued to the base, sometimes you're taking training courses or recertifying your skills, and sometimes you're out in the field. There was little consistency other than you were typically away from home more than 250 days a year. Today's warriors may be away even more.

Officially, the reason was that the United States needed a counterterrorist force on standby that wasn't committed to the Gulf War. Had there been an embassy raid or terror attack, there needed to be assets not tied up in that theater. And, of course, being that we were relatively close to Washington, DC, and other major strategic military areas, I imagine politicians and top brass liked having us nearby.

I remember thinking it was both sad and ironic that the nation's top fighting force watched the Navy band assemble, get on an aircraft, and go to the Persian Gulf before we were called to action. Hey, I love our fight song, "Anchors Away," as much as the next sailor. But . . . they saw desert, and we did not.

Service to country.

I was elected to the Montana State Senate in 2008 to represent District 2, a district that is 1,882 square miles. In Congress, I represent a district approximately the same distance as from Washington, DC, to Chicago. I am used to big districts. The day I walked into the state house in Helena as a newly minted Republican senator—my heart proud but racing, I confess—I joined an old and honorable group of fifty men and women who meet once every two years for ninety session days. As a Montanan, I worked hard and I worked well with my colleagues across the aisle, and also with the one hundred members of the other part of our bicameral legislature, the Montana House of Representatives. We were all citizen legislatures, we all had our own constituents and agendas, but most of us never forgot this: we were also elected to serve the people and not ourselves. I was fortunate enough to have some great political mentors along the way who placed higher purpose above self. Local community heroes like State Senator Bob Depratu, who was a Ford Dealer; State Senator Bob Brown, who was a teacher; and Charley Abell, who ran the local credit union. Ordinary citizens who made an extraordinary difference.

As thrilled and honored as I was to be a senator, as humbled as I was every single time I walked into the great domed chamber, as determined as I was to give my all to serve the people who had cast a precious vote on my behalf, one aspect of my new job was immediately familiar: I was part of an elite group with its own traditions, rules, and codes of conduct. That part, at least, was extremely familiar to me. I slipped into my new team as though I was putting on my old, comfortable beach recon hiking boots. The marines have a saying that I like very much: "Once a marine, always a marine."

That's very true. I was able to bond quickly and tightly with my fellow senators because being part of a special team was already familiar to me. For more than two decades, I had been learning to lead when it was essential, follow when it was necessary, and stand shoulder-to-shoulder with fixed bayonets when that was the call. The senate was just a different kind of team waging a different kind of war—purse strings instead of territory, infrastructure instead of supply-line logistics, quality of life instead of life itself.

The challenge of politics is that while there are rules, there are also backroom deals. What you see on C-SPAN—for those of you who have the interest and patience to watch elected officials stand at a podium and drone or shout or implore for hours—is the proper, formal face of governance. Once those heavy oak doors close on committee meetings, though, the shirtsleeves get rolled up, the harsh words and foul language kick in, pizza or salads are sent for, and real struggles take place.

I was good with that too. Heck, I enjoyed it. That was like the difference between drilling on-base and going out into the field to face the unknown.

I found that there are two kinds of people who do politics well. One is the "wonks," the accountants or lawyers or surgeons who have logical minds and stick to the ideas or programs they've crafted. Follow the map, and you never lose your way.

Me? From the get-go, I have never been that kind of politician. Under that broad banner of "service," service above all, I follow my gut and look for opportunities to strike to make a difference. In that respect, I have a strong core of "cowboy," as we say in Montana. When I was with the SEALs, though, there was those who followed all the rules and played it safe, and there were those who used unconventional tactics to win.

We called them "pirates."

THIRTEEN

GOOD LUCK, LIEUTENANT

WHEN I DROVE THROUGH THE SECURITY CHECKPOINT at the secretive SEAL compound on a memorably balmy day in 1990, I was introduced to a world that had nothing—and I truly mean nothing—to do with the navy white uniform world I had experienced to that point. And I don't say that in a demeaning way: I love my neat, starched uniform as much as the next serviceman or woman.

But this wasn't that.

When I got to the base, I couldn't find the command. You'd think there would be signs, like at every other naval base I'd been to. Nothing. I stopped in building after building—poked my head in the Landing Signal Officers School and a construction office, asked sailors in the courtyards—not one of them could tell me exactly where the command was. They didn't even *ummmm* or *ahhh* or "let-me-think;" they did not know. It was as though I'd asked them to direct me to Mars.

Though it was perplexing, this was the kind of intel-gathering I actually loved. Later, in Iraq, I would remember this experience and refer to it often, remind myself I had to keep hunting calmly but with firm resolve. I would buttonhole every uniform I met, if necessary, but I would achieve my goal.

After about three-quarters of an hour wandering—during which time I'd mentally divided my unexpected field of operations into quadrants—I spotted what looked a lot like an ammunition bunker and an old fountain cigarette boat on a trailer. I drove toward the facility and stopped at a gated fence. The gate opened and I thought, *They must know that I am here.* I was wrong. The gate opened, but not for me. Two guys on a Harley-Davidson, complete with Ape Hangers, drove out the gate in a cloud of dust. I didn't say two sailors because they didn't look like me in my whites, clean shaven and looking like something as pure and clean as Montana air. No sir. They looked like outlaw bikers with scruffy beards, long hair that would have looked more suitable on Axl Rose, and then there were the earrings and tattoos. This was years before everyone except newborns was wearing ink. It was still a relative novelty.

I stopped and looked and wondered how the heck these guys made it through the front gate. All of that I took in at first glance, which took about a half-second. The second half-second—and yeah, you learn to do quick studies that fast—I noticed the guy on back had an M60 machine gun complete with belts of 7.62mm ammo wrapped over his shoulders like Pancho Villa! I invested another second to make an assessment: threat or non-threat. It was not uncommon for gangs to plant members in the military so they could get their hands on sophisticated ordnance. Did these two have an inside man? Do I approach and challenge, or do I report this pair to the shore patrol? As I watched, having eased into the shadow of a nearby shed, the armed men on the Harley-Davidson roared off toward a gun range I spotted earlier.

Before that, I had been on alert. Now I was just confused. I was starting to realize I had just arrived at a different type of command than I had ever been exposed to before. Later, I found out that I had just been introduced to the Pirates. The Pirates also had a reputation as being the "porthole to hell" for officers.

The gate remained open and I drove a few yards to the guard shack. Two guards walked out, looked at my uniform, and asked, "Are you here to check in?" I replied, "Yes, sir." "The building you want is over there. The last officer didn't even make it long enough to unpack. Good luck, Lieutenant." I had arrived at the right place.

Later, after I had checked in, I found myself in a place that looked like a rec room, but was also, I kid you not, a "wrecked" room. There was a white drop-ceiling that looked as though it had never been painted, and with good reason: it had actually split in spots from the weight of the empty beer bottles that had been stuck up there. I could see the necks of the bottles poking out—that is, where said bottles hadn't fallen to the floor.

Incredibly, as I was about to learn, I found what I had been looking for. This was the "team room," the gathering and staging area for the assault teams that make up the core fighting unit. And the men who were lounging in vinyl-covered seats were my new colleagues. What I can tell you is that in 1991, the team was carved into different assault teams. It's changed since, but at the time the three assault teams made up the backbone of our nation's maritime counterterrorist force. Within the assault teams even their rivals conceded that the Pirates were "the most piratical of all Pirates." But before one could join one of the assault teams, the first test that all had to pass was the training team. And not every SEAL did. In fact, the attrition of specially screened SEALs who had previously proven themselves was as high as 50 percent at times. The distinguisher was really the ability to quickly identify a threat versus a non-threat and pull the trigger or not. When it came to kill or be killed, the decision to engage and the skill required to hit what you're aiming at separated those who would be assigned to one of the training teams, and those who would return back to regular SEAL teams. The original assault teams made up the core of the "meat eaters" at the command. There were other personnel attached to the command, affectionately known as "plant eaters," that provided support in the form of communications, administration, logistics, and a host of other critical tasks. Each group could not survive without the other.

Turned out that the "meat eaters" were similar in capability but distinctly different in personality. One team, known as the Redman or the Indians, was the "train harder not smarter" team—when it went on operations, you could count on those operations being full of explosions and action. They were the knuckle draggers, the over-the-top weight lifters. I started out with the Redman.

Another team, known as the Crusaders, was made up of the "sunshine pretty" boys, triathletes in polo shirts and Dockers but who just happened to be deadly. This team's temperament was on the quiet side, and their tactics using silent runs and low-light night-vision reflected it. Crusaders were cold, calculating killers.

The last of the teams was also known as the Pirates. True to the *Jolly Roger*, this crew was amazingly talented and "the most piratical of this team of Pirates." Many had been at the command since Captain Marcinko had the helm and they were set in their ways. On operations, there were two teams. One was an extraordinary feat of swash-buckling excellence; the other was an unmitigated disaster. The problem was it took a roll of the "bones" to determine which team showed up.

The assault team was my new crew and life was good.

I have seen a lot in my life, especially on the battlefield. But nothing has impacted me quite the same way as seeing the ordinary where I was expecting to find the extraordinary. It would be like going into the locker room at a body-building competition and not finding a single sculpted bicep. Or a bakery without a cake. It was just bizarre. In my experience, even new recruits in civvies had a certain respectful decorum about them. These men? It was like some bizarre roadside bar where Vikings, soccer dads, and blue-collar workers somehow socialized.

Everyone here, men and officers, were in civilian clothes. They were casual and relaxed. Only later did I learn that their appearance was carefully chosen and their "characters" scrupulously rehearsed so that they would be able to blend in with the local populace during covert operations in some of the most unwelcoming and hazardous environments on planet Earth.

Those guys who had biked off when I arrived? Their beards blended in with most biker bars and drug lords south of the border. Today, beards blend in well for the Middle East. (A side note: believe it or not, as you move from province to province in some Middle Eastern countries, you have to be aware of your beard length. In Islamic law, a basic beard of at least a fist-length is *wajib*, or "mandatory." But within that there's a bunch of leeway, and different groups—certain bandit bands, for example—identify themselves by subtle differences in that length. If you're collecting HUMINT—human intelligence—on the ground, you have to make sure you move through groups that require longest beard to shortest, since it's faster to trim one than to sit around waiting for one to grow!)

Anyway, I stood there in a naval room in my navy whites with my short blond haircut and squared shoulders, feeling more like an outsider than I had ever felt in my twenty-nine years on sweet Mother Earth. The external qualities that I had always thought defined "navy" made me feel positively out of step in the headquarters of the US Navy's most elite warriors. Right then and there I traded the uniform for a pair of khaki pants and never looked back.

Yet that was just the first of the many speed bumps I would hit. You want to know what kind of seagoing individual I was about to become?

You guessed it. A rogue warrior. Committed to the mission and committed to make sure that we win. If that is the definition of a rogue warrior, I will take it.

I have worked with the Army's counterpart and every component within the Special Operations family. Each member of the larger team supports the greater effort of America's Special Operations Forces. Whether it is Army Special Forces, Rangers, or the Marine Special Operations Component, each is to be respected and feared by the enemy. The SEALs historically have focused on maritime targets and Delta on land targets. Since 9/11 all Special Operations Forces and their Tactics, Techniques, and Procedures (TTP) are nearly interchangeable on land. No unit is more important than any other and every unit is critical to victory on the battlefield.

But the navy's elite SEAL Team was unique. It was wild and unbroken, at times savage. From day one of this unit's training, they were told they were special. Making it to the team proved it. They were cocky, confident, and deadly in a fight. From the moment I pulled up to the gate, the throttle was on full. We did everything harder. We trained harder, deployed longer, and viewed the conventional rules as guidance rather than the law.

I quickly learned that the typical military hierarchy was inverted. The senior enlisted men who had come in under Lieutenant Commander Richard Marcinko (the unit's commanding officer) basically ran the day-to-day operations. That's different than the way things are done in the conventional navy. Because of the bond that existed among the enlisted ranks—well, let's just say there was strength in numbers and it was unwise for an officer to go against the will of those who were technically junior in rank but more experienced in warfare. They had been there longer, knew more about tactics, and remained at the command long after an officer departed for other assignments. Being an officer meant that if I didn't show respect for, and win the respect of, the enlisted personnel under me, my career as an officer would end. That took some getting used to. I probably felt similar to how some of those old industrialists did in the first half of the twentieth century when workers were unionizing and owners found their power diminished. I was there to listen, learn, and provide the men with tools to win. One Master Chief expressed it best when he said, "Officers rent their lockers, we own ours." Good point.

This is a good place to take a walk around the question of workers unions. Back then, they were needed. They still are. Every system needs its checks and balances. But when a unit—say, a military unit—goes from necessary offense to conquest, it becomes an entity that ceases to function for the good of the community. It becomes what it was conceived to dispel. Too many unions and union leadership have become more interested in power and control over service. I have been a union member and have always believed a principle role of a union is to protect and promote its membership by ensuring that the organization is value-added to industry or society. Unions have the advantage of being able to develop training programs and securing good-paying jobs through collective bargaining. Protecting US jobs and promoting a highly skilled labor force is honorable. A union worker should be better trained and offer better value. The rub is when unions fail their own membership by not providing quality labor at competitive contracts. Our society depends on America being competitive. It's like any institution that separates itself from society and ceases to be concerned with its role *in* that society. Can you imagine a school dictating to parents, *"You're asking your children to learn too much," "We want to serve caviar at lunch," "We think the school day should be halved to keep the kids from having to actually learn math and then science and then history"*?

It's absurd. Everything in moderation. Many unions have forgotten that and, in so doing, have created an adversarial role with the very people they were formed to protect. Those rifts are not only dangerous to a nation, they are fatal. Especially when you add stranglehold demands to those of other self-interested groups, every hyphenation out there. Instead of having a nation of proud, well-integrated communities, you end up with something akin to the Middle East, a world of warring tribes with greedy warlords. Some of you may remember when we were, say, Irish-American, Italian-American, Polish-American on one big, celebratory day each year. We had a parade and then we went back to being "just" plain old Americans the other 364 days. Talk about "union"? That nationalistic quality is fading. We don't happily make room and try to learn from the other guy or gal and the group to which they belong. We take offense at the drop of a questionable word or thought. People see a stereotype in an old movie and instead of using it to educate about the way things were and how far we've come, they boycott the station that showed it. We are "pro" this or "anti" that but with a completely deaf ear. I don't like everything unions do, but I want to listen to them, hear from them, consider what they have to say. I want them to extend the same courtesy and concern for their fellow Americans. That's how reasonable global solutions are achieved.

That said, let me get back to my indoctrination and a guy who broke a lot of those rules I just laid out.

The guy who spoke for the senior enlisted men was Command

Master Chief Fred Fritsch, and he was the guy you absolutely did not want to cross. Fred was hard. I mean, like concrete. He was a former member of the Navy's Olympic bobsled team and looked like he was still competing. The rest of the enlisted men were hard as concrete too, but more forgiving. If you did something wrong, by accident—not maliciously—they took the time to identify why it was a mistake and they made sure you didn't make it again. If you did, you had to answer to Fred. What that meant, ironically, was that you *didn't* answer to him: he didn't talk to you, period, till you straightened up. The silent treatment made you an outcast.

Mind you, the officer corps with us was no more run-of-the-mill than the enlisted men. Every officer was specially screened and selected. The competition was keen with less than a handful of SEAL officers even getting past the first interview. In many cases you were asked to join them and not the other way around. It was no secret that an officer who was selected to the command and able to make it through the selection process would be promoted faster than his peers. If you were invited back for a second tour of duty you were recognized as the best of the elite. There were many pitfalls for an officer too. If something went wrong, which it often did, it was the officer who took the fall, as he was in charge. An officer was always in charge when anything went wrong and was only present went the operation went right. Those were the terms of being selected and I gladly accepted the condition of service.

And right there was my problem in a thimble: I was in charge by rank but not in action. I had to earn respect in a way that was different from anything I'd experienced in "big navy." My rank, my uniform, meant nothing to these Pirates. What impressed fellow teammates was a strong work ethic and an ability to get the job done.

My work was cut out for me. That first day, walking into that room, I felt as though I'd been handed a plastic knife to cut marble.

It wasn't just the enlisted men who represented a challenge, though. It was the collective mind-set against big navy. I'll give you an example. The facilities were extremely unusual by traditional standards. At my previous command, reflecting what was going on in the "real" world, the US Navy had undertaken a serious effort to get rid of alcohol from its bases. Just as the old "smoke 'em if you got 'em" mantra was dead and buried—the mind-set that once encouraged combat soldiers to relax and have a cigarette—the higher-ups had decided that drinking and soldiering were not a good fit. Maybe so. I'm an everything-in-its-time-and-place kind of guy myself, and, besides, I don't like playing nanny to grown men and women. But I wasn't the secretary of the navy, so the service was trying to phase alcohol out.

Not here.

Among the SEALs, alcohol was used as frequently as firearms and chewing gum. There was a bar in every team room. Despite that, no man drank on duty. Never mind that he could get himself killed by mishandling explosives; he would endanger the life of his teammates. But once that beer lamp was lit, man, these guys drank like Prohibition was right around the corner.

"We drink like it's our last," one guy admitted to me that first week I was there. "Because in our line of work, it might very well be."

Even though Marcinko had departed a couple of years before, the team was still basically an operation living under rules he had laid down. Let me pause here to tell you a little about that man, about the kind of clout his shadow still carried. During the Iran hostage crisis in 1979, when Tehran was holding fifty-two of our embassy personnel—and didn't relinquish them for a staggering 444 days—Marcinko was one of two Navy guys placed on a Joint Chiefs of Staff task force called the Terrorist Action Team. TAT was tasked with the job of coming up with a plan to free those hostages. The result was Operation Eagle Claw, which foundered in just about every way a military operation could go bad. After that humiliation, the Navy realized they had to have a force that could go into action swiftly, dynamically, and effectively. They asked Marcinko to come up with that team. His response was an elite group of SEAL warriors.

You can begin to get an idea of the tactical brilliance of the man just from that designation. The navy had a pair of SEAL teams: One and Two. That's it. But Marcinko felt that by jumping up the numeric ladder, he would confuse the Soviet Union and other enemies into believing the navy had such teams. They would not only overestimate our response capabilities, they would also waste precious time and manpower trying to find SEAL Teams Three, Four, and Five. Anytime enemies are exposing themselves to that kind of recon, the greater the likelihood they'll slip up and you'll get them. So it was a double stroke of genius.

Marcinko personally chose the team members from the entirety of the navy's Special Operations commands. He handpicked the best of the best, and his SEAL team became the navy's standout premiere fighting force.

Dick Marcinko remains controversial even today. There was little doubt that he was a rogue warrior in that he found rules to be "guidance" and was unafraid to run against authority. The navy eventually went after him and he was convicted of taking a small kickback on an ammunition contract. He went to prison. I don't give judgment, but what I do know is those who served under him remain loyal and would fight with him again given the chance.

This seems like a good place to comment on some of the other responsibilities that come with the uniform. It has nothing to do with risking your life or learning your skills better than any human beings ever have in the history of warfare—which is itself a pretty heady thought. The years of effort you invest *are* a potent and constant reminder that *this is your life*. It's no different than becoming a doctor, except for the number of lives that depend upon you at any given time.

No, this has to do with family and the price *they* pay being married to a SEAL.

People like to ask government workers, especially government workers in sensitive or essential positions, whether their family or their country comes first. There will always be people who disagree with you, no matter what answer you give. On these shores, ever since that fateful day in 1776 when Nathan Hale uttered his immortal, "I only regret that

I have but one life to lose for my country,"[1] the primacy of life or family or country has been an awful choice many patriots have had to make. Another quote, not quite so lofty but no less true: in John Wayne's *The Alamo*, Davy Crockett said something about his life before that fateful commission. "None of it seemed a lifetime worth the pain of the mother that bore me. It was like I was empty. Well, I'm not empty anymore."[2]

Yes, sir. If we make this commitment, we will never be empty again. But there is a price. Either sadly or reassuringly—depending on your point of view—for most of us in the military, and particularly in special ops, the choice is made when they sign up: "Country comes first."

Sometimes, though, the choice is worse than simply having to miss a sister's wedding or a child's confirmation. Sometimes, you are forced to make a decision that the devil himself must have crafted.

FOURTEEN

LOLA'S BIG STORM

IN 1997, MY WIFE, LOLA, AND I, ALONG WITH OUR TEENAGE daughter, Jennifer, our toddler, Wolfgang, and our newborn, Konrad, were living in base housing near the shores of Virginia. The house was built in the '50s and only a small sand dune separated the beach from the backyard. It was actually our second time in Virginia; we'd been there three years before, when Lola and I were engaged but not yet married.

During our first go-round in Virginia, in 1991, we had been giving our relationship a one-year engagement period. When the wedding date was set, the boys on the team ensured that the occasion would be memorable by preparing an elaborate pulley system in the ocean surf zone using truck wenches and line attached to old pier pilings. My hands were tied behind my back and I was provided with a lifejacket and a pair of goggles and then attached to the line. The boys then positioned themselves on the beach with MP5 submachine guns loaded with paint rounds, while the wench operator proceeded to make me a floating "rubber duck" shooting arcade. They must have spent hours setting up the system. I am guessing they did not see the memo on the navy's hazing policy but I was glad to help them improve their shooting. Nonetheless, I survived and Lola and I were married on August 8, 1992. Mind you, we were both being extremely cautious. Both of us had been married before, and Lola was a widow whose husband had died. So Lola was bringing up Jennifer as a single mother, and doing a really good job of it.

The point is that we wanted to be methodical about making sure we could forge a strong relationship. We were going to face stresses Ozzie-and-Harriet-type families don't. Lola knew what my priorities were going to have to be, regardless of how I felt about my loved ones. She knew that in military families, every time the kids get sick, or a dog gets run over, or a house gets broken into, it's the non-military spouse who has to deal with whatever needs to be dealt with.

SEAL team marriages have an even greater set of stresses because of the nature of the mission and the people it takes to do it. We are not just guys who signed on for tours of duty; we are also all Type-A personalities. "Take charge" and "Never quit" are in the basic job description. And I have to confess, we also were used to enduring a whopping amount of physical and emotional abuse, especially during training. In those times, it's a SEAL wife who often plays a big role in either nursing her husband's wounded ego when things go wrong or reining it in when it gets out of hand. Keep in mind that when our egos take a beating it isn't like a traditional bad day at the office. You fail at some task and you come away questioning your very self-worth, asking whether you deserve the job, the respect of your comrades, or even the love of the woman you're with. It's a far-reaching, *deep*-reaching doubt.

Apart from those challenges, SEALs spend a lot of time away from home on missions or training. Sometimes, they leave with no notice. You walk in the door, grab a go-bag, kiss your wife, and—with your brain already on the mission—walk back out the door. If you remember to say good-bye, that's a plus. Because the majority of operations are classified, wives of team members often don't know where their husbands are or what they're doing. And there's one set of stress that comes from wondering if their husbands are going to be late coming home from work and quite another that comes from wondering if they're in a hotspot somewhere, and whether they'll ever see their husbands again.

Lola and I once figured out that for a time I was spending two hundred nights out of the year away from her and the kids. It takes someone special to be a SEAL; it takes someone even more special to be a SEAL's wife.

So you have SEAL team husbands coming back after being away for a while, and they're returning to households where the wives have had to step into household mother and father roles . . . plus celibacy, which presents its own nasty issues. Sometimes you come back from war and there are kids running around, sometimes there are teenagers being teenagers, and all of a sudden this knucklehead shows up saying that he's the man of the house, and the wives who have been dealing with the usual family drama say, "Wait a second! The crown is not yet yours!" There's definitely an adjustment period.

When you're in a leadership position, there's another consideration. Even when you're home, your mind may be elsewhere. You're thinking about past missions and training—what went right, what could have gone better. You're planning for future training and missions—your own, and especially the men under you. You're considering your team's shortcomings and how to shore them up. You're thinking about the complexity of the mission and the cost of failure to your men and their families. You are responsible to make sure everyone comes home. Try reading Dr. Seuss to your kid with that on your mind. And more often than not these considerations aren't things you can share with your wife, so she can't do much but be supportive in a general way.

What's even worse for a SEAL wife is that they're not supposed to know about the missions their husbands are on, but if you suddenly start growing a beard or tanning, they can get a pretty good sense of what you're going to be doing. Quite frankly, however, the spouse's intel network is oftentimes better than the team members'. When your suitcase is already packed when you get home, they know. And sometimes they'll turn on the TV and see reports about specific military operations, and even though there's no specific mention of SEALs they'll know SEALs were involved . . . and if you happen—*happen*—to steal a moment to call, they can't ask any questions. They have to know without being able to comment on it. There's a lot that can't be shared between spouses.

It takes a pretty special person to realize this is the sort of life they're going to be in for, and then to be able to make it work. And I'll be frank here: a lot of SEAL team marriages fail. It's ironic when you think of all the time and money that goes into turning man to superman, yet the hidden cost is structural damage to the human parts of us. I truly do not believe it is possible to avoid that. The way you *live* with it is through the strength of your partner. Our marriage has been one of the strong ones, and Lola has been well more than half of the reason why.

If anything, we put our engagement through more tests than most. As I mentioned, the first time I was stationed in Virginia, Lola and I weren't married. We were engaged, we knew we were really good together, but we hadn't formally taken our vows. We didn't know it when we first moved there, but the fact that we weren't married was going to make life more difficult for her than it otherwise would have been. Fiancées were not considered a "fully vested" part of the command. They could go to Christmas parties and picnics and other social functions, but without the title and the marriage certificate they weren't really taken into the heart of the community. They did not have access to naval facilities or command services.

They've since loosened the rules in an attempt to accommodate the demanding lifestyle. But those changes came after the first time Lola and I were there, unmarried, and before our return, when we were already married. By that time she had already been around the base enough that they weren't going to do the introductions for her. She sort of slipped between the cracks, and that wasn't easy for her either time.

I liked living on-base near the beach. I was close to work, and during the second time we were there the kids were young enough that they could run around on the base without getting into anything that would compromise security too much. Jennifer was very happy with her high school friends, Konrad—who had recently been born—was still in Lola's arms, and as for Wolfgang, well, a three-year-old's curiosity is mostly limited to what he can get from the Navy Exchange in the way of toys or candy.

When the team was on standby and held hostage to staying within forty-five minutes of the command, the kids literally grew up on the compound. Since we lived on-base, nearly every time higher headquarters needed an answer or had an inquiry I was called and asked to go into the operations center and answer the mail. After all, "He lives so close." As a result, I was always on the compound on the weekends and typically brought the kids in tow. Wolf and Konrad would play hide and seek in the locker room and between the equipment cages filled with gear. They knew how to shred paper and what not to touch. They knew where the boneyard was and what not to touch. Looking back on it, it was just nice to be a dad.

If there was a downside to living on the beach, it was that we were occasionally in the path of Atlantic storms. For the most part, this wasn't too bad: base housing could stand up to a little wind and rain. The house was small but cozy, I could walk to work, and except for a few of my colleagues speeding through the neighborhood, I loved living there. It was like living in a 1950s community, right out of the pages of *Leave it to Beaver*.

It was there that we went through one of the more trying times in our family life. There was a tropical depression that pretty much overnight turned into a tropical storm, which then quickly turned into a hurricane—one heading right for the base, and our home.

But Lola and I talked about it, and we agreed that while the storm might crack a window or two, it wasn't anything to worry about. I assured her that we were going to get through it together.

Turned out the command had other plans. The military was not going to risk its most valuable assets getting damaged if the destruction was avoidable. If a terrorist organization seized a ship at sea or took hostages on some foreign shore, a storm of this size might prevent the team from being able to respond immediately. We were the nation's 911 force and could not be delayed should we be called. Word came down from the command that certain assets had to be moved and sheltered away from the storm's path. Those assets included SEALs, but they did not include the SEAL families.

Boy, that really puts the question on its ear: What comes first—country or family—when the military could accommodate both but chooses not to for reasons they did not care to share with us? I was not comfortable with the idea of heading for safety and leaving my family in potential danger.

In this case, barring being brought up on charges of insubordination, I didn't have a choice. The storm was upgraded in the morning. The team was ordered to move out in the afternoon, and on the evening before the storm was supposed to hit I moved out with them. Hurricane Bonnie was about to show the full force of nature at her toughest.

The command did what it could to make up for ordering the SEALs off-base. Seabees assigned to the command—members of the US Naval Construction Forces, or Construction Battalions—came in and sandbagged the houses, boarded up the windows, and otherwise did what they could for the SEAL families living on-base.

But at least a lot of them were together. I was now away from danger with the rest of the team in Florida, and Lola and the kids were in the house bracing to face the storm alone.

If you've ever been in a hurricane, you know that you don't as much see them as you do hear them and feel them. If you're in the middle of a hurricane, hopefully you're in an inside room, one without windows. So you while you can't see what's going on, you can probably hear the wind and the rain. Sometimes, you can feel the house you're in rattle, and there's the occasional thump as something—a heavy tree branch, a garbage can someone has stupidly forgotten to secure—hits your house. And wind is loud too: there's an overused cliché about wind howling, but when you're in the middle of a hurricane or a tornado, you realize that *howl* or *shriek* are the right words. The weather becomes alive, and it's not very happy. It eats things too. Like phone and electrical wires.

With a hurricane, there's a double blow. If you're directly in its path, when you're hunkered down you'll hear all the howling, and you'll feel the thumps and shaking. Then there will be a period of calm, which is deceptive—sometimes deadly so. This isn't the storm's end; it's the eye—a bit of calm in the center before the eye passes over you and the wind and rain starts up again.

The eye of the storm was predicted to hit landfall a few hundred miles away and the intensity of the hurricane at the base was predicted to be not much more than a storm. The predictions were wrong. The hurricane winds increased as the storm turned toward land. Hitting the roads was risky alone with children, so Lola stood fast and hunkered down with our three kids—including two who weren't three yet. She was waiting out the storm, and when the calm came of course the kids got restless and she had to keep them waiting . . . and keep them from going nuts when the noise started again. The power and phones went out and the line between the ocean and house became blurred.

None of this I knew while it was happening. For all I knew, the house had collapsed with them in it.

Hurricane Bonnie made landfall on August 27, 1998, achieving wind gusts of up to 104 miles per hour. Close to 950,000 people were evacuated and total damage exceeded one billion dollars. Lola showed her grit and braced herself and the kids in the bathroom. The house flooded, the power went out, but the plywood that the Construction Battalion had screwed on the windows held. Nobody died, thankfully. But I can tell you that it hasn't been easy to know I wasn't with my family, especially since not being with them wasn't my choice.

One thing I do know is that Lola is a trooper.

FIFTEEN

THE LAST OF THE
PIRATE RAIDS

SO THERE I WAS, HANDED THE BEST OF THE BEST AND given the order: lead. It's one thing to take new recruits and drill bad habits out of them. But to take knife-edged professionals and tell them to do things *your* way? That's like telling a tiger to be a canary. Wasn't gonna happen, and I was smart enough to see that on minute one of day one.

I worked tirelessly to acclimate and gain the respect of the men. That meant, first and foremost, I had to work harder than my teammates and look for opportunities to excel. And not just figuratively. I drilled with the team, making certain every training revolution was better than the last. I spent sleepless nights on the sea, bouncing all the hell over rough seas while chasing down ships. I exercised like a demon, the same way I had in high school and college, ignoring the pain and savoring the burn. I flushed every naval regulation I ever knew about proper grooming. In those years before rampant political correctness, I called myself the Last of the Mohicans. At my wedding, I had a small ponytail. Minus the tattoos, I began to look like the two Pirates on the Harley.

I worked nonstop to be one of the guys, and you know how I knew I'd made it? When they finally gave me a nickname. They called me "Z Man." I liked it, and the name stuck.

That was it. I was in. All those qualities of service I talked about before, of the importance of working with and caring about the people around you? I had that now to a degree I never thought possible. "Brothers" doesn't come close to describing the bond. And I'll tell you this: that's the difference between us and most of the enemies we fought in the Middle East, the same ones who terrorize defenseless families, who bind and execute helpless, blameless individuals. We weren't motivated by hate or visions of conquest. We were obsessed with duty and honor and uplifting the lives of those we served at home and also abroad. That was as true in the field as it is—at least for me—in the halls of Congress.

Service.

That simple idea is why we win, why we will always ultimately win.

It is why terrorists and despots who may bloody our noses or slaughter their own people always fall.

The wild and woolly culture of the SEALs had its advantages. It was more flexible and in many ways more effective than "big navy." It could get in and out virtually unseen, complete a mission before an enemy even knew it was underway. But there were problems, too, as there are in any organization. A decade before the strain of long, sustained combat began in the aftermath of the September 11, 2001, terror attacks, an internal bloodletting had begun in the SEAL teams . . . and it came from a most unexpected source.

A success.

As I rose in seniority, I was asked if I would take over leadership of the team on my second tour. I had earned a reputation of working hard and leading from the front. While I could handle a rifle, I never was a sniper, and, more importantly in the eyes of the headquarters, I had been previously assigned to a unit other than the Pirates. It was an honor to even be considered and I took my new role seriously. My job was to ensure the men at the front of the battle's edge had everything they needed to win. The team had gone through a rough patch and had lost the commanding general's confidence by under-delivering on a couple of high-visibility training exercises. It was more bad luck than anything else, but there was never any room for even the slightest excuse for failure. I was sent in to restore confidence and faith to the Crusaders. I would start by focusing on the right training, the right equipment, and the right plan to dispatch the enemy and come home.

Some of the best SEALs have what I call "outlier" personalities. They may have come from the school of hard knocks, or they may have something smoldering deep down inside them. They may not have been academic or athletic superstars, but they had incredible drive and they were tough. Very tough.

A lot of discussion has been made over SEAL selection. *Can you tighten up the initial screening so that the attrition is less? Can you predict success or failure?* Judging from the backgrounds of the current master chiefs, I would say those who don't fit the mold push the team forward. It's easy to record the number of push-ups, difficult to screen character and drive, and impossible to predict greatness.

As it happened, there were characters on every SEAL team. Take "Blake Edwards" for instance, who was in training class with me. Blake had been assigned to an East Coast team and had seen action in Panama. He was a phenomenal shot and enjoyed life on the road. He used to go out on training trips and pick up local girls with his sidekick and fellow SEAL, "Vic Ferraro." They couldn't say they were with the SEALs, of course, so they'd concoct a story of being part of the Coors Light jump team, or some other outrageous cover. Even his choice of their cover names indicated they were brazen.

That was only the start of the stories they used to make up on the fly. They rarely got called out on his stories, of course, and they were never traced back to the command. How could anyone trace back his wild tales when he told any girl he met in a bar that his name was Blake Edwards? For those of you too young to remember him, Blake Edwards was an actor and director made famous for films such as *Breakfast at Tiffany's* and *10*.

Blake had always been a wild man, even when stateside. He once picked up a girl; I have no idea if he was Blake Edwards at the time, and it really doesn't matter. He decided he was going to take a blue chem light—like those day-glow light sticks you get at parties, except a lot more powerful—crack it open and, become the original "Blue Man" when they were both under the covers.

God only knows what that chemical is inside those lights. Blake certainly didn't. It took a few minutes before it began burning him, and by the time he and the girl realized it was not a good idea, it was too late but that didn't stop Blake from telling the story after he got back from the hospital.

I had what you could call an interesting conversation with Blake later, when I was the operations officer. I got a call from one of the master chiefs, telling me he'd received a letter from Blake's wife stating she had a problem with his pay. On issues of family and pay, I took the issue seriously. Blake had been shot in Somalia months back during the infamous mission portrayed in the book and movie *Black Hawk Down*. Due to his wounds, he was assigned to the operations department while recovering. Somehow, he dropped off the radar.

"Okay," I said. "How's Blake doing?"

"You should know," the Master Chief said to me. "He's assigned to you."

At that point, I hadn't seen Blake for months. In fact, I could not remember the last time I saw him and had not realized he had been assigned to me. I hadn't seen his name on any paperwork, and the team had been traveling a lot, so I wasn't around much. But the navy thought Blake was still assigned to me, and there was a trail of direct deposit paychecks to prove it.

Nobody knew where his pay was going. Blake's wife certainly didn't; she hadn't seen any of it for her bills or expenses. She thought he was still in the team area, and we thought he was rehabbing or had been assigned somewhere else.

We contacted the bank where his paychecks were being deposited, and from it got an address for him in North Carolina, where he was living off the grid, yet on full active-duty pay.

I was able to find his number and gave him a quick call. That was a fun conversation.

"Uh, hey, man, how's it going?" he said upon answering the phone.

"Hey, Blake. It's good here in the navy. You're still part of it, and you've got to come back to work."

"Well, I've got a lot of things going on, Z Man. You know how it is."

"Yes Blake, I know how it is. I also know the navy and you are still in it. It's Monday. You have until next Monday to be back on the job. Your decision matrix is either: a) you're going to come back to work, permanently, or b) you're out of the navy. You have zero leave left, you're not on rehab, and you have to support your wife."

Blake came back, at least for a little bit. We weren't going to bust him. He had been shot, been stuck in rehab, and decided to go fishing for a while. Quite frankly, given the circumstances of being overrun in Somalia and the amount of time that a team guy is deployed, I was willing to work with him. But he knew that he no longer had the passion and soon got out of the navy, which was a shame. He was a good SEAL and an excellent shot. He just couldn't do it anymore, and found other interests.

At least Blake was entertaining to be around. Unfortunately, every organization has them. The SEALs have more than our share. When you're in charge of a SEAL assault team, you potentially have one of the best jobs in the world. You have plenty of money, great guys, cool equipment, and you're in fantastic shape. You should feel like you were on top of the world.

But there is always one guy in any organization whose personality clashes with the rest like oil and water. I had mine with "Old Two Grit." We called him that because he was the sand that got everywhere and rubbed everybody wrong. He hated officers, and the men hated him. Even his own mother, rumor had it, didn't tell him when she was coming into town. Maybe it was me, maybe it was our egos, but the lesson learned was "cut bait early."

I will say this about Old Two Grit: when it came to battle, he left his bull behind. He'd fight with people in the team room, and he'd fight with them in planning sessions or during training, but when we were out in the field, he was a SEAL warrior alongside the rest of us. I guess he always needed to be fighting someone, and if an enemy wasn't handy, we were it.

Other guys were more in the mold of just being fun to watch talent work, like "Scotty," who served with me throughout my career. He was savagely unorthodox, and savagely deadly in combat. You couldn't really train guys like this. They'd learn the basic lessons, but most of the time they were driven by instinct, and their instincts were excellent.

Scotty was near perfection when it came to close-quarters battle work. He instinctively knew when to press ahead, and when to slow down and assess the field of battle. People around him learned quickly that when Scotty slowed down, they'd better slow down too, because he was probably seeing something you were not. I don't even think he knew how he knew this. He just did it based on pure instinct. You can't teach that; you can only hope to recognize and refine it. For me, I was in awe of his talent and remain so today.

Scotty usually wasn't the best athlete on the field at any given time, although, of course, he was pretty good. But he was a great shot, and he had the right mental software to be a SEAL. He had enormously powerful and accurate decision-making capabilities for assessing threat/non-threat situations.

I did have a glitch in my record. Call it bad judgment or a bad habit; it was one in the same. My first tour was characterized as the Pirate era. Members traveled and trained where they liked and navy oversight was little or none. While the open throttle years of Dick Marcinko had passed, the legacy was still there. The team was in the early stages of a transition from pony tails and earrings to getting haircuts and returning to uniforms. I transferred about the same time that Eric Olson came in and changed the culture. When I came back to senior leadership in my team, the command had changed, but I had not. As team leader, I was in charge of determining the training schedule based on meeting critical skill requirements. I took every opportunity to go out west to find training sites and look for opportunities for my team. As areas of Montana are nearly indistinguishable from the forests of Bosnia or the hills of Afghanistan, it made sense. Selecting training sites was a privilege that had been afforded to every team leader before me. I had bought my grandparents' house and decided to restore it rather than sell the family seat of generations. It seemed like a perfect match to travel to Fort Harrison, Spokane, Glasgow, and other training areas and go on leave. We conducted weapons and explosive training in Yakima, Washington, and conducted fire and movement in the hills of Montana. Why not? I was in charge and that was standard operating procedure. The problem was autonomous travel was no longer authorized and the rules had changed. Every travel claim for the past seven years was reviewed and every training trip was scrutinized. I felt like Captain Drake being tried for piracy in England after he fought for the Crown. It wasn't pretty but I did not get hung. I ended up having to repay $211 in unauthorized expenses, but the biggest penalty was being embarrassed for wrongdoing. Lesson learned, all of us are accountable to someone. Even the President and Congress are accountable to the people. It was a hard lesson to learn and likely put a cloud over me making flag officer. When I transferred, I was still given the highest recommendation for early promotion, assigned as executive officer, promoted to full commander, and later assigned multiple tours as the Naval Special Operations Forces Commander in Kosovo, and later acting Commander of Special Operations Forces in Iraq. The incident was a "shot across the bow" for sure, and I have to say I got the message.

Then there was my association with the Pirates. The damn-the-torpedoes guys. Most of the time, if you gave them a training assignment, they'd pull it off brilliantly, but every once in a while they'd be absolutely horrendous. And you never knew which group of Pirates would show up.

Now, if you had a high-risk, high-action mission, any of the teams (with the exception of the training team, of course) could have accomplished it, but the Pirates would be the ones who were really pissed off that they didn't get first crack at it.

The Pirates pulled the assignment to demonstrate at-sea techniques for boarding fast-moving ships using high-speed boats with monster outboard engines, and helicopters, something that not only had never been done, but it was considered damn near impossible. But we had been tasked with being ready to counter any terrorist threats against the 1992

Barcelona Olympics, particularly aboard the cruise ships that were acting as floating hotels for the Olympics.

The Pirates were game, of course, and got the call to demonstrate their capability. After parachuting the boats and men at sea, they banged over the rough seas and approached a big, smooth metal wall several stories high: the side of a cruise ship the navy had rented, along with a full crew and extras who would play enemy personnel and vacationers aboard the ship. It wasn't just an exercise in skill, daring, and machismo, and the techniques would have benefits well beyond the 1992 Olympics. Since the hijacking of the *Achille Lauro* in 1985, the Special Operations tactics to board a ship at sea needed to be developed and trained. Today, with the threat of weapons of mass destruction being transported on the high seas, the mission remains critical to national security. This technique was like hooky bobbing but with guaranteed deadly consequences if it didn't work out. The slightest mistake in a small boat next to a large ship in high seas might mean the boat and men being taken under by the current and crushed by the steel hull or the ship's propeller. Either way, the result was an "E" ticket to Davey Jones' locker.

The night of the "ship attack" was dark and the seas were about ten feet high. Right on the edge of possible they were at their best. Helicopters appeared out of the dark skies and the boats seemed to rise from the seas alongside. The masked men in flight suits came in, guns blazing, and every one of their shots hit the targets we'd set up.

The day's glory went to the men in the boats. These pirates' pirates made a parallel run at the cruise ship that was dazzling. They used grappling hooks and caving ladders to secure themselves to, and then ascend, the wet, slippery hull. We were tense and sweating just watching them work it from our positions on the deck. The rush of the men descending from the helicopters and climbing from the boats made me proud to be a SEAL. After what seemed like an hour—but was just under two minutes—the guys hauled themselves onto the pitching and rolling deck and fanned out to take control of the entry points. It was impressive: the only person who ever looked better climbing out of the sea was Ursula

Andress in the beginning of the James Bond movie *Dr. No.* And she wasn't nearly as well armed as my guys.

Through the glass of the bridge windows, several senior officers and I watched through binoculars. On the deck, my job was to narrate the action to the VIP dignitaries watching. I had arrived just weeks before and had yet to prove my merit as a "meat eater." I was the outsider, the liaison between the Pirates and the brass. I was also forced into an ad hoc diplomatic role. In addition to the US fleet admiral, we had our commanding officer (CO) and command master chief, who were almost inseparable. In my role as an ad hoc diplomat, I was the "expert," but, in actuality, I knew very little at the time and watched with equal amazement. In addition to US dignitaries, there were flag officers and diplomats from Spain to include rivals from the Spanish naval headquarters in nearby Rota, Spain, and Spanish air force in Madrid. In short, it was a "dog and pony" show on steroids. I later had "inside baseball" experience with the rivalries between the Spanish navy and air force.

These two branches of the Spanish military hated each other: apparently more than forty years before, Spain's General Francisco Franco had been denied a ride from the navy and the two services were still at odds with each other. I was assigned to negotiate a Memorandum of Understanding between the two parties and the US in regard to establishing a Naval Special Warfare Unit in Rota. During the negotiations, the Spanish navy admiral would say, in English, "Inform the Spanish air force that our position is . . ." and the Spanish air force general in return would say, in English, "Inform the navy that our position is . . ."

Both the base's executive officer and I tried to navigate that particular minefield of territorial pissing while getting our unit established. Neither of us were fluent in Spanish, but we received a master's in Spanish politics in getting the unit approved.

All the brass were watching the assault team from the deck. They were supposed to be there to observe the tactics and techniques of a maritime assault that may be needed for Olympic security, but they spent at least half their time glaring at each other.

As soon as the team had swiftly taken charge of the major control points of the vessel, you could tell the dignitaries were impressed. Ideally, the team would have gotten back on their boats and headed back to Rota once the exercise was completed. But there was a wrinkle: among the role players serving as the crew and cruise ship passengers were women, and the boys in the team weren't going to pass up a chance to mingle with them and tell tales. They hadn't discussed this with anyone in advance, of course.

My other role in the exercise was to ensure the hook from the boat was secure, crack a chem light to signal that the hook and ladder was secure, and then get out of the way and let the assault teams do their work. No, in a real scenario there wouldn't be anyone checking the security of the ladder, but we made this allowance: we weren't going to risk killing any of our guys for a little extra unnecessary verisimilitude. I also had the task of entertaining and answering questions from the distinguished visitors on board. At the time I knew just enough to be dangerous. In my role as liaison, I was standing next to the fleet admiral, the commanding officer, and his command master chief. When the ship was secure and the exercise was wrapping up, the admiral turned to me and asked if he could say "Bravo Zulu" to the men before he left. Since he was "the admiral," it was hardly a request and I obliged. I turned to both the CO and master chief and said in very loud and clear tone that the admiral has asked to say hello to the men and I am taking him down to the "Pursers locker" to see them. I stared right into the master chief's eyes, nodded, and repeated it twice because I knew the Purser's locker was a bar, and more importantly I knew the Pirates knew it too. The admiral and I departed and I took him on a circuitous route into the bowels of the ship, pointing out all the hook points and control points along the way. When we arrived at the locker, even I was not prepared for what was next. The Pirates had found the bar, removed their masks, and created a scene that looked like it was straight from Disney's Pirates of the Caribbean. I remember even hearing a muted "F**k you, admiral" from someone deep inside the crowd. Like the short calm before the storm, I prepared for heavy rolls.

"My navy?" I remember the admiral asking, "These guys are in *my* navy?"

Hardly another word was spoken as the visitors departed the ship bound for Rota. I was not invited to join them. I just stood there, trying not to recall tactical details of the impressive performance the team had done. The admiral was not as impressed as I was. His navy was the US navy and not Jean Laffite's!

Within days of that triumph, the naval equivalent of breaking the sound barrier, came what I called the "great bloodletting."

Turns out that big navy and the joint forces commander did not want their SEAL units to be *too* special. It didn't want pirates; it wanted traditional, neat, respectful sailors. Sadly, it wasn't just the look they disapproved of. In fairness, I could understand how the long hair and attitude would draw fire, and agreed that change was needed. It was possible for any Pirate to be good and to look good at the same time.

The edict came through channels, and it was like a change in tides. Absolute and impossible to stop. The age of the Pirates as I knew it had come to an end.

The man tapped to do the initial housecleaning was Captain Tom Moser. Moser had been previously assigned to Joint Special Operations Command (JSOC) and was fully briefed on what he faced as the new commanding officer. He rapidly changed grooming standards and reintroduced the men to the navy uniform. Perhaps it was fear or just his leadership style, but he sent a video down to the Pirates' team room rather than go in person. It was the early '90s, and Moser was at the forefront of using new media—not just to communicate but also to create a permanent record and make an indelible impression. Whenever he had a new policy to share, he didn't go over to the team rooms to brief us. He made a video, which we all were required to watch. Either way, they got the word. After all, where could they go? Moser was followed by

Admiral Eric Thor Olson, who made the transformation from Pirate to professional complete and permanent. Olson, now retired, was a thirty-eight-year veteran who rose higher than any other SEAL before—all the way to four-star admiral, the navy's highest rank.

He remade the SEALs all right, and he did it in a way that the big, loud, fearlessly brazen Richard Marcinko never did: Admiral Olson never ever raised his voice. Not once. That was one of the most useful tactics I have ever encountered. To hear him, we had to stop whatever we were doing and listen. You ever see the way guests on political talk shows shout to be heard over one another? If you talk softly when you speak, people have to be quiet or they'll miss what you're saying. They can't respond to what they don't hear. With Olson, you had to be comfortable with silence.

In Congress, I've never had to board a cruise ship from an inflatable. But let me tell you, Admiral Olson's "speak softly" approach is a skill I use to this day in politics.

Olson made several lasting changes. All SEALs under his command would be in uniform while on duty without exception. Regulation haircuts were once again mandatory. Jewelry was banned. Navy policy about smoking, drinking, and other health and quality-of-life issues was adopted at once. Olson made the changes in culture as well as drove changes in tactics. The team commenced a review and update of every tactical procedure and leveraged emerging technologies as appropriate. The chasing down of vessels at full throttle was changed to reflect advances radar signatures and stealth technology. Flashlights were replaced by night-vision optics and the boneyard was retired.

It was pretty brilliant. In retrospect, I couldn't understand why any of us college-educated wunderkinds hadn't had the intestinal fortitude to do that before.

Within a few short years, almost all the "founding members" had either transferred or retired. Sad to say, tens of millions of dollars of training and experience left with them. It was a real loss, though there was no way to break the downtime habits and the traditional way of doing business. It's kind of sad, when you think about it, since while we were all being shaved and shorn of our piratical earrings, everyone from metropolitan police to gridiron stars were starting to adopt the look.

Back then, I was not sure whether removing all the previous culture was the right or wrong thing to have done. I was too busy to give it much thought. I'm not sure that it improved the way we did our jobs but there is no doubt it improved the image in the eyes of those who would approve and authorize the missions and provide the money. I mean, I'm not aware of any Super Bowls that were lost on account of hair.

A new SEAL team culture began to appear, and quickly, that won the hearts and minds of big navy and the joint commanders. It was more by the book, and reflected the US Army's elite SF approach of the "quite professional" rather than the celebrated crew of the Queen Ann's Revenge.

The army's elite force was having their issues as well. US Army Rangers, known for following procedure, were winning a battle for control with the Army SF ranks at the expense of the more unconventional-minded Special Forces. On every front, the rogues were endangered. By the end of my second stint, they were extinct. The old days of the Pirates were over.

But, obviously, it wasn't my call.

The funny thing is, it didn't close the cultural gap that had always existed between regular and irregular (Special) forces, between the guys who sailed the seas and the guys who killed terrorists in their beds. But I was surprised and proud to see the well-oiled machine that command had become. Full disclosure time here: Even though I was "Z Man" to the enlisted men, I was always "one of those guys" to the senior leadership. And they were the ones who controlled assignments and promotions. They were right in that my loyalties lie with the men more than with the institution. I was always the first to go to the gap. I had done two tours of duty at the command, been ground force commander, elements and team commander, current operations officer, and had been privileged to lead some of the most complex operations our military had ever executed. I was not the best, but I always knew who was and was just honored to be with them.

SIXTEEN

THREAT–NO THREAT
(LIFE OR DEATH)

AS MUCH AS TECHNOLOGY HAD CHANGED IN THE YEARS since I first saw those "bikers" heading out to the gun range, the SEALs' ability to function in the field is unchanged. And it was tied to their trigger finger. If you're an adversary and you are not compliant, there are ways of making you comply. Even if you are resistant, you can be "persuaded." But if you're a clear and present threat in any environment where SEALs are functioning, you will die in a hurry.

I cannot emphasize enough how, in the mind of every SEAL in combat or working a sensitive operation, rapid calculations are always going on. This is true of police officers as well, whenever they enter a house or answer a 911 call. The difference is that for police, there may be danger, possibly *mortal* danger. For SEALs, that's a given. And we must react accordingly. What goes through our minds is a brutally fast, instinctual threat/non-threat analysis, and it boils down to this one idea: Is that potential target presenting himself as a threat? Honing this ability to a razor's edge quite literally takes thousands of hours of training in a "Kill House" training facility. There, SEALs learn to be aware not only of potential hostiles but of each other. One of the great tragedies of any engagement is what the navy calls "blue on blue," inadvertent fratricide: the accidental killing of a brother. Those extremely long hours—often with no sleep, since you may find yourself in a combat or escape situation where sleep is not possible—are imperative to the survival of every SEAL and those at his side.

An example. We're all aware, now, of how the team took out Osama bin Laden in the bold compound raid in Pakistan on May 2, 2011. That is the perfect example of the lightning-fast "threat/no threat" calculation. If we allow that just being around the terror mastermind was not in itself a crime, you have a situation where you have to decide: Who is a threat? Who is an innocent? Who is at the wrong place at the wrong time?

Bin Laden presented himself as a threat and they took the shot and killed him. I can tell you with certainty, the man who pulled that trigger was so well trained that he never even thought about it until after bin Laden was dead. Yet there were many others in the walled compound who were not shot. It is a supreme credit to those guys on the ground there that zero civilians were killed during a high-adrenalin operation.

But frankly, the way the raid and those who were on it were talked about makes me a little uneasy. I've said it before and I'll certainly say it again: Too much media attention on current SEAL operations—from magazine articles to Hollywood films—is a booby-trapped gift, a necklace with a sharp, rusty edge. In the case of bin Laden, disclosure of which unit was responsible came from the top. On a raid of that magnitude, once the media is given a little light, they will pursue it right down to who pulled the trigger. And they did. I don't judge those who were on the mission for deciding to put the record straight, but I do take issue with administration policies that are more about taking the credit than keeping America and our forces safe. More recently, senior officials have tipped the media on special operations while they were still on the target! Sure, the taxpayer has a right to know and America sleeps better knowing that we have capable forces on watch to protect us. But the military and civilian leadership has the responsibility to protect the forces who are assigned the difficult mission as well. Tactics should be protected so that disclosure does not jeopardize any current future operations. Yes, the story should be told but only after it is vetted and well after the fact.

The glamorization is understandable but inaccurate. People forget how tough the job is when you're not on a mission, when you're just training. You're not fast-roping from choppers every day. There's a certain grind to it. Worst of all, being a SEAL means a *lot* of time away from your family, leaving them to wonder where you are and *how* you are, and the divorce rate is really high. The number of days deployed remains well over two hundred, and that—*that*—is the real job. The job most civilians and journalists don't know about. The SEAL community is tight, but let me tell you, there is a world of sadness in the community. Not just the long hours and physical taxation, not just the time away from loved ones, not just the reality of the hazards you face. There's also an ever-present sadness over how many SEALs we've lost, of how many husbands and young fathers and only sons we've lost. There is also the strain of being deployed so many days a year. What is normal and what is not? Guys returning from overseas are wound tight when they come home, as being in war is now the norm.

I extol beyond all measure service to country. But, Lord, I never said it comes without a price.

The first time was as an instructor, and the second was as an executive officer. I've mentioned that the majority of my SEAL career was spent either conducting operations in a SEAL team or training young SEALs at either Basic Underwater Demolition/SEAL (BUD/S) training or the Advanced Training Command, which I was a founding plank owner, meaning I was one of the men there when it was created. I would have to say being an instructor was the most enjoyable.

I was able to influence SEAL training the most when I was an executive officer of Naval Special Warfare Center. I ran the basic and advanced training command in Coronado, as well as the sixteen different training locations, each of which had its own set of missions and environments. A lot of what I was doing was creating and applying standards, such as where, how, and at what level SEALs should train; who should be responsible for each phase of training; and what standards of skills SEALs should possess when they are deemed ready for war.

At the time I took it over in 2001, a lot of this training was pretty patchwork. Training programs are like that; you discover what you need as you go along and add it, without a whole lot of attention being paid to the best way of putting it all together. But the changing nature of warfare meant that SEAL teams and their counterparts would increasingly be working together, and would be working with other military assets as well. Joint operations involving SEALs were becoming more common, and the mission got more challenging.

Bringing cohesion to all of these operations meant applying at least some standards to weapons and communications operations, as well as reporting formats for intelligence operations, especially if our pegs of intelligence would be filling the holes—square, round, and otherwise—of other commands.

Initially, everyone learns the same elements: learn your positions; learn the weapons systems; learn the basic skills. But officers quickly have a bunch of other considerations added to their drills. They are required to know what training and equipment their men will need for a variety of situations, what the rules of engagement for various situations are, what support systems will be needed and how to coordinate them, and a variety of advanced tactics and longer-range planning.

A SEAL officer may not be the one leading the charge, but he's going to have to be able to see the breadth of the battlefield, as opposed to just his specific part. The demands for greater communication and coordination on the battlefield were increasing and the skill set to plan complex operations required more training. His men have to know that if they're focused on kicking in a door, the officer is mapping their physical position and momentum, where the medical support elements are, how far out the extraction units are, and whatever the next command call on the mission execution checklist is. Those aren't considerations door kickers should have cluttering their mind if they're going to perform their own tasks to the best of their ability. It's like being a conductor in a band: each player has a role and all must work in concert.

While I didn't create it, I am a big fan of one of the exercises that tests SEALs' abilities to quickly assess the threat level of a situation. That would be the hooded box drill—which is exactly as grim as it sounds. In it, the SEAL is brought into a room with a hood over his head. The room is padded, which means if he chooses to fight, he can. The hood is lifted, and he's presented with an immediate scenario—an advancing person, a retreating person, someone without a gun, two people, low visibility, or any combination of these—and the SEAL has to quickly determine how to react.

In a variation on this, a small tactical element is led into the room—an officer and a few enlisted men. They're then presented with a scenario and stress is induced, and the instructors watch to see what choices the officer makes under pressure, and how the enlisted men follow his instructions.

While instructors watch every aspect of the drill, they're usually paying special attention to the relationship between the officer and his men—whether the unit operates with cohesion or as individuals, what determination the officer makes about close-quarter battle and fields of fire, and generally how that officer reacts to stress while commanding. And yes, sometimes the "right" answer is not to engage at all.

When would-be SEALs graduate BUD/S, their journey is just beginning. The clay has only just been made, not yet formed. They're going to receive layers of advanced, and very expensive, training. When I was running training, the cost for just basic training for a single SEAL graduate was over a million dollars. Coupled with the cost of advanced training in weapons and explosives, it's no wonder the obligation of service is fifty-two months *after* receiving a Trident. For a SEAL unit, it takes as long as five years before the member has the requisite amount of training and experience to assume a leadership role.

All too shortly after they've been in the field, they'll have to start giving back to the program by training the next generation of SEALs. Technology advances quickly, and the value experienced SEALs can offer younger trainers is drawn from their experience, which those younger SEALs can then apply to the advanced systems they'll be training on.

Even the nature of what a SEAL does has changed. In my case, there was a psychological buffer. That is, I spent most of my time preparing for the possibility of war, preparing others for that possibility, considering and examining theoretical future requirements, making sure equipment was available and that it would be appropriate for new tactics and procedures, and then and only then dealing with the occasional skirmish. SEALs today have entered their service in a time of war, a war that will no doubt be with us for decades. They are much more likely to spend their entire career being deployed in dangerous situations where there are active enemies. You enter that training today with a different edge: the enemy has a face and a mission, and more than ever before a SEAL *must* be ready to fight and win.

That's not the only change new SEALs are facing. Modern warfare has become more complex: SEALs need to be able to integrate weapons systems in an asymmetrical battle environment. A SEAL candidate today would have a great deal of difficulty succeeding without being computer literate. In an earlier era, that would not have been a defining skill, but today SEALs have to have the sort of intelligence that allows them to quickly grasp these systems.

There's one more major change between yesterday's and today's SEALs, and I sometimes wonder if it handcuffs one of our most valuable fighting assets. We're asking these highly trained warfare specialists to operate within the confines of political correctness, in a zero-tolerance environment for many things that weren't even considered punitive a few years ago.

Frankly, that's a very dangerous enemy.

The pursuit of political correctness does not allow honest mistakes. A SEAL can now get busted for a single drinking incident, even if it's a birthday or some other major life event celebration. There's been a change to what constitutes an infraction in the way men and women interact. Obviously, I'm not talking about any sort of sexual misconduct. I am talking about "perceived" misconduct. SEALs are trained about the rules of engagement in warfare, and the same basic humanity is expected for interpersonal interactions.

But there's a difference between decency and basic human behavior and the minefield that now makes up over-sensitized interactions. Highly trained warriors aren't going to be all things—diplomats, intelligence agents, lovers, and killers rolled into one—and the very inclinations and skills that make them excellent military assets come with a cost. I keep hearing of wanting to create "the whole" man concept and pre-screen candidates based on a mortality test. Duty, honor, country—I think that is enough.

War is inherently brutal, and it's also unfortunately very unforgiving. It's not pretty when you err on the side of caution and your side—your team, your friends, your country—takes a hit. Expecting a spoonful of sugar in every setting, on every occasion, from the greatest war technicians the world has ever seen, is unrealistic.

Having said that, the nature of people trying out for SEALs changed between when I was a trainee and when I became an executive officer. Back in the 1980s, SEAL candidates had still been influenced by members of the Greatest Generation—those men and women who instilled the beliefs of getting ahead by working hard, having commitment, conforming to the system, and climbing gradually up the ladder of success. It is the classic Protestant work ethic. While you were supposed to function as a member of a team, you were ultimately responsible for your own successes and failures. There was no such thing as social promotion and affirmative action. You got ahead because you deserved to get ahead. Period.

The newer generations of SEAL candidates are different. Call them X-generation or millennials; they are different. There is that awareness of ever-present war, as I said. They still work hard, and they still are highly motivated and embrace a lot of essential skills, but they are less willing to take responsibility for their own actions. If they smoke—and I actually have heard this—it's the fault of the tobacco companies for putting their product where, by golly, you see it and just have to try it and find out what the fuss is about. First Lady Nancy Reagan took a lot of guff for her allegedly simplistic "Just Say No" campaign about drugs, but what was wrong with that? What happened to individual backbone? I've actually been around SEALs who guzzle sugared, caffeinated sodas, but then beg off when a cracker has gluten. We bring our backgrounds and upbringing with us, wherever we go, and when the military shoulders uniformity aside to make room for personal expression, the entire purpose of a unit, a platoon, a squadron, goes out the window. Just look at the squabbles that go on in the locker rooms of professional sports because "m-e" have become the dominant letters in "team."

Today's SEALs are groomed in school to be more community oriented, but that also means the community is somehow responsible for their personal wrongs. At a recent high school graduation I attended, there were twenty-four valedictorians. Everyone who had an A average was a valedictorian regardless of curriculum. There are schools that count culinary arts as a science just to keep moving the kids through a broken system. The schools have promoted that everyone is a winner and everyone is to receive a participation award. A downside to community-based thinking is that it is difficult to hold anyone accountable for group action. And, of course, if you're part of a desired demographic, you're given a do-over when you screw up. That's just wrong.

In fact, look around you. Today's younger generations are practically programmed to expect second chances. When they don't measure up, they go into a litany: "I've had a chance to think about what happened. I know what my successes and failures were. I've accepted feedback and conducted self-criticism to learn to be better, and I am ready to go back and be the best possible candidate. So when can I start again?" They have all the right phrases but all the wrong actions.

Fortunately, there is still one place where there is a hard line drawn. When a SEAL trainee rings that bell three times, there are no second chances. You don't get to dry off, sleep, and eat, while your fellow candidates are still pushing themselves, and then have seller's remorse. I've gotten a lot of blank stares in disbelief when I've told candidates that they're not coming back into the program they just left, because in many cases it's the first time in their lives they've not been given a second chance.

What's amazing is they had to have known this was the case going in. For all I'm complaining about this aspect of today's SEAL candidates, they also are superior to previous generations in terms of their ability to use technology and gather information. They have the opportunity to be the best classes of SEALs ever, especially regarding the intelligence-gathering functions, and they cut the ground out from under themselves by not taking personal responsibility. The world is moving faster and this generation is moving with it. Where my generation saw learning basic tactics as critical, the new generation values innovation and speed. In today's world of technology, the ability to rapidly leverage the cutting edge gives you the advantage.

In fact, the newest SEALs' entire generation has the potential to be the next greatest generation. They are less rigid in thinking, can adapt to changing technology, and don't like to be told what to do. The last part is embedded into their American DNA and may be their greatest asset. The drive toward innovation and the ability to "think out of the box" runs square in the face against big government and centralized control.

The few who get through the program are exceptional, and I don't want to see any lessening of its standards based on either physical or attitudinal shortcomings.

Some wise person—I wish I could remember who; maybe it was one of my history teachers—once pointed out to me that before the American Civil War, citizens used to say, when referring to this country, "The United States are . . ." After the Civil War, recovering slowly from the pain that we had perhaps inevitably inflicted on ourselves, citizens began to say, when referring to this country, "The United States is . . ."

It's a subtle difference but a significant one. The crucible of combat, that left no state unscathed, had hammered us for the first time into a true union. A collection of states "are." A nation "is."

I thought of that idea often during my time playing sports and training to be a SEAL. We all went from "are" to "is," from individuals to a unit. The benefit of that is not just apparent in combat. As I've said elsewhere, it makes you a permanent member of that group. Everyone who comes after you will do essentially what you did, will meet a lot of the people you know, will go through the same physical and emotional transformation you endured. It's like an athlete watching a game he used to play or a dancer going to the ballet. It's in your blood; you get it in your brain, heart, and soul.

My point here is that even though I am retired, there is not a news story about SEALs that doesn't get me where I live. As you might imagine, one of those towers high over all the others.

I want to talk about that because of the impact a handful of good men and an incredible support structure made on the world.

A lot has been written about, talked about, and debated about the SEAL team raid that took down one of the most hunted individuals in history: Osama bin Laden. Most of you already know the general facts of the mission.

I want to take a fresh look at that, not only because I have heard some fascinating details from SEAL friends but because it is a master class that illustrates a lot of the qualities, attitudes, and skill sets I have been talking about. Even though I wasn't there, I know what it took to succeed—both the mission and the terror leader. Meaning, no disrespect, the word that keeps coming to mind—even today, when I hear about it or read about it or talk about that event—is:

Jesus. There was a huge amount on the line that day, and I am grateful to God for the help in completing that mission.

The crew of the team knew that this was the real deal when they got the order to load out and be ready for the mission. From the countless many who had joined the military since 9/11, to the tens of thousands who had attempted to become SEALs, to the roughly 2,500 active SEALs in Special Operations Command, these guys were the "A" team, the proverbial best of the best. And finally, after ten long years they were chosen to get not only a high value target (HVT), but The HVT.

Many different versions of the events that unfolded have been written. That's understandable. In the fog of war, people perceive things differently. From different perspectives, people see and hear things differently. Thanks to the rush of adrenalin that turns every moment into a lifetime, people remember things differently.

What is not disputed in any version is that SEAL team had been flown to a compound in Abbottabad, Pakistan, to kill or capture bin Laden. Members of the team believed they were going on a one-way mission whether they killed him or not.

The mission started off inauspiciously when they crash-landed one of their helicopters in the compound outside, barely surviving the infiltration (infil). The element of surprise they so desperately needed was now at risk. As the team piled from the downed helicopter, they knew they had to move quickly and efficiently to "clear" the compound and locate their target. Their satellite intel told them that if bin Laden was there he would be in the main house, likely on the top floor, where images had been seen of a tall man dressed in robes pacing the roof.

Like a finely tuned machine, they quickly and methodically moved through the area. The team was on the ground with only one objective. You wreck an aircraft just outside the target area, the enemy is going to know you're there. The occupants of the compound were now clearly awake and waiting for them. All enemy firepower would be in hand, and any traps like mines or blinding flash-bang grenades rigged to doors would already be set. There was no backup, no air support, no nothing. The only thing that separated the members of SEAL team from a six-foot hole were they themselves.

They cleared the outlying buildings in the compound surrounding the main house and killed the sole male occupant of the smaller structure, who had demonstrated hostile intent rather than submission. They secured the women and children easily and safely.

The door to the main house was blown open and they were then immediately running upstairs through the home where bin Laden was believed to reside. Three men, single file, weaving their way up the stairs.

The years of training and developing tactics, techniques, and procedures paid off. Every rifle covering a different direction, as the counterattack could come from anywhere. Surprising thing is, in many ways your brain checks out at times like these. You aren't a pack animal; lions and wolves don't have compassion. SEALs do. They must if they're going to live with themselves post-mission. But you are running on muscle memory, sensory input, and threat/non-threat instinct. That's the entirety of who and what you are at that moment.

Sensory input—it's more than just seeing, hearing, smelling, touching, even tasting. (Certain kinds of fuses, powder, and metal actually make an impression on the tongue without ever coming into contact with it.) It's about a thousand or so stimuli assaulting your body.

Which matter? Which don't? Is that a guy sweating with fear around the corner, or just someone who hasn't showered? Was that meal cooked on a hot plate, is there an aura of "burn" around it, or was it brought in from somewhere else? Are those dogs or children whimpering? Is that shadow a crouching target or a pile of clothes?

All of that—every particle of input—is being processed and used or discarded as you move.

Threat/non-threat.

Laser sights move through the area constantly, with team members' trigger fingers resting lightly on the edge of the trigger guards to avoid accidental discharge, yet ensure maximum speed and efficiency. They scan 360 degrees of the house that is now a battlefield.

Thousands of hours of training, millions of dollars spent on each human "asset," and it comes down to a moment in time. A second—if that. A face appears behind a door above them in the stairway. All that can be seen is that the individual is a tall male looking down the stairway directly at them from behind the entrance to the room. They cannot see his hands or body, but must assume he is armed and dangerous. That doesn't necessarily mean a gun; it could be a knife, an explosive vest, a hostage—anything.

THREAT—NO THREAT (LIFE OR DEATH)

Let me tell you what the lead man was feeling right then. All of those guys were pretty amped, and if there weren't the possibility that bin Laden had been armed, if he would have been very complacent, I think we would have had a live bin Laden in Guantanamo Bay. We could have interrogated him. But these guys, when you're a fighting force— emphasis on the "fighting"—I cannot overemphasize not only the need but the ability of them to make a decision. When you get in that close proximity to your target, and your training quickly starts peeling back the options, you're left *only* with threat/non-threat.

We know the answer to that.

Controlled shots taken by the lead man in the group within milliseconds of processing the single thought.

The bullets hit the intended target within inches of one another.

The threat was neutralized.

Bin Laden was no more.

SEVENTEEN

TACTICAL AND
STRATEGIC FAILURES

NOW LET ME DO A PIVOT HERE AND TALK ABOUT AN
operation that didn't happen but should have.

Benghazi.

Maybe you're tired of hearing about the deadly attack on our embassy
and its personnel—the hearings, more hearings, the allegations of par-
tisanship against the Obama administration, the e-mails that confirm
lies were told for political gain—for example, knowing that Al-Qaeda
was behind the planned attack, yet insisting it was a spontaneous reaction against an irreverent YouTube film that wasn't kind to Islam. (And
let me digress here to say that I saw that film and I didn't like it, but my
not liking it does not mean it is unprotected by the First Amendment—
the right to free speech. The notion that a filmmaker should have been
interrogated and arrested for exercising that right is more than repre-
hensible. It goes against the very thing that every SEAL who ever lived
has fought to defend: our Constitution and our freedom. So you are not
going to find a sympathetic voice in the discussion that follows.)

But I will tell you why I will never tire of making sure this country
does not forget what actually took place there. It is because we did *nothing* to attempt to assist Americans once we knew they were in trouble.
This is the core of our being. One might also ask: Isn't this the same thing

we have done to all of our allies in the Middle East, as well as in the rest of the world?

As we now know, our ambassador, J. Christopher Stevens, made repeated requests for additional security at an extremely vulnerable compound. It was not provided, apparently, because the narrative promulgated by the Obama administration was that the overthrow of the Libyan tyrant Muammar Gaddafi had not only been a success, it had resulted in a free and more stable Libya. A security posture that showed strength and demonstrated superior firepower would not support the new narrative of Islamic peace and understanding.

My eye. That was right up there with the fantasy about Yemen being a model state and not the new home of Al-Qaeda.

Benghazi did not have to end the way it did. It *should* not have ended the way it did. The embassy did not have local air assets for evacuation. Fine and understandable. But when you've got between 125 and 150 masked gunmen converging on your position, you don't sit on your damn hands. You simply do not. We had a GPS position, and the United States had a whole arsenal in the region. I mean, pick one. You can put a fast mover on it, everything up. It's not as though we didn't have an array of choices. It's not like we didn't even have time to deploy them. We did. The raid was actually multiple attacks that took place over the course of *thirteen* hours! Here's what the asset map looked like at the time. A team of "operators" was shifted from central Europe to a US naval base in Sigonella, Italy. Guys who could have turned the battle were an hour's flying time from Libya. For support, they had fueled fighter jets. Even a low flyover would have been something. I have also been informed that diplomatic and military channels were being worked so that the United States would have permission from Libya to enter their air space. Permission from whom? Our ambassador was dead, and we were asking permission? Outrageous.

Nothing.

The frustration to any professional fighting man or woman involved in that had to be intense. The reality is, however well trained you are, however ready to go you are, that command must come from someone else. You may have *service to country* tattooed on your soul, but without the launch order, it is not an actionable concept. I present, without comment, the famous quote from General Douglas MacArthur: "It is a dangerous concept that men of the armed forces must owe their primary allegiance to these temporary occupants of the White House, instead of to the country and the Constitution to which they have sworn to defend."[1]

I'm not advocating reckless behavior. Of course not. That was discredited in 1876 when George Armstrong Custer led his 7th Cavalry blindly into a vastly superior force of Lakota, Northern Cheyenne, and Arapaho in my home state. (By the way, that hasty action is not the same as 185 heroes electing to face thousands of the enemy at the Alamo forty years prior. There's a difference between knowing heroism and ignorant vainglory.)

Just reading about Benghazi, or even hearing about it, makes me cringe. In Congress, I am forced to do both. Know this, though: I would have given anything to be leading a team to that site. I was personally involved in the training that went into the creation of two of the warriors lost there, Glen Doherty and Ty Woods, both former SEALs.

We are set up to fight wars within moments anywhere. Shipboard ordnance can reach targets that personnel cannot. Special operators are currently on the ground in places that would surprise you. And there, in Benghazi, we had an immediate and accessible target, we had the exact location on it, we had powerful assets available . . . and we did nothing.

While I'm on this subject of things we can't or won't do, look at what is still happening in Afghanistan with our troops. The rules of engagement are so ridiculously restrictive that we are no longer on the offense. And with terrorism, being on the defense is not just a disadvantage, it's flat out stupid. You've got to keep them on the run, keep them disorganized, and you've got to pursue them with all vigor. When we're hunkered down and can't engage targets—or the only way we *can* engage is by bringing in a group through operational security that is either undermanned or nonexistent—there's a lot of frustration. Even assuming the best course is to leave the country—and I am not advocating that—while you are still there, you push the enemy as hard as you can, as often as you can, and then you leave. But you don't do what we were doing: hash out all kinds of crap politically and leave the enemy in an advantageous position as you make your way to the exit door.

This hearts and minds stuff? Winning over the population? That's good in theory. But we can all agree, I think, that you are not going to change the mind of fanatics like the Taliban. You are not going to change the Taliban's philosophy and you are not going to change the way they operate. The only way you eliminate the threat to the population is to hunt the enemy down individually and destroy them. That is what creates positive change. You want hearts and minds? As soon as villagers see what we're doing, see where we're going, know that we will be there to help and protect them, they will start sending their daughters to school, which is forbidden by the Taliban. They will start using the roads we built for commerce, not flight. They will help us.

These people only want to survive. Turning tail does not accomplish that.

Many politicians say that the United States cannot be the world's police force. I don't think those people understand this: if we don't fight these monsters there, we fight them here. That's more than policing. That's common sense.

Now we have a situation in Iraq, and arguably the entirety of the Middle East, where the United States has simply given up on leading the war against radical Islam. We left Iraq, and the result was the collapse of the local forces and the loss of the entire northern region to a new set of Islamic terrorists who call themselves ISIS.

Arguably, the destabilization we have seen from our lack of leadership has caused and/or contributed to the collapse of Libya and the civil war in Syria. Either way, the lack of leadership (by this administration and Europe) has led to a refugee crisis, the likes of which we have never historically witnessed in the past—*ever*. Does this crisis ultimately lead to the collapse of the European Union as we know it? One could make an argument it is a very real possibility. Personally, I think it's inevitable, particularly after what we recently witnessed in the Paris attack in which more than 130 unarmed people were slaughtered by Islamic terrorist elements, including "refugees." The recent attacks in Brussels are more evidence of the same.

While the ultimate outcome of recent world events, and the collapse of "states" as we have known them, is yet to be written, one thing is certain. When the United States is weak in its leadership role, the world suffers. That is a fact. Unless and until the United States is replaced by some new "shining light" on the world stage, it is our job, if not our "manifest responsibility" to operate as the leader of the free world. I am here to tell you that I am in wholehearted agreement with Ronald Regan that there is no other "shining light" in the world, and if we do not make our stand here for freedom, there will be nothing left to stand for.

I believe this to the core of my soul.

EPILOGUE

AS SCOTT AND I ATTEMPTED TO PULL THIS SERIES OF stories of my life together, I often thought, *What did I want to accomplish with this work?* I set out to attempt to define the panorama of why I felt this country, and the men and women I have trained and with whom I fought side by side, were so exceptional. Have I accomplished this task? That is for you, the reader, to decide. But one thing I certainly feel I have done is to be clear that I have the greatest admiration and respect for those who have been willing to take up arms, and lose life and limb, in the defense of this great nation.

General Mattis had it right.

"For whatever trauma came with service in tough circumstances, we should take what we learned—take our post-traumatic growth—and, like past generations coming home, bring our sharpened strengths to bear, bring our attitude of gratitude to bear. And, most important, we should deny cynicism a role in our view of the world."[1] I ask that you take a moment to think about this simple and yet brilliant message. Three aspects of this quote are particularly important to me: (1) it acknowledges our current and historical losses of life and limb, aka "trauma"; (2) it compels us to learn and grow from this; and (3) it asks us, as a people and a nation, to move forward with this knowledge—but without cynicism.

That is the only way I can get up in the morning and continue my fight to bring this nation back to the greatness I have seen in her past, and of which I know she is capable in the future.

I have no doubt that this great nation is fixable—if each of us are willing to do our part. I hope this story has given you incentive to do yours.

NOTES

FOREWORD

1. Authors' Note: In the interests of full disclosure and review requirements, this manuscript and related photos were submitted to the Department of Defense for redaction of any material and/or descriptions deemed "classified." Certain parts of the manuscript and the foreword reflect the redactions made.

PROLOGUE

1. "Sexual Violence in Bosnia," https://www.srebrenica.org.uk/what -happened/sexual-violence-bosnia/; http://womensenews.org/2000/07 /bosnian-rape-camp-survivors-testify-the-hague/.

CHAPTER 1: AL-SADR'S BOOKKEEPER

1. "The Life and Thought of Edmund Burke," https://www.washcoll.edu /live/news/6314-the-life-and-thought-of-edmund-burke.
2. A side note here: Beheading, which gained popularity during the First Chechen War between Russia and Chechnya from 1994 to 1996, was mostly reserved for men. The reason for this was as simple as it was grotesque: as video camera and Internet technology grew, those images made for sick, terrifying videos. Over the years, helpless Russian conscripts, bound American and European reporters, and contractors were all gruesomely dispatched on camera. However, very few women were beheaded. Though women are considered second-class citizens in many Middle Eastern nations, there is a conversely twisted reverence

for motherhood that risked local backlash if women's heads were both uncovered . . . and severed.

CHAPTER 2: FALLUJAH: A WAREHOUSE OF DEATH

1. James N. Mattis, "The Meaning of Their Service," *The Wall Street Journal*, April 17, 2015, http://www.wsj.com/articles/the-meaning-of-their-service-1429310859#:WapTtENWG6oszA.

CHAPTER 3: ABU GHRAIB

1. *The New York Times*, June 2, 2003, https://georgewbush-whitehouse.archives.gov/news/releases/2003/09/20030929–14.html.

CHAPTER 4: SMALL-TOWN AMERICA

1. Montana Historical Society, "Homesteading Women of Montana," http://test.mzartstudio.com/category/women/.
2. Montana Historical Society, "Homesteading Women of Montana," http://test.mzartstudio.com/category/women/.

CHAPTER 5: EARLY TEAMWORK

1. http://www.theodore-roosevelt.com/trenv.html.
2. http://ngm.nationalgeographic.com/2015/04/pine-beetles/rosner-text.
3. http://naturalresources.house.gov/newsroom/documentsingle.aspx?DocumentID=398568.

CHAPTER 6: GO DUCKS

1. http://www.inspirationalstories.com/quotes/t/i-ching-on-thought-thinking/.

CHAPTER 7: THE ENERGY PLAY

1. Russell Gold, Amy Harder, "Fracking Has Had No 'Widespread' Impact on Drinking Water, EPA Finds," *The Wall Street Journal*, June 4, 2015, http://www.wsj.com/articles/fracking-has-had-no-widespread-impact-on-drinking-water-epa-finds-1433433850.
2. http://www.quotes.net/quote/41878.

NOTES

CHAPTER 12: INTO THE FIRE
1. http://www.rense.com/general77/ted.htm; https://thehornnews.com/theodore-roosevelts-ideas-on-being-an-immigrant-and-an-american-in-1907/.

CHAPTER 13: GOOD LUCK, LIEUTENANT
1. George Dudley Seymour, *The Familiar Hale* (New Haven, Connecticut: The Yale Publishing Association, 1907), 12.
2. Richard D. McGhee, *John Wayne: Actor, Artist, Hero* (Jefferson, North Carolina: McFarland & Company, 1990), 200.

CHAPTER 17: TACTICAL AND STRATEGIC FAILURES
1. http://www.plaintruth.com/the_plain_truth/2010/06/firing-a-general-its-been-done-before-by-another-lousy-president.html.

EPILOGUE
1. James N. Mattis, "The Meaning of Their Service," *The Wall Street Journal*, April 17, 2015, http://www.wsj.com/articles/the-meaning-of-their-service-1429310859#:WapTtENWG6oszA.

ABOUT THE AUTHORS

RYAN ZINKE IS A MONTANA NATIVE AND THE FIRST NAVY SEAL commander to serve in Congress. During his twenty-three years as a SEAL, he was commander at the country's most elite SEAL Team, acting commander of Special Forces in Iraq, and was awarded two bronze stars. Congressman Zinke serves on the House Armed Services Committee and is an expert in emerging threats, terrorism, and national security. He holds a degree in geology, an MBA in finance, and a masters in global leadership. He and his wife Lolita Hand have three children and two grandchildren.

SCOTT MCEWEN LIVES IN SAN DIEGO, CALIFORNIA, where he began writing while practicing law. He grew up in the mountains of Eastern Oregon where he became an Eagle Scout; hiking, fishing, and hunting at every opportunity presented. He obtained his undergraduate degree at Oregon State University and thereafter studied and worked extensively in London, England. Scott works with and provides support for several military charitable organizations, including the Seal Team Foundation. Scott's interest in military history, intense patriotism, and experience with long-range hunting rifles compelled him to accurately record the battlefield experiences of Chris Kyle, the most lethal sniper in United States military history. He continues that message here with the story of Ryan Zinke.